LOVE CONQUERS THE WORLD!

LOVE CONQUERS THE WORLD!

Love Is The Answer For Racial And Societal Healing And Reconciliation

AUGUSTINE SENGULAY

XULON PRESS

Xulon Press
2301 Lucien Way #415
Maitland, FL 32751
407.339.4217
www.xulonpress.com

Paperback ISBN-13: 978-1-6628-0612-4
Dust Jacket ISBN-13: 978-1-6628-0613-1

Ebook ISBN-13: 978-1-6628-0614-8

Quote

"Alexander, Caesar, Charlemagne, and I have founded empires.
But on what did we rest the creations of our genius?
Upon force.
Jesus Christ founded his empire upon love; and at this hour millions of men would die for him."
(Napoleon Bonaparte, French Military Leader – 1769-1821)

Dedication

This book is dedicated as a first fruit offering to the glory and honor of our God and Father who has created all men and all the races equal in His own image and likeness, and with whom there is no racial superiority or inferiority but equality; and who loved the world so much that He sent His only begotten Son to die for the sins of the world that whosoever believes in Him shall not perish but shall have everlasting life! And to our Lord and Savior Jesus Christ who came down from heaven to announce His universal "Emancipation Proclamation" of true freedom, justice and love, and the abolition of slavery of the entire human race in the devil's plantation of sin and bondage; and has broken down the middle wall of racial barriers and prejudices and has nailed the enmity to the Cross; and has reconciled all men and all races back to God as one new man and one new race saved by grace alone under God, indivisible and invincible by His death on the Cross! And to the Holy Spirit who has come to convict the world of sin, of righteousness, and of judgment, and to point all men and all races to Christ on the Cross as the only Savior of the world!

Table of Contents

Acknowledgements

In writing this book, there are some very important and very special people in my life that I would like to acknowledge and honor. And the first of such persons is my leprous mother, Monday, who is the greatest influencer and heroine in my life. My mother was stark illiterate and leprous, but her love for me was not illiterate nor leprous, but rather, it was rich and prosperous. She was the one who chased me to school, chased me to church, and eventually chased me into the very hands of God! She was a chaser! She was the one who prayed prophetically into my life and all those prayers have been answered. I am what I am today because of her mother's endearing love and prayers. Even though she's gone to be with the LORD now, I would forever express my deepest love and appreciation for her for all her selfless sacrifice and sufferings. Thank you, Mama. I love and miss you and will see you in heaven!

The second most important and most special person in my life that I would like to express my deepest love and appreciation for is my most precious and beautiful wife, Queen Esther. She is a very special and precious gift from God to me. And I would like to thank her for entrusting me back into the hands of God and moving out of the way so that I will be free to do the works that Christ has called me to do. She is more than a wife to me: She is my best friend, companion, confidant, sister, mother, intercessor, co-laborer, helpmeet, a great lover and a great caretaker. She is a woman with an extra-ordinary inner and outer beauty and humility and a saintly character and honor. She is truly a Proverbs 31 wife to me. And to her and to our beautiful children: Zion, Fanta, Gideon and Augusta, I would like to express my profound love and appreciation. You are most loved and cherished!

I would like to express my deepest love and gratitude to my spiritual mother, the Rev. Lola Oyebade for her wise spiritual and motherly counsel, prayers, and support, and for reading through the original manuscript and writing the foreword. I appreciate you, Mama. My deepest love and appreciation also go out to our adopted White mother, Mama Mildred Poehner for her precious love, friendship, prayers, and support.

I would also like to acknowledge the wonderful friend-ships, fellowships, prayers, and support of the following very special people in my life: Mrs. Olga Maria Moigbe and family, Deacon Desmond & Monica McCormack, Pastor Kofo Padonu, Bro. Hector & Philomena Obeng Asamoah, Pastor Phyllis Ellis, Apostle Bobby & Prophetess Teresa Hogan, Bro. Jim & Kathy Ferguson, Dr. Perry & Lori Meyer, Bro. John & Cindy Reichardst, Papa David & Tracy Ruleman, Bro. Steven & Maryann LaVine and the wonderful brethren at The Gate DC, Pastor David & Maureen Freshour, Rev. Dan C. Cummins, Apostle Jeff Johns, Pastor Pitts Evans, Dr. Corinthia Ridley Boone, Pastor Brad Wells, Apostle Emmanuel & Pastor Chiquitta Kamara, Bro. Moses & Georgette Bukenya, Bro. Saidu Bangura, Min. Mama Lorraine Boesman, Deacon Jina & Bridget Vandi, Papa Harold Jean, Bro. Wayne & Jenese Garland, Dr. Virgil Roberts, Jr., Pastor Anita Henry, members of the Bride of Christ Global Prayer and Intercessory Team, and to the Unknown Prophet.

I would also like to express my profound gratitude to all my numerous family members and friends whose names I could not possibly mention here, for all their prayers and support. Finally, I would like to thank the editorial team and publishers at Xulon Press for reviewing, editing, and publishing this book. May God bless them all!

Foreword

I t is an honor for me to write the foreword to this book, "Love Conquers the World." Reading this timely book is a reminder that in a nation that sets the pace for others to follow, a nation that gives comfort to their persecuted brethren across the world, a nation of refuge to many, the same is now faced with an unprecedented crisis. To a broken, wounded, bleeding, hurting, and divisive America, this book offers an insightful knowledge into the ancient solution and promises you a moment of understanding on the subject – Love that conquers the World.

Rev. Augustine Sengulay calls us to do the main thing, and that main thing is love. The book is explosive and very educative with facts to discover or be reminded of. That agelong wisdom and practical counsel awaits you in this book as you learn of God's heart for the world through the Church that has received love from God and is called not to owe any man anything apart from loving them.

Yes, that age-long message of Christ telling you to love your neighbor as yourself is presented in this book as God's answer to all violence and racial prejudice.

As you open this book to read it, you are about to share the burden for revival that is indeed around the corner in America.

For truly, from the book, it is sure to note that revival is around the corner in America.

The message is timely and on point for this hour! Even though written to address the timely issues in America that sure needs to experience the love of God, but then it is not only America. I believe the truth presented to you in this book cuts across the world even as you read this book from wherever you are in the world. The entire world must experience the love of God again from those who have received God's love.

Humanity is now torn apart and is in need of the love of God, and America, given her leadership role in the world, must receive love to give love as written in Love conquers All!

Thank you, Rev. Augustine, for bringing us to the central message of the Gospel which is the love of God and the love from God that conquers the world.

And as he has said, "The Cross is the bridge for racial reconciliation in America." Once America leads on the topic, it will sure affect the whole world for good.

Highly recommended! And I believe reading this book will change your mind on the issues that are causing lawlessness on our streets.

Rev. Lola Oyebade Senior Pastor
House On the Rock International Church
London, UK

Introduction

The whole world is in turmoil and in distress, and America is racially, socially, economically, and politically, broken, wounded, and hurting. America is on edge and pent-up and is facing a "perfect storm" of gigantic proportion with dark cumulonimbus clouds of racial, social, and political thunderstorms and thunderbolts rumbling over her skies with gushing winds of civil unrest and upheaval blowing across the land and dumping hailstorms of street protests, rioting, looting, shooting, burning, killing, anarchy, and lawlessness!

Not only that, but America has also become a racially, socially, culturally, politically, and denominationally divided nation and a house divided and turned against itself and up in arms against itself, with her greatest enemies being the very members of her own household. The America that is called one nation under God, indivisible and "invincible" with liberty and justice for all has now become a nation under many competing and confusing gods and goddesses, patrons, and matrons, divisible and "vincible" with partisan politics and racial and social injustices for many!

The land of the free and of the brave has now become the land of her own slaves and of her own demise and of her own grave prepared by her own politicians and physicians and sounding her own death knell. America has become her own very existential threat! The Lord Jesus has said that a house divided against itself cannot stand, and America is not only a house that is already divided against itself, but it is also a house that has turned against itself, and up in arms against its own, and is already standing on a precipice, tilting precariously.

America is now a broken and divided nation. The center can no longer hold, and things are falling apart because her biblical, godly, spiritual, and moral foundations have been broken and destroyed. As a result, America is now a nation that is tottering in her steps and stuttering in her speech and is losing both her national and global equilibrium!

Racism and the race issue, especially in America, has become highly sensitized, highly politicized, highly divisive, highly polarized, highly antagonized, highly volatile, and highly explosive! The racial, social, and political atmospheric tension is densely saturated with a thick smog of offenses, hurts, pain, anger, hatred, bitterness, resentments, hostilities, divisions, disunities, polarizations, distrusts, intolerance, grudges, unforgiveness, and revenge. Great fears and anxieties have gripped the hearts and minds and homes of many.

And it is as if Lucifer, the Devil himself, has landed on the American soil and has put both feet on America's neck, and America is being racially, socially, politically, economically, and spiritually asphyxiated, and is gasping for breath! It seems as if the poem by Emma Lazarus at the base of the Statue of Liberty in New York that says, *"Give me your tired, your poor, your huddled masses yearning to breathe free,"*[1] and the final heartbreaking words of George Floyd, "I can't breathe," are, to me, spiritually speaking, symbolic and symptomatic of the state of condition of our nation.

America is referred to as a melting pot that is supposed to have melted and blended all the different cultures and races and colors of people into one homogeneous nation. However, it seems as if that melting pot that once held us as "One nation under God, indivisible with liberty and justice for all" has now become a boiling cauldron seething with racial, social, cultural, and political tensions, civil unrest, strife, divisions, and polarization. This melting pot has become like a pressurized cooker and it seems as if the tragic death of George Floyd in particular, was like a tipping point that has lifted off the lid from that pressure cooker and a violent steam of rage, anger, bitterness, resentment, and hatred was vented out and spewed into our streets, communities, and cities all across America.

It is as if the enemy has thrust a sharp double-edged sword deep inside the very soul of our nation and many lives, homes, families, marriages, communities, neighborhoods, cities, the police, the government, and our nation as a whole are deeply broken, wounded, hurting, and divided.

And only JESUS can crush that serpent's head and thrust the devil's feet off the neck of America and breathe upon her a fresh breath of life to revive her so that she might breathe and live once again, yet for a season and for a time. And that is, if she repents and returns back to the God who founded her and crowned her with beauty for His glory as a beacon of light and hope to the world to proclaim freedom, liberty, and justice for all and to all!

The Background to The Writing of This Book

The writing of this book came about by divine revelation and inspiration from God Himself. In 2015, the LORD woke me up one night to pray and then He began to deal with me about the issue of racism and all its attendants racial, social, societal, economic, educational, and political injustices, inhumanities, inequalities, and discrimination; its generational effects especially on the Blacks; its effects on the race relations in America especially between Blacks and Whites and other people of color; its effects on society, the government, politics, the economy, education, our nation, the world, and on humanity as a whole.

Moreover, the LORD showed me the hatred, anger, bitterness, grudges, resentments, offenses, unforgiveness, and the racial, social, and political tensions that are dividing and destroying America. But at the same time the LORD also showed me how He wants to bring a revival of love and healing and reconciliation in America. And as the LORD was laying these things in my heart, He began to fill my spirit with divine revelation and heavenly download, and then He breathed this book in my spirit for me to write.

And then in 2017, the LORD gave me a dream in which He showed me an explosion of racial, social, and political tensions and civil unrest coming to America. In the dream He brought me in front of a young Black African American man who was filled with rage and anger, hatred, resentment, bitterness, revenge, and murder.

He was very angry about all the racism and racial, social, and political injustices and inequalities in America. And then he said to me that the only answer and solution to all these problems is war. I told him that war is not the answer, but that love is the answer, and that Jesus is the answer. And when I said that to him, he then dragged out a huge luggage bag and dropped it in front of me, and pointing at it, he said to me very angrily that this is the only answer to the problems in America.

And when I looked inside the bag, it was full of all kinds of weapons, including guns and machetes.

And then in the dream, something supernatural happened. I felt the power of God coming upon me, and I bent over and picked up the bag full of weapons. And with some supernatural power, I broke them into pieces with my bare hands and threw them to the ground. I then said to him that there is no need for any more bloodbath because much blood has already been shed, and that it must stop now. I told him war is not the answer, but that love is the answer. He protested and shouted at me that war is the answer! I told him no, love is the answer.

As we were going back and forth, suddenly, I was overwhelmed by some kind of a strange supernatural love and compassion for him. And I began to share with him about the love of God as demonstrated through His Son Jesus Christ on the Cross. I told him how God loves him, and how that love is the only answer for racial, political, and societal healing and reconciliation in America and in the world.

I told him that all that is needed is a change of heart. I said to him that he may not understand what I am saying to him right now, but that there is coming a great revival in America that is going to change the hearts of the Blacks and the hearts of the Whites, and the hearts of all the other races and colors of people, and that God is going to bring healing, restoration, and reconciliation. I told him that this is the reason why God has brought us to Washington, DC.

And as I was sharing the love of God with him, suddenly, something supernatural happened. The power of the love of God came upon him and he started weeping as God began to break and to melt his heart and taking away all the anger, rage, hatred, bitterness, resentment, unforgiveness, revenge, and murder.

The power of the love of God instantly healed him and set him totally free, and there was a sudden change in his countenance. A supernatural healing and deliverance and transformation has taken place in his heart and he was filled with God's love, joy, and peace with a bright smile radiating in his face. And then with tears in his eyes, he said to me that yes indeed, that love is the answer, and that Jesus is the answer.

And then he told me something incredible that only God could have revealed that to him. He said to me that by the way, the book that God has given me to write is going to be very powerful. I knew immediately that he was referring to this very book. I was amazed when he said that, because in the dream I did not tell him anything about the book.

I woke up from that dream knowing fully well without a shadow of a doubt that this is God revealing and confirming these things to me and directing me to write this book.

And then came 2020, the perfect storm began. We began to see the explosion of racial, social, and political tensions and civil unrest with nationwide protests, rioting, looting, burning, toppling, shooting, killing, anarchy, and lawlessness, just as the LORD showed me. It was then that the LORD told me that now is the time to write and to publish this book.

And as I started writing, something happened. The LORD brought back to my remembrance the dream about the young African American man. In that dream, He showed me the outward manifestations of the anger, rage, hatred, bitterness, resentment, unforgiveness, revenge, and murder that was coming out of him. But now, as I was sitting right in front of my computer writing, the LORD opened my spiritual eyes and began to show me the inside of this young Black man's heart. And what He showed me, crushed my heart! God showed me how this young

Black man's heart has been badly broken, crushed, bruised, wounded, and deeply hurting on the inside!

The LORD then said to me that this young Black man represents the vast majority of the African American people that have gone through centuries of deep physical, emotional, mental, psychological, racial, social, economic, educational, and political injustices, inhumanities, inequalities, and discrimination. He showed me that many of them are deeply broken, crushed, bruised, wounded, hurting, angry, and offended deep down on the inside because of the centuries of slavery, racial segregation, institutional racism, racial injustices, discrimination, and inequalities that began since the time of slavery in America.

And God showed me that all of these pain, hurts, wounds, anger, and offenses have become generational in them; and that they have been passing it on to their children generation after generation, and that they have not yet been totally healed and set free. And when the LORD showed me these things, it crushed and broke my heart, and I literally wept in front of my computer, because it was as if I could feel the hurt and the pain deep down inside me. I wept just as Jesus wept for His friend Lazarus who had died.

And what the LORD told me about these things becoming a generational stronghold that has been passed on from generation to generation is true. I myself have actually come across many African Americans who are carrying these pain, wounds, hurts, anger, and offenses deep down inside them. They have told me that they are even teaching and passing on these things to their children. This is how deeply broken, wounded, and hurting the Blacks are, and how deeply divided America is! And no government or politician or man is able to heal these wounds but God alone!

But then the LORD took me even further and deeper and began to show me other kinds of injustices and inhumanities being perpetrated not only in America, but all over the world. He showed me sexual injustices, political injustices, religious injustices, economic injustices, social injustices, human trafficking, sex trafficking, organ trafficking, modern day slavery, abortion, and many other societal and global injustices and inhumanities.

He showed me how sin, evil, wickedness, immoralities, perversions, hatred, violence, terrorism, and lawlessness have taken over the world because the love and affection of men have grown cold, and their hearts have become evil and wicked just like in the days of Noah.

God showed me how the lives of millions and even billions of men, women, and children are broken, wounded, bruised, hurting, voiceless, powerless, helpless, and hopeless and are crying for help, and how He has heard their cry and is going to send a revival of love, healing, restoration, salvation, deliverance, reconciliation, justice, freedom, peace and unity!

I was very heartbroken when the LORD showed me all these things. And for me, it was like when God appeared to Moses on Mount Horeb and said to him:

"I have surely seen the oppression of My people who are in Egypt, and have heard their cry because of their taskmasters, for I know their sorrows. So, I have come down to deliver them out of the hand of the Egyptians, and to bring them up from that land to a good and large land; to a land flowing with milk and honey...Now therefore, behold, the cry of the children of Israel has come to Me, and I have also seen the oppression with which the Egyptians oppress them. Come now, therefore, and I will send you to Pharaoh that you may bring My people, the children of Israel, out of Egypt." (Exodus 3:7-10 NKJV)

Today figuratively and spiritually speaking, the whole wide world is referred as "spiritual Egypt," in which the devil is holding millions and billions of souls in slavery and bondage and oppression. And that is where God is sending me with His message of His conquering and redeeming love to deliver His children that are being oppressed and held in bondage and captivity by sin and by the devil in every nation, and tongue, and tribe, and people, and race!

The background and timeliness of this book and its message of love is further supported by the fact that my first ever divine encounter with God as a 4 to 6 years old child was with His love. I grew up in abject poverty and hatred, rejection, hurts, and trauma as a child. And I remember when out of sheer hatred one of my older stepbrothers landed a vicious kick on one of my legs and broke it. I dropped to the floor and fainted, and unable to cry because of the impact of that kick and the excruciating pain that was going through my tiny body. It was then that my dad came and carried me on his back to the hospital that was just about three blocks away.

But as he was carrying me on his back, something happened. Suddenly, all the excruciating pain that I was experiencing seemed to have left me, and deep down inside me I started crying for a father's love, of which I have never experienced as a child, and I was desperately yearning for it. I thought my dad would hear my cry from deep down inside my broken, wounded, hurting, rejected, hated, and traumatized childhood heart. But he never did!

Shortly after that, the next traumatic thing in my life as a child was me standing in front of my dad's dead and lifeless body in a coffin. He died never hearing my cry for a father's love.

At that time, I didn't know anything about God whether He existed or not. My mother was a leper and we have never been to a church. But then, it was shortly after these two traumatic childhood events in my life that one night, I had a dream. It was the first ever memorable dream that I had as a child.

And in that dream, I found myself being carried high up into the heavens above in the tender, loving, caring arms of some supernatural being that I did not know. He was rocking me back and forth as a parent would rock a child. He cuddled me close to His heart, and when He did, I then felt what seems like bolts of electricity going through me. I felt a surge of warm currents of love like electricity being transmitted from His heart and flowing into my tiny body.

And then suddenly, without Him saying a word to me, I was instantly filled with His love, and with the divine revelation knowledge of God, and I immediately knew that it was God. He didn't say a word to me, but His love spoke and spilled trillions of eternal life-giving and heart-comforting words into my spirit and soul and gave me meaning for life and reason for living!

And I woke up from that dream knowing without any shadow of a doubt that God has revealed Himself to me as a tender, loving, and caring Father. Even though my earthly dad did not hear my cry, but my heavenly Father heard my secret cry for a father's love, and He answered me. And He revealed Himself to me and showed me His love and acceptance at a time when I was being hated, rejected, and traumatized as a child.

And so, the first ever divine revelation and supernatural experience that I have of God as a traumatized, wounded, hurting, hated, and rejected child was with His amazing heavenly Father's love. And that first deposit and experience of His love and revelation knowledge has never left me ever since. He still carries me in His tender, loving, caring arms and has never dropped nor abandoned nor forsaken me!

And this is that same tender, loving, and caring God and heavenly Father who has heard your cry for a father's love, and for justice, and freedom, and who wants to carry you in His tender, loving, caring, and healing arms. For in His hands, He's got the whole wide world!

Not only that, but also the first message that God ever gave me to preach as a child of about 10-12 years old was about His love as demonstrated through His Son Jesus Christ on the Cross. And now the first book that He has ever given me to write is again about His love. And for me, these things are not mere random probabilities or coincidences, but rather, they are the unveiling and unfolding of the perfect plans and purposes and divine timing of God.

The Purpose for Writing This Book

"LOVE CONQUERS THE WORLD," is about the all-powerful, all-conquering, all-redeeming, all-healing, all-reconciling, and all-life giving Love of GOD that is the only answer for all our racial, social, societal, cultural, political, moral, and spiritual problems in America and in the world!

The book is not a historical discuss or a chronological narrative about these racial, social, societal, cultural, and political issues which have already been written about, taught about, talked about, debated about, campaigned about, legislated about, adjudicated about, protested about, and rioted about.

Rather, the writer takes a different approach by addressing these societal issues with the all-conquering and all-redeeming Love of GOD that is the only answer and solution that can bring about a radical life-changing spiritual, moral, racial, societal, cultural, political, governmental, national, and global transformation and reformation, with great conviction, repentance, forgiveness, healing, deliverance, salvation, restoration, reconciliation, justice, freedom, peace, joy, unity, hope, and comfort to our deeply broken, wounded, hurting, and divided America and the world!

It is against this backdrop therefore, that the book addresses the scourge of racism and the cancer of hatred and all their attendant evils of racial, social, societal, economic, educational, political, and religious injustices, inhumanities, inequalities, and discrimination being perpetrated against all races and all colors of people not only in America, but all around the world.

The book addresses the cry of all those who have suffered from all kinds of racial, tribal, ethnic, social, societal, political, and religious injustices and inhumanities being perpetrated against them simply because they are of another race, or skin color, or tribe, or ethnicity, or nationality, or religion, or creed, or politics, or age, or gender, or because of their status or fetus in society.

It is in response to the cry of all the vulnerable, helpless, powerless, and voiceless voices who have been oppressed, suppressed, repressed, depressed and brokenhearted, shattered, battered, crushed, abused, bruised, molested, shamed, violated, hated, rejected, wounded, and hurting arising from every home, every street corner, every ghetto, every slum, every village, every neighborhood, every town, every city, every nation, every continent, every island, and from the uttermost ends of the earth to God! Their cries have reached the ears of God, and have touched the heart of God, and have moved the hand of God!

The book also addresses the great racial, societal, and political rifts and deep fractures as well as the deep-seated hurts, wounds, pain, hatred, anger, bitterness, resentments, offenses, malice, grudges, intolerance, unforgiveness, and revenge plaguing our nation with violent eruptions of civil unrest.

Of course, these racial, social, and societal issues of injustices and inhumanities are not unique solely to America. They are even far worse in other parts of the world. However, America, of all nations on planet earth, stands more accountable before Almighty God, and has been weighed in the balances and found wanting! And this is because America was founded and called by God to be a beacon of light and of hope to the whole world to proclaim freedom, liberty, justice, and equality to all! The Lord Jesus said that to whom much is given much is required. And much has been given to America, and much will be required of America! This is the guilt of America before Almighty God, and unless she repents, otherwise!

Therefore, it is for such a time as this when there is so much racism, hatred, offenses, anger, resentments, bitterness, intolerance, revenge, unforgiveness, brokenness, wounds, hurts, pain, sufferings, distress, fears, anxieties, perplexities, uncertainties, and confusions all over. It is for such a time as this when there are rising tidal waves of racial, social, societal, cultural, religious, ethnic, tribal, national, and global tensions.

And it is for such a time as this when there is a global pandemic and pandemonium with economic meltdowns, COVID-19 lock-downs, shutdowns, isolations, emotional breakdowns, mental breakdowns, psychological breakdowns, family breakdowns, governmental breakdowns, societal breakdowns, with a sense of helplessness and hopelessness all happening at the same time in our nation and around the world, that God has seen it fit for me to write this book and its message of His conquering and redeeming love to go out all across America and to the nations of the world to bring healing, restoration, reconciliation, deliverance, salvation, peace, unity, joy, freedom, liberty, justice, comfort, and hope to all peoples!

And I believe that in the midst of this perfect storm facing our nation and the world is also the perfect hour and the perfect timing for the Church of Jesus Christ to arise and shine, for her light has come, and the glory of the LORD is risen upon her. For behold, the darkness has covered the earth, and gross darkness the people. But the LORD will now arise over her, and the glory of the LORD will be seen upon her, and the nations and kings, and sons and daughters will come running to the brightness of her light! (Isaiah 60:1-3)

And that is why the message in this book is to help bring about God's healing, salvation, deliverance, restoration, peace, unity, reconciliation, love, joy, freedom, hope and comfort to the broken and hurting hearts, broken and hurting lives, broken and hurting marriages, broken and hurting families, broken and hurting homes, broken and hurting communities, broken and hurting societies, broken and hurting governments, broken and hurting America, and to a broken and hurting world!

Therefore, in this book, people are going to discover the origin of racism and of all evil. They will discover how that racism is not a Black and White or a race or skin color problem but a heart and a sin problem. Readers will learn about the original Equality Act of God for Mankind and of the commonalities of the human race and how all the races and languages came about, and the importance of words in our communications and race relations.

People will learn why the Blacks are not yet free and what are the root causes for the continuing racial, social and political tensions and civil unrest in America. With a national and global cry for freedom, justice, and love, readers will discover what is true freedom, what is true justice, and what is true love.

They will learn how that it is love that conquers the world and the hearts of all men, and how love is the antidote and panacea for all evils, hatred, racism, and injustices.

They will discover how love is the answer for racial, societal, political, and national healing and restoration.

People will learn about the power of unconditional love and forgiveness and how and why America and the rest of the world desperately need unconditional love and forgiveness. They will learn how God wants to send us a revival of love to heal our racially, socially, economically, politically, denominationally, and morally broken, wounded, hurting, and divided nation and the nations of the world, and much more!

Since God deals with the heart of all men, and since the problem of mankind is a sin problem of the heart, therefore the message of this book is a heart-to-heart message from the heart of God the Father to the hearts of all men through His only begotten Son Jesus Christ, the Savior of the world!

Therefore, do not judge this book by its color, but by the contents of its message; and do not judge the author by his race or the color of his skin, but by the content of his character. Therefore, I would encourage you to lower your guards and lay aside any preconceived idea or perceptions for a moment, and with an open mind and a humble heart, glean through the wheats of truths in this book and see how it will end up with you.

My earnest prayer for you is that as you read through the pages of this book and digest its message, that you will experience a personal divine encounter with the supernatural power of the love of God and with the God of love Himself that will radically change your life forever!

I strongly believe that God is able and willing to do what He has promised, and that is why He has asked me to write this book for such a time as this. And I believe that God is going to use this book and its message of love as a harbinger of His coming revival in America and in the world because love is the very heartbeat of God toward all mankind: "For God so loved the world!" And because love is the central message of the Gospel: "That He gave His only begotten Son!" And because love is the redeeming message to a sinful, fallen, broken, wounded, hurting, and a lost world: "That whosoever believes in Him shall not perish, but shall have everlasting life!"

This is our only hope for America and for the world. And this alone can bring about a genuine and lasting inward and outward supernatural, spiritual, moral, ethical, racial, social, societal, economic, cultural, educational, political, governmental, national, and a worldwide revival, transformation, reformation, healing, restoration, reconciliation, peace, unity and a great awakening in America and in the world.

CHAPTER ONE

Tracing The Origin Of Racism And Of All Evil

I have observed that when people talk about racism, they always see it as a Black and a White thing or something that is between the races and colors of people, but they never go beyond that to try and find out the real root causes and origin of racism. And I think it is very important that if we want to fight racism and all other racial and societal injustices, inequalities, discrimination, and inhumanities not only in America but also around the world, then we must try to understand the origin of racism and of all evil because racism is just one evil among a plethora of evils in our societies and in the world.

Militarily and spiritually speaking, you cannot effectively fight an enemy that you don't know much about or that you don't have some strategic knowledge and intelligence information about. This is the same principle whether you are fighting a spiritual or a military warfare. We must first know our enemy and then choose our fight. That is why in this first chapter of the book, we are going to unmask the devil who is enemy number one of the entire human race, and then trace the origin of racism, hatred, and of all evil.

Racism and the race problem, especially in America, has become highly sensitized, highly politicized, highly polarized, highly divisive, highly antagonized, highly volatile, and highly explosive. It has even become a political race and campaign card for our politicians and activists. Racism seems as if it is something that has been pitched especially between Blacks and Whites. And sadly enough, many people have bought into that myth and fallacy, thinking or believing that the race issue is a Black and White or a race or a skin color problem. But I beg to differ and politely ask to dismiss this myth and fallacy that has been diffused for centuries.

That is why one of the aims of this book is to expose and to dispel this ancient lies and fallacies about racism as being a Black and a White, or a race or a skin color thing. Racism in America, and in any other part of the world for that matter, is not a Black and White thing, or a race or skin color problem. This is a myth that has been sold and bought wholesomely and gullibly swallowed and has falsely pitched races against each other for centuries and must be exposed and be dispelled now.

For centuries and millennia, the devil has been throwing this bait into the sea of humanity and societies, and many have gullibly or ignorantly swallowed that bait wholesomely, hook, line, and sinker. By exposing and dismissing this myth and misconception will help set people free from this racial, emotional, mental, psychological, cultural, societal, and political stronghold and entanglement that has been strangulating our societies and nations for centuries. Exposing and dispelling this myth will help people to understand that racism is not a Black and White thing, nor is it a White against the Black thing. Neither is racism a race or a skin color thing.

Now, I know this may sound like a bombshell to many minds and intellectual reasonings. And it is indeed a bombshell exploding with the truth that will set people free. If racism is to be defeated and sent back to the bottomless pit of hell from where it came from, then someone must be willing to not only take the bull by its horns, but to confront the devil himself right up in his face. And that is exactly what I intend doing in this book and in life! For it is only the eye of childhood that fears a painted and a defeated devil! And Satan is a painted and an already defeated devil masquerading around like a wounded, hungry, and angry roaring lion seeking whom he may devour. As it is said, a hungry man is an angry man, and so is the devil! He has been devouring the human race for too long and must be stopped with the truth that sets free! Woe unto the inhabitants of the earth and of the sea! For the devil is come down unto you having great wrath, because he knows that his days are numbered! (Revelation 12:12)

I strongly believe that if we are to fight and defeat the evil scourge of racism and the cancer of hatred and all other societal injustices and inhumanities, the first place to start is when all the races: Blacks, Whites, Native Indians, Hispanics, Africans, Europeans, Asians, Jews, Arabs, Chinese, and all the other races of people come together and have a common understanding that racism is not a Black and White, nor a race or skin color problem. Only then will they have a common ground to stand to fight against a common cause and against a common enemy. The Bible says, *"My people are destroyed for lack of knowledge, because you have rejected knowledge."* (Hosea 4:6 NKJV)

Indeed, ignorance destroys! And that is why in this first chapter of the book, we are going to talk about the evil origin of racism and of all evils, and how it all started with the devil in heaven, and how it is a spiritual thing and not a social, cultural, or political thing. In this chapter, we are going to discover how racism is not a Black and White thing or a race or skin color thing, but a heart and a sin problem thing that has been affecting the entire human race over six thousand years since the fall of Adam. Let us understand that racism is not as recent but as ancient as the devil!

The Fall of Satan

Let me start by making this indictment upfront, that Lucifer, also known as Satan and the devil, is the originator of racism and of all evils and injustices and inhumanities in the world! The devil is a sinner, racist, rapist, supremacist, and is the father of racism and supremacy and of all other evils!

The Bible says that the devil is a thief, a liar, a deceiver, a hater, a murderer, and a destroyer, and is the father of them all!

But remember though, the devil was never created like that in the very beginning. In fact, he was never called a devil or Satan when God first created him. His original created name was Lucifer, which, in the original Hebrew word means, "shining one." His name means "a light-bearer." He was created perfect, with no sin in him. But pride, arrogance, envy, jealousy, and ambition caused him to sin and fall from grace to disgrace and to racism.

Here is how the Bible describes Lucifer before he became known as Satan:

"You were the model of perfection, full of wisdom and exquisite in beauty. You were in Eden, the garden of God. Your clothing was adorned with every precious stone – red carnelian, pale-green peridot, white moonstone, blue-green beryl, onyx, green jasper, blue lapis lazuli, turquoise, and emerald – all beautifully crafted for you and set in the finest gold. They were given to you on the day you were created."

"I ordained and anointed you as the mighty angelic guardian. You had access to the holy mountain of God and walked among the stones of fire. You were blameless in all you did from the day you were created until the day evil was found in you. Your rich commerce led you to violence, and you sinned. So, I banished you in disgrace from the mountain of God. I expelled you, O mighty guardian, from your place among the stones of fire."

"Your heart was filled with pride because of all your beauty. Your wisdom was corrupted by your love of splendor. So, I threw you to the ground and exposed you to the curious gaze of kings. You defiled your sanctuary with your many sins and dishonest trade."

So, I brought fire out from within you, and it consumed you. I reduced you to ashes on the ground in the sight of all who were watching. All who knew you are appalled at your fate. You have come to a terrible end, and you will exist no more." (Ezekiel 28:12-19 NLT)

The Bible went further to say this about Lucifer:

"How you are fallen from heaven, O Lucifer, son of the morning! How you are cut down to the ground, you who weakened the nations! For you have said in your heart: 'I will ascend into heaven, I will exalt my throne above the stars of God; I will also sit on the mount of congregation on the farthest sides of the north; I will ascend above the heights of the clouds. I will be like the Most High.'"

"Yet you shall be brought down to Sheol, To the lowest depths of the pit. Those who see you will gaze at you, and consider you, saying: 'Is this the man who made the earth tremble, who shook the kingdoms, who made the world as a wilderness and destroyed its cities, who did not open the house of his prisoners?" (Isaiah 14:12-17 NKJV)

From the above two scriptural passages, we see clearly that Lucifer, who is also now called Satan and the devil, was created perfect with splendor and beauty. But the Bible says that he became prideful, arrogant, envious, jealous, ambitious, and thirsty for power and superiority over God who created him. The devil did not just want equality with God, but supremacy and superiority over God. The Bible says:

"What is causing the quarrels and fights among you? Don't they come from the evil desires at war within you? You want what you don't have, so you scheme and kill to get it. You are jealous of what others have, but you can't get it, so you fight and wage war to take it away from them. Yet you don't have what you want because you don't ask God for it. And even when you ask, you don't get it because your motives are all wrong-you want only what will give you pleasure." (James 4:1-3 NLT)

And that was exactly how the devil felt, and that was exactly what he did. He was not only dissatisfied with the way God created and positioned him, but he was also jealous and envious of God. He wanted power. He wanted to become not only like God, but wanted to be supreme and superior over God, and that became the origin of sin and of supremacy and racism and of all evil.

It is interesting to note that while Christ Jesus did not consider it robbery to be equal with God, but laid down His equality and glory and power and humbled Himself as a servant, even unto death for the sins of the world, on the contrary, Satan considered it a robbery that he was not created equal with God and so he had to fight for not only equality, but superiority and supremacy over God, and he must have it at any cost, by hook or by crook!

And here is that contrasting nature between Jesus and the devil. The apostle Paul wrote,

"You must have the same attitude that Christ Jesus had. Though He was God, He did not think of equality with God as something to cling to. Instead, He gave up His divine privileges; He took the humble position of a slave and was born as a human being. When He appeared in human form, He humbled Himself in obedience to God and died a criminal's death on a Cross. Therefore, God elevated Him to the place of highest honor and gave Him the name that is above all other names, that at the name of Jesus every knee should bow, in heaven and on the earth and under the earth, and every tongue confess that Jesus Christ is Lord, to the glory of God the Father." (Philippians 2:5-11 NLT)

What a contrast! Jesus, though God, did not think His equality with God as robbery or something to cling on to; whereas Lucifer, though created, thought his inequality with God as something to fight for. This is the origin of sin and of the spirit of hatred, racism, supremacy, superiority, and of all evil.

It is a prideful thought of self-importance and self-exaltation of oneself above another or others. It is the most preposterous, most presumptuous, and most disastrous of all pride and arrogance! And it is delusional and psychotic. It is a dissatisfaction with who one actually is and a delusion of who one is factually not. And the mental and emotional collusion of these two produces a psychological ideology of superiority or supremacy over the other or others. This is the origin of the doctrine of racial superiority, supremacy, inferiority, and inequality of the human race and of all evil.

After Satan's foiled coup in heaven, he was cast out of heaven and came down to the earth as a defeated, disappointed, discontented, disgruntled, angry, wrathful, and revengeful devil. He came down to the earth to take out his wrath and revenge on the human race. The Bible says, *"Woe to the inhabitants of the earth and of the seas! For the devil is come down unto you, having great wrath, because he knows that he hath but a short time.*" (Revelation 12:12 KJV)

And so, Satan, which means an adversary or enemy of God came down and deceived Adam and Eve with the same temptation of wanting to become like God. Just listen to the diabolical dialogue between the devil and the woman in the Garden of Eden:

"*Now the serpent was more cunning than any beast of the field which the LORD God had made. And he said to the woman, "Has God indeed said, 'You shall not eat of every tree of the garden'?" And the woman said to the serpent, "We may eat the fruit of the trees of the garden; but of the fruit of the tree which is in the midst of the garden, God has said, 'You shall not eat it, nor shall you touch it, lest you die."*

Then the serpent said to the woman, "You will not surely die. For God knows that in the day you eat of it your eyes will be opened, and you will be like God, knowing good and evil."

So, when the woman saw that the tree was good for food, that it was pleasant to the eyes, and a tree desirable to make one wise, she took of its fruit and ate. She also gave to her husband with her, and he ate. Then the eyes of both of them were opened, and they knew that they were naked; and they sewed fig leaves together and made themselves coverings."

(Genesis 3:1-7 NKJV)

Did you hear that: you will be like God? It was the very same spirit of wanting to be like God that the devil tempted the woman with. Sadly, Adam and Eve were also deceived into wanting to become like God, knowing good and evil. They ate of the forbidden fruit of the tree of the knowledge of good and evil with devastating effects to the entire human race. Like Lucifer, who fell from grace to disgrace, to racism and depravity, Adam also fell from grace to disgrace, and to racism and depravity. Thus, sin entered the human race.

Jesus said to the Jews who wanted to kill Him,

"For you are the children of your father the devil, and you love to do the evil things he does. He was a murderer from the beginning. He has always hated the truth, because there is no truth in him. When he lies, it is consistent with his character; for he is a liar and the father of lies." (John 8:44 NLT)

Furthermore, the Lord Jesus said that the devil has come not, but to steal, to kill, and to destroy. (John 10:10). Jesus calls the devil a thief, a liar, a hater, a murderer, and a destroyer of the human race. So, we now see very clearly that the devil is not only the originator of sin, racism, and of all evil, but he is also the progenitor or father of all sinners and evildoers. He is the embodiment of all evils and devils and vices. He is called the devil because he is evil and the father of it!

Racism and all other forms of racial hatred, supremacy, superiority, discrimination, segregation, prejudice, racial profiling, racial inequalities, and all other societal injustices, inhumanities, immoralities, perversions, addictions, oppressions, suppressions, repressions, and depressions are all from the devil, of the devil, and by the devil!

Darwin's Theory of Evolution of the Species and the Descent of Man

Charles Darwin's theory of the evolution of the species and natural selection also became the basis for the theory of the evolution of the ideology of the superiority and inferiority of the human races. According to Webster's New World Dictionary, racism is a doctrine or teaching, without scientific support, that claims to find racial differences in character, intelligence, etc., and that asserts the superiority of one race over another or others, and that seeks to maintain the supposed purity of a race or the races, and that racism is any program or practice of racial discrimination, segregation, etc., which is based on such beliefs.[2]

In his book, The Descent of Man, Darwin talked about the supremacy and superiority of the White race (Europeans) and the inferiority of all other races, including Australians, Mongolians, Africans, Indians, South Americans, Polynesians, and even Eskimos as "savages." He justified violent imperialism as he wrote, "From the remotest times successful tribes have supplanted other tribes...At the present-day civilized nations are everywhere supplanting barbarous nations." Darwin's theory applies survival of the fittest to human races, suggesting that extermination of non-White races is a natural consequence of white Europeans being a superior and more successful race than other races of people.[3]

It was from this scientific racism that the Atlantic Slave Trade and European conquest, colonization and imperialism started because Blacks and all other races were considered inferior, so therefore must be colonized and enslaved.

While slavery was the degradation and dehumanization of a person's or a group of peoples' self-identity and dignity, and the violation of their created and human rights, on the other hand, colonization was the deculturalization of the people colonized by their colonists. It is the destruction of the culture of the dominated group and its replacement by the culture of the dominating group.[4]

Therefore, slavery, colonialism, imperialism, and racism were all under girded and propagated by the same evil ideology of White supremacy and superiority.

Adolf Hitler's Aryan Master Race

Adolf Hitler was one of the world's most notorious eugenicists, who drew his inspiration from social Darwinism for his Aryan Master Race, which was a belief in "racial purity" and the supremacy of the Germans and other northern European people who were deemed the highest in racial hierarchy. The Nazis began to put this ideology into practice with the support of German scientists who believed that the human race could be improved by limiting the reproduction of people considered "inferior." Forced sterilizations and operations were performed, making it impossible for victims to have children. The elderly, the blind, the deaf, the mentally and physically handicapped, the Gypsies, Jews, Africans, and other races of people were defined as being racially inferior and non-Aryan and were thus considered to be a danger to the Aryan or Germanic master race.[5]

And I want to personally believe that this ideology of the purity of the races and the purging of the undesirable ones might have led to the holocaust which saw the cold-blooded massacre of over six million Jews and others.

Margaret Sanger's Planned Parenthood

It is from this same set of beliefs and practices of eugenics that aimed to improve the genetic quality of a human population, historically, by excluding people and groups judged to be inferior and promoting those judged to be superior that Planned Parenthood was founded by Margaret Sanger, who was believed to have been a eugenicist and a racist.[6]

And all other supremacist and racist groups have their origin from these doctrines and ideologies. The Civil War in America was fought over slavery. The Jim Crow laws were racist laws of oppression against the Blacks in America. For how can two races be equal but then one is segregated and discriminated against? Apartheid in South Africa was a racist institution and instrument against Black Africans. As we have seen, the devil is the originator of racism and of all evils. The doctrines and ideologies of racism, racial inequalities, racial inferiority, colonialism, imperialism, eugenics, etc., are all supported by the idea and belief of White supremacy and superiority. But racism is a much deeper and more complex thing. Its root cause is spirit and is spiritual. Over the past centuries, it has evolved into so many diverse racial stratifications and classifications and has spread out its tentacles to include racial hatred, racial discrimination, racial segregation, racial profiling, racial inequalities, racial injustices, anti-Semitism, apartheid, xenophobia, genocides, ethnic cleansing, euthanasia, infanticide, terrorism, sex trafficking, human slavery, etc.

But what I have found even more troubling is the fact that this ideology of racial supremacy, superiority, and inferiority are all concepts that are deeply embedded in the minds and hearts of people. And this is because for centuries, these doctrines and ideologies have been taught in the dormitories and corridors of our schools and universities, and they have been inculcated, indoctrinated, institutionalized, politicized, formalized, and normalized in our cultures and societies.

Our cultures and generations of children have been taught, especially the racial superiority of the White race and the inferiority of the Black and other races. It is deeply seated in the hearts, minds, thinking, and the psychology of people. Therefore, racism is an indelible mental and psychological tattoo and a societal taboo that has stained the minds of the oppressed and the oppressors alike, which tattoo, and taboo can only be eradicated by the blood of Jesus Christ and by the supernatural transformation of the heart and the renewing of the mind.

Racism is a spiritual, mental, psychological, and emotional stronghold. And I would like to believe this was what the late Bob Marley had in mind when he sang, "Redemption Song" urging people to *"Emancipate yourselves from mental slavery -None but ourselves can free our minds."*[7] Jamaica itself was a slave colony. Unfortunately, man is not capable of emancipating himself from any spiritual, mental, emotional, or psychological slavery. Only Jesus can!

But even more so, racism is a spiritual thing with a spirit entity behind it – Satan. This is what makes it very difficult to fight racism by just using human means. And that is why the only way to eradicate racism and hatred in our society is to first eradicate it from the hearts and minds and psychology of the people. And that can only happen by the supernatural transformation and reformation of the heart and the renewal of the mind through the conquering and redeeming love of God.

There is no superiority, inferiority, or inequality of the human race in love, and there is no racism or racial discrimination in love. That is why the apostle John wrote and said,

"Dear children, do not any one lead you astray. He who does what is right is righteous, just as He is righteous. He who does what is sinful is of the devil, because the devil has been sinning from the beginning. The reason why the Son of God appeared was to destroy the devil's work. No one who is born of God will continue to sin, because God's seed remains in him; he cannot go on sinning, because he has been born of God. This is how we know who the children of God are and who the children

of the devil are: Anyone who does not do what is right is not a child of God; nor is anyone who does not love his brother.

This is the message you heard from the beginning: We should love one another. Do not be like Cain, who belonged to the evil one and murdered his brother... Anyone who does not love his brother remains in death. Anyone who hates his brother is a murderer, and you know that no murderer has eternal life in him." (1 John 3:7-15 NIV)

The Bible further states that, *"If someone says, "I love God," and hates his brother, he is a liar; for he who does not love his brother whom he has seen, how can he love God whom he has not seen? And this commandment we have from Him: that he who loves God must love his brother also!"* (1 John 4:20-21 NKJV)

From the above scriptural passages, we see that the Bible clearly states that anyone who does not love his fellow human being is a hater, a racist, and a murderer. To not love is injustice in itself because love is justice. Racism is a crime against humanity and against God who created all men equal in His own image and likeness out of love! The Bible says for us not to think of ourselves more highly than others: *"For I say, through the grace given to me, to everyone who is among you, not to think of himself more highly than he ought to think, but to think soberly, as God has dealt to each one a measure of faith."* (Romans 12:3 NKJV)

Do we now see how that Satan is not only the originator but also the embodiment of sin, racism, supremacy, pride, hatred, lie, murder, theft, and of all other evils, wickedness, injustices, and inhumanities in the world? Therefore, racism is a much bigger and complex problem than we think. It is not just a Black and White thing, neither is it a political thing.

Racism is a Luciferian spirit bearing the mark of the devil himself! Therefore, when we talk about fighting racism and all other societal injustices and inhumanities, we are talking about fighting a spiritual battle with the devil himself and his wicked world system. The Bible refers to Satan as the god and ruler of this world:

"If the Good News we preach is hidden behind a veil, it is hidden only from people who are perishing. Satan, who is the god of this world, has blinded the minds of those who don't believe. They are unable to see the glorious light of the Good News. They don't understand this message about the glory of Christ, who is the exact likeness of God." (2Corinthians 4:3-4 NLT)

Indeed, the devil, who is the god of this world, has deceived and blinded the eyes and minds of many to The Original Equality Act of God and to the commonalities and dignity of the human race. In direct opposition to God's Original Equality Act for the human race, the devil has injected his own doctrines of racism and racial supremacy, superiority, inferiority, inequality, hatred, disunity, discrimination, injustice, inhumanity and all other evils.

Racism is "hate-ism." And unfortunately, the flames of racism and of hatred, especially in America, are being fanned by politicians and the main-stream media. But behind it all stands an unseen spiritual force that is playing the diabolical chords of racism and hatred to which many are made to unwittingly listen and dance to. The devil himself is the DJ and spin master!

CHAPTER TWO

Racism Is Not A Black And White Or A Race Or Skin Color Problem But A Sin And A Heart Problem

R acism is not a Black a White, or a race, or a skin color problem. Rather, racism is a sin problem and not a skin problem. It is a heart problem and not a race problem. Again, according to Webster's New World Dictionary, racism is a doctrine or teaching, without scientific support, that claims to find racial differences in character, intelligence, etc., and that asserts the superiority of one race over another or others, and that seeks to maintain the supposed purity of a race or the races, and that racism is any program or practice of racial discrimination, segregation, etc., which is based on such beliefs.[8]

It is true that the doctrine of racism that claims to find racial differences in character, intelligence, etc., and asserts the superiority of one race over another or others, and the inferiority of one race to another or others, cannot be scientifically proven or measured. And this is because racism is a sin problem and not a skin or a race problem, and sin cannot be scientifically measured because it is spiritual with a spirit entity behind it- Satan!

Sin is found deep down inside the heart of man where it is conceived, concealed, incubated, hatched, and dispatched to commit evil. That is why in Shakespeare's "Macbeth," King Duncan said that "There's no art to find the mind's construction in the face. He was a gentleman on whom I built my absolute trust."[9]

In other words, King Duncan is saying that there is no skill or technique to tell what lies deep down inside a man's heart and mind or what he is thinking just by looking at him. Even man himself sometimes finds it difficult or impossible to know exactly what lies deep down inside his own heart. It takes only the all-knowing and the all-seeing Omniscient God, who alone sees and knows the true state and condition of the heart of man and his thoughts, motives, intents, and their outcomes.

The Wickedness of the Heart of Man

God Himself has said this about the heart of man, that: *"The human heart is the most deceitful of all things, and desperately wicked. Who really knows how bad it is? But I, the LORD, search all hearts and examines secret motives. I give all people their due rewards, according to what their actions deserve."* (Jeremiah 17:9-10 NLT)

There is nothing hidden from God. He knows every thought and motive and intent of the heart. The Bible says, *"And God saw that the wickedness of man was great in the earth, and that every imagination of the thoughts of his heart was only evil continually."* (Genesis 6:5 KJV)

The depraved and sinful heart of man has become the factory of all evil imaginations, machinations, motivations, intentions, and inventions. And racism is an evil imagination, machination, invention, and intention of the thoughts of the heart of man. Therefore, racism is a sin problem and not a skin problem, and it is a heart problem and not a race problem. Racism is an ungodly, unjust, unrighteous, and inhumane evil spewed from the very bottomless pit of hell and deposited into the depraved and evil imaginations and thoughts of the hearts of men! The assertion of supremacy and superiority of one race to another or others is a hellish, devilish, demonic, diabolic, and satanic doctrine. And its evil tentacles have spread out to include all kinds of racial and societal hatred, racial prejudice, racial discrimination, racial segregation, racial profiling, racial inequalities, racial stratifications, racial experimentation, racial colonization, racial imperialism, racial repression, racial oppression, racial suppression, racial injustices, racial inhumanities, racial wars, racial slavery, racial holocaust, racial apartheid, racial genocides, racial ethnic cleansing, political, social, religious oppressions and persecutions, human trafficking, sex trafficking, etc.. It is a plethora of evils!

Therefore, when we talk about racism, it is not just a Black or White or Brown or Red or an American thing. It is a sin problem and a heart problem of the human race and it is a global cancer of society. And that is why, in spite of all the huge leaps and bounds in our educational, intellectual, scientific, technological, economic, political, cultural, and societal advancements and achievements, modern man is still spiritually, morally, ethically, mentally, emotionally, and psychologically bankrupt, deficient and insufficient! Otherwise, we would not be dealing with racism and societal injustices and inhumanities in this our 21st-century modern world.

The heart of modern man is no different from the heart of the heathens or savages. They all have the same heart infected with the leprosy of sin! While the brain of the modern man has advanced and progressed more intellectually, scientifically, and technologically, however, his heart has continued to degenerate and degrade into a spiritual, moral, and ethical decadence. Even the Lord Jesus has said that sin will continue to increase and the love of many will grow cold: *"And because lawlessness will abound, the love of many will grow cold."* (Matthew 24:12 NKJV) And a heart that has grown cold in love is a breeding and spawning ground for the infestation and manifestation of all sins and evils and devils and vices!

Jesus even went deeper to say that it is not what goes in a person's belly that corrupts him, but what comes out of his heart is what corrupts him: *"Do you not perceive that whatever enters a man from outside cannot defile him, because it does not enter his heart but his stomach, and is eliminated, thus purifying all foods? And He said, "What comes out of a man, that defiles a man. For from within, out of the heart of men, proceed evil thoughts, adulteries, fornications, murders, thefts, covetousness, wickedness, deceit, lewdness, an evil eye, blasphemy, pride, foolishness. All these evil things come from within and defile a man."* (Mark 7:18-23 NKJV)

Do you now see how that the heart of man is where all sins and evils are conceived, incubated, hatched, and dispatched to commit wickedness? And racism is a sin and an evil. It is not a skin problem but a sin problem, neither is it a race problem but a heart problem. Therefore, what needs to change is the heart of man and not the skin color of man. What mankind desperately need is a spiritual heart-transplant with transformation and reformation. The heart of man is sinful and spiritually degenerate, morally depraved, and desperately wicked! Therefore, the heart of man cannot be modernized nor improved upon by any scientific, technological, intellectual, cultural, or political advancements. What the heart of man desperately needs is a spiritual and moral revolution, regeneration, and renewal. And this can only happen by the washing and cleansing power of the blood of Jesus Christ and by the infusion of God's love!

Having lived in three continents of the world: Africa, Europe, and North America, I have come to understand that the race problem is a very complex and intricate one. I have come to discover that there is racism in every culture and in every race of people all over the world. There is no culture, or race, or tribe, or tongue, or people, or nation where there is not found some form of racism, prejudice, discrimination, tribalism, nationalism, and even xenophobia.

I have even come to discover that there is racism not only between the races, but also within the races. And by this, I mean there is racism among Blacks, Whites, Browns, Reds, etc. In fact, I myself have personally experienced some form of racism and tribalism in my life, both in Africa, Europe, and in America. It is a sin and a heart problem and not a skin or a race problem.

It is the Heart of Man that Needs Changing and not One's Race or Skin Color!

And so, what God requires is a change of the heart and not a change of one's race or skin color. God has said, *"Can an Ethiopian change the color of his skin? Can a leopard take away its spots?"* (Jeremiah 13:23 NLT) The answer is no, because both the Ethiopian and the leopard were created that way by God. In other words, God is saying that just as it is impossible for the Ethiopian to change his race and skin color, and the leopard its spots, so also it is impossible to change one's race and skin color.

God is saying that you cannot change your race and the color of your skin, but you can change the color of your heart that has been stained and darkened by sin. And only the blood of Jesus is able to do that. All hearts of men need to go through the deep cleansing blood of Jesus Christ, the Redeeming Lamb of God! Even as your dentals need some deep cleaning and you go see your dentist or periodontist, so also does your heart needs some deep spiritual cleaning, and you must go see Doctor Jesus, the greatest Physician of the human heart and of the human race! That is why God has said, *"Come now, and let us reason together, saith the LORD: though your sins be as scarlet, they shall be as white as snow; though they be red like crimson, they shall be as wool."* (Isaiah 1:18 KJV)

From this scriptural passage, we see how God has extended an invitation to you and me and to all fallen sinful mankind to come and have their sinful hearts washed and cleansed in the blood of Jesus, the Lamb of God, who was slain for the remission of the sins of the world. Nothing else in the whole wide world can wash away our sins but the blood of Jesus, even as the hymn writer wrote, "What can wash away my sins, nothing but the blood of Jesus."

It is sad though, that the color of one's skin or race has become a parameter for racial, social, economic, educational, political, and religious stratification and classification that has led to racism and all kinds of racial discrimination, segregation, profiling, prejudice, inequality, persecution, injustice, and inhumanity. But God doesn't look at your race or the color of your skin. He looks at the color of your heart. God is a God of diversity and of colors. Just take a look at the beautiful unity in diversity of His creation: the flowers, the trees, the plants, the birds, the fishes, the insects, the animals, the stars, the planets, and over and above all, the human race. God appreciates and respects each and every race and skin color. He is not a respecter of persons and shows no partiality.

Therefore, I would say, change the color of your heart and keep your race and skin color. If you are Black, be proud of your blackness, because black is beautiful! If you are White, be proud of your whiteness, because white is beautiful! If you are Brown, be proud of your brownness, because brown is beautiful! If you are Red, be proud of your redness, because red is beautiful! Whatever the color of your skin, your race, your tribe, your ethnicity, or your nationality, be proud of it without any apology!

All skin colors are beautiful, therefore, let us celebrate and compliment the diversity of our races and skin colors. And stop spending and wasting your money on bleaches and other skin products just to try and change your skin color. For what? One of the weapons against racism is discovering your self-identity and self-worth of who you are and whose you are. If you truly know who you are and whose you are, and not what society is saying who you are, then you will help free yourself from mental, emotional, and psychological slavery and bondage and be proud of yourself, appreciate yourself, and celebrate yourself!

God has made all things beautiful. Therefore, appreciate, celebrate, and enjoy your created beauty and dignity and self-worth. And if you ever try to blend all the different races together, the result is one beautiful super-human race made in the image and likeness of God. And if you ever try to blend all the different skin colors together, the result is dust. For dust is what we all are made of, and to dust we shall all return. At death, your body returns to the dust, but your heart, which is your spirit and soul, returns to God for some question and answer (Q&A) time on how you treated the love of God, which is Christ, and how you treated others.

Yes! ALL LIVES MATTER! But it is the color of your heart and not the color of your skin or race that matters in the eyes of God. Jesus said, *"Blessed are the pure in heart: for they shall see God!"* (Matthew 5:8 KJV) Did you hear that? Jesus said only those whose hearts are pure and without sin, shall see God. And that purity of heart means a heart that has been washed, cleansed, and made pure by the blood of Jesus Christ. Therefore, is the color of your heart pure or impure? Purity is the color of the heart that God is looking for, and not the outward beauty. Man looks on the outside, but God looks in the inside, because a pure heart is a heart that is filled with the pure love of God. Love is pure and holy, righteous, just, harmless, and blameless. There is no racism or evil in love. Therefore, only the pure in heart shall enter heaven and shall see God.

The Bible says, *"Who may climb the mountain of the LORD? Or who may stand in His holy place? Only those whose hands and hearts are pure, who do not worship idols and never tell lies. They will receive the LORD'S blessing and have a right relationship with God their Savior."* (Psalm 24:3-5, NLT)

Therefore, what is the color of your heart? Is it pure, spotless and without blemish or wrinkles of sin, hatred, racism, prejudice, grudges, bitterness, resentments, malice, envy, jealousy, unforgiveness, injustice, immoralities, and impurities? Your skin color may be well toned and well massaged, spotless, smooth, wrinkle-free and without blemish. But what about your heart? Is it pure, spotless, without blemish, or wrinkles of sin? In the eyes of God, it is the color of your heart that matters, and not the color of your skin or race. If racism and all other societal injustices and evils are to be eradicated, it must first be eradicated in the hearts and minds and psychologies of men! Therefore, change the color of your heart and keep the color of your skin, and celebrate your race and who God has created you to be!

Take Off the Devil's Ugly Mask of Sin, Hatred, and Racism and Put-on Jesus' Beautiful Royal Robe of Love, Purity, and Righteousness!

The Bible says that we all have sinned and fall short of the glory of God. This means that not only have we all sinned, but that sin has also stained and defaced God's original created glory and beauty in us. This means that sin has made us ugly, and we have changed from the glory and beauty of God to the ugliness of sin and of the devil. Sin is ugly! In other words, we have put on the devil's mask of the ugliness of sin, racism, hatred, and evil. This means that the entire human race became sinful and depraved not by the color of their skin, but by the evil nature of their hearts.

This is exactly what happened to our first parents and ancestors, Adam and Eve. The moment they sinned, the glory of God, the light of God, departed from them, and they were overcome by pitch spiritual, moral, and intellectual darkness and ugliness, in so much that when they saw their own ugliness of sin for the first time, they fled from the presence of Holy God and hid themselves.

Not only that, but in an attempt to cover up their nakedness and ugliness, the Bible said that they sewed up fig leaves and made themselves aprons to cover themselves. And those aprons became a spiritual and moral generational mask of the fallen human race that has been passed unto the entire human race from generation to generation. The entire human race is living under a mask, and every man, woman, child, and race, black, white, brown, red, have all been wearing and carrying

this generational mask of the nakedness, shamefulness, guiltiness, ugliness, condemnation, accusation, and curse of sin over
their lives. The entire human race is a facade and a masquerade!

And the reason why Jesus came to the world is to unmask
the entire human race of this ugliness, nakedness, shamefulness, guiltiness, condemnation, accusation, and curse of sin
and of the devil over their lives; and to clothe them with His
own beautiful royal robe of holiness, purity, love, joy, peace,
righteousness, justice, truth, redemption, salvation, healing,
freedom, eternal life, and eternal hope.

Therefore, take off the devil's mask of sin, and ugliness,
guilt, condemnation, shame and of racism in your life, and
put-on Jesus' beautiful royal robe of love, joy, peace, holiness,
purity, righteousness, and salvation! And this will have to take
place inside your heart, by inviting Jesus into your heart to
purge and to cleanse it with His blood.

The changing of the color of your heart is a spiritual thing
that can only be done by the supernatural washing and cleansing
of your heart with the blood of Jesus Christ. It is sin that has
stained and made impure the heart of man, and there is nothing
in the whole wide world that can wash it away but the blood
of Jesus! And that means that you must repent of your sins and
ask God to forgive you, and then ask Jesus to come into your
heart and beautify it with His blood.

The Bible describes this supernatural spiritual and moral
transformation and reformation of the human heart when it
says, *"Therefore, if anyone is in Christ, he is a new creation;
old things have passed away; behold, all things are become
new!"* (2 Corinthians 5:17 NKJV) And this is talking about the
brand-new you with a brand-new heart that has been washed,
cleansed, purified, beautified, and glorified by the cleansing
blood of Jesus Christ. That is why the Bible says, *"So now*

there is no condemnation for those who belong to Christ Jesus. And because you belong to Him, the power of the life-giving Spirit has freed you from the power of sin that leads to death." (Romans 8:1-2 NLT)

And this means that you are now saved by grace alone and not by race or any good thing in you. This is the only supernatural change of the heart of man that can bring about a radical spiritual, moral, ethical, racial, cultural, political, governmental, economic, and societal revolution, transformation, and reformation in our lives, communities, societies, our nation, and in the world. Before kingdoms or nations can change, men must change first from within their hearts. It is an inside-out revolutionary and transformational change.

Therefore, let us leave all our racism behind us and let us race to the cross to receive grace from the Throne of Grace, that we may obtain mercy and find grace to help in this time of great distress and need in America and in the world!

(Hebrews 4:16 NIV)

America and the world are indeed in great distress and in dire need of God's mercy and grace and help! The human heart has been infected and made leprous by sin, and only Jesus can change the leper's spots of sin in our hearts and our nation. And love is the antidote to hatred and to racism, and is the answer for racial, political, societal healing and reconciliation in America and in the world. Therefore, let us stop playing the race card and let us start playing the grace card because America and the world can never be saved by race but by grace alone! And hatred can never save America and the world, but LOVE alone can!

CHAPTER THREE

The Original Equality Act Of God For The Human Race

O ne of the problems of the human race and of racism today is that there is a problem of identity crisis. And it is an identity crisis that began over six thousand years ago in the Garden of Eden when Adam and Eve sinned and fell from the original creative glory of God to depravity. It was since then that the devil has been distorting and messing up with the true racial and creative identity of the human race. And I would say that the entire human is struggling with a racial and creative identity crisis.

Racism itself is a distorted and stolen identity crisis. And that is why in this chapter, we are going to talk about the original Equality Act of God for the entire human race as diametrically opposed to the erroneously held psychological notion of racial superiority and inferiority of the races. This is extremely important because this will help people rediscover who they truly and really are and to recover their stolen creative racial identity, individuality, and dignity. People will come to understand that their true identity is not in the racial and cultural image of the devil and of society, but in the beautiful image of God. And that truth itself can bring about freedom and deliverance and healing and restoration to those that are bound and are struggling spiritually, emotionally, mentally, psychologically, intellectually, racially, culturally, and physically with their racial identity crisis. It is the truth that sets free!

The Bible describes this original Equality Act of God for the human race in the very first chapter of the Bible and of the creation story. Here is what it says:

"Then God said, "Let Us make man in Our image, according to Our likeness; let them have dominion over the fish of the sea, over the birds of the air, and over the cattle, over all the earth and over every creeping thing that creeps on the earth." So, God created man in His own image, in the image of God He created him; male and female He created them. Then God blessed them, and God said to them, "Be fruitful and multiply; fill the earth and subdue it; have dominion over the fish of the seas, over the birds of the air, and over every living thing that moves on the earth." (Genesis 1:26-28 NKJV)

In a very precise and concise form, the above scriptural passage describes the original Equality Act of God that He has designed for the entire human race as the Almighty Creator. And it is an immutable, immortal, and eternal Equality Act that is divinely enshrined in the Holy Constitution of Heaven. There are several things we are told in this original Equality Act of God.

And the first thing that we are told in this Equality Act of God and by God Himself is that God Himself said to Himself that they should come together and make man in the image and likeness of God Himself, and not in any other image or similitude or form, but in the very image and likeness of God Himself as a highly intelligent moral being with a spirit, soul, body, and mind with a conscience and a free will. And in this image of God is found the true original and creative identity, individuality, and dignity of every man, woman, and child and of the entire human race as specially and uniquely different from all animals and other created things. And this means that it is a God-Identity and not a racial or cultural identity. And this means that every man, and woman, and child is made in this selfsame God-Identity.

The second thing that we are told in this Equality Act of God and by God Himself is that God Himself in creating man, He created them male and female, a man and a woman. And this means that from the very beginning God the Creator and Designer of the human race created two distinct sexes of the human race: a man and a woman.

The third thing that we are told in this original Equality Act of God and by God Himself is that God Himself commanded Adam and Eve, the first male and the female that He has created for them to procreate by bringing forth children after their own kind: male and female, after the likeness of their biological parents.

The fourth thing that we are told in this Equality Act of God and by God Himself is that He created both the male and the female equal with no superiority or inferiority. And this means that God has created all men equal in His own image and likeness, both male and female, and never unequal or superior or inferior. And this means that all babies are created, conceived, and are born equal. From the womb to the tomb, from the cradle to the grave, from birth to death, and from conception to resurrection, all babies are born equal!

The fifth thing that we are told in this original Equality Act of God and by God Himself is that God Himself commanded man: both male and female, to have dominion over His creation:

over the fishes, the birds, the cattle, and over every creeping and living thing that creeps on the earth, and never dominion or control or supremacy over their own fellow human beings.

The sixth thing that we are told in this Equality Act of God and by God the Creator Himself is that after He has created Adam and Eve, He commanded them to be fruitful and multiply and fill the earth with the human race. This means that man was given command to give birth to children and to populate the earth with mankind and never to depopulate it by killing other human beings made in the image and likeness of God.

The seventh thing that we are told in this original Equality Act of God and by God Himself is that, after God has designed this Equality Act for the human race, God Himself concluded that it was very good, and the Bible declared: *"And God saw everything that He had made, and behold, it was very good!"* (Genesis 1:26-31)

And so, we see that this was a comprehensive Equality Act for the entire human race that God put together. However, after the fall of Adam and Eve, we have seen how this original Equality Act of God has come under attack both from the devil and from mankind himself. And this has led to a massive breakdown and distortion of the human race, whereby now we are faced with racism and all kinds of racial supremacy, superiority, inferiority, inequalities, discrimination, injustices and inhumanities.

But in the beginning, it was not so. God never created racial superiors or inferiors but equals. God never created racists or supremacists, and neither is any man born a racist or a supremacist. All racists and supremacists are made by men and indoctrinated in the halls and dormitories of our educational institutions and in the corridors of power of our constitutions.

What makes the American Constitution the greatest in the world is its belief in the equality and inalienable rights of all men. Its article on the Declaration of Independence states: *"WE hold these Truths to be self-evident, that all Men are created equal, that they are endowed by their Creator with certain unalienable Rights, that among these are Life, Liberty, and the Pursuit of Happiness."*[10]

The foundation of America's democracy was built upon these solid godly principles of this original Equality Act of God the Almighty Creator who has created all men equal and endowed them with the unalienable rights of life, liberty, happiness, dignity, and respect. God never created a superior or an inferior human being. Therefore, there is no superiority of any one race over another or others, nor is there any inferiority of any one race to another or others. America owes her greatness, affluence, opulence, and influence in the world because of these great eternal truths of the Equality Act of God.

Living in an "Orwellian" World of Inequalities!

But like I have said, since the fall of Adam and Eve, men have tried to alter and to redefine this original Equality Act of God and to reclassify the human race into what I would call an "Orwellian Classification," as described in George Orwell's "Animal Farm," with its own 1st Amendment of the seventh commandment that says that "ALL ANIMALS ARE EQUAL," but has now been amended to read, "ALL ANIMALS ARE EQUAL, BUT SOME ANIMALS ARE MORE EQUAL THAN OTHERS!"[11]

What a 1st Amendment! But doesn't that sound ironical, paradoxical and even confusing? For how can all animals be equal but at the same time some animals are more equal than others? This to me, is definitely not animal equality but animal inequality and discrimination!

And doesn't that sound familiar with the Jim Crow Laws of racial segregation in America and apartheid in South Africa? If you have read George Orwell's Animal Farm, you will come to understand that this was a political maxim cleverly designed by Napoleon and his political spin master and propagandist, Squealer, on behalf of one special class of animals –the Pigs, who asserted that they were more superior than all the other farm animals. The pigs claimed to have more superior brains and intellects than the rest of the animals. They also claimed that because of their superior brains and intellects, they should do all the critical, analytical, political, bureaucratic, administrative, intellectual, and scientific thinking, planning, and decision-making.

And with such assertion of superiority, the pigs cleverly devised some political tactics and antics to control all the other animals to believe in their superiority and should therefore be accorded and awarded with special preferential treatments and privileges for their hard thinking. And any animal that dared to challenge or oppose them was considered an enemy of the state.

I would imagine that the pigs used the weapons of political correctness, mass media propaganda machinery, intelligence surveillance and media censorship to ruthlessly suppress and silence their opponents, such as poor comrade Snowball, who opposed their tyranny, and was therefore chased out of the farm and banished into exile. Doesn't that sound familiar with our world today?

To me, this very maxim that all animals are equal, but some animals are more equal than others is a vivid depiction of the world in which we are living in today. To me, even though Animal Farm was a political satire lampooning the era of Soviet

Stalinism or communism, however, one can deduce from this Orwellian maxim that "ALL RACES ARE EQUAL, BUT SOME RACES ARE MORE EQUAL THAN OTHERS!" Or "ALL HUMANS ARE EQUAL, BUT SOME HUMANS ARE MORE EQUAL THAN OTHERS!"

This is exactly the world in which we are living in today whereby the original Equality Act of God that states that all men are created equal, has now been changed to classify all races and humans as equals, but some races and some humans are more equal than others. And since man is a political animal, therefore, this political maxim has become the political, ideological, cultural, educational, scientific, social, economic, intellectual, psychological, and racial perception and assertion held by many in the world today.

It is an ideology that borders on the superiority and inferiority of the human race from which stems racism, racial inequalities, discrimination, segregation, slavery, colonization, imperialism, and racial injustices and inhumanities. Racism, slavery, the Jim Crow laws of racial segregation, institutional racism, apartheid, genocides, holocaust, ethnic cleansing, tribalism, and all other forms of racial, tribal, ethnic oppressions, suppressions, repressions, inequalities, discrimination, tribalism, injustices, and inhumanities, are all depictions of the maxim, "All races and all humans are equal, but some races and some humans are more equal than others!"

This is not only diametrically opposed and antithetical to the original Equality Act of God, but it is also an aberration of the article on the Declaration of Independence, and an abomination in the eyes of God who has created all men equal. In God's original Equality Act, there is no superiority or supremacy or inferiority of the human race, but equality. Not only are all men created equal, but all babies are born equal, therefore, ALL LIVES MATTER to God!

All Lives Matter to God and All Souls Belong to God!

And since all men are created equal, and all babies are born equal, therefore, all men and all babies have the right to life, the right to live, the right to breathe, and the right to exist! There should never be any existential threat posed against any human life and against any human being, from conception to birth and to death because ALL SOULS BELONG TO GOD AND ALL LIVES MATTER TO GOD!

Yes! It is true that not all men or babies are born with the same equal privileges, same equal opportunities, same equal luxuries, same equal environments, and same equal parents. Some may have been born with "silver spoons in their mouths," while others, like me, may have been born with what I would call "wooden spoons in their mouths." Some may have been born in mansions and fashions, while others may have been born in the ghettos and gutters. Some may have been born in cradles, while others may have been born in animal stables like the baby Jesus. Nevertheless, and notwithstanding all these environmental and circumstantial differences in birth, yet still, that doesn't make any one race or person or human superior or inferior to another.

The environment or circumstances of one's birth does not determine their racial superiority or inferiority. Whether one is born in a palace or a stable, in a mansion or a ghetto, poor or rich, they are all equal! And I say this of the entire human race: That from conception to resurrection, from the womb to the tomb, from the cradle to the grave, and from birth to death, all men and all babies are created equal, born equal, and will die equal!

Therefore, a child's or a person's circumstances at birth, parentage, sex, gender, race, color, ethnicity, education, disability, and their status or fetus in society should never be used as a scientific, psychological, sociological, cultural, or political parameters to measure the social or racial stratification and classification of that child or person!

Neither should they ever be used as parameters to determine their racial superiority or inferiority; nor should they ever be used as parameters for racial profiling, discrimination, segregation, inequality, and racial injustice!

No man, or woman, or child should ever be racially prejudiced and discriminated against just because they are of another race, or skin color, or tribe, or clan, or ethnicity, or nationality, or gender, or age, or creed, or religion, or because of their status or fetus in society. Never!

No matter the status or fetus or condition of a child or a person in all their stages of development in life, they have the God-given inalienable divine right to be conceived, be born, be loved, be seen, be heard, be accepted, be respected, and be treated equally with dignity and equity, and with freedom and justice because they are our fellow human beings created in the image and likeness of God and not our fellow "animal beings" or "guinea pigs!" God never created dustbins or trash bins where we can dump and trash the least underprivileged and unfortunates in society! There should be no UNWANTED child or person in the world!

It was said of Jesus, "Can there any good thing come out of Nazareth?" (John 1:46 NKJV) Now, today in our times that could have been labeled as a racially motivated and prejudiced statement to make. But the truth is that even Jesus Himself, from conception to resurrection, from the womb to the tomb, from the stable to the grave, and from birth to death, was confronted with racism and racial prejudice, hatred and extermination from the devil, King Herod, the high priests, Pharisees, Sadducees, scribes, and from the Jews and Gentiles. His parents had to flee with Him to Egypt to escape the racially and politically motivated massacre of the innocent children by King Herod. The prophet Isaiah said that He was despised, hated, and rejected by men.

But even right now, even after two thousand years since His death and resurrection, Jesus is even more so now being racially despised, hated, insulted, blasphemed, cursed, mocked, dishonored, disrespected, evicted out of our public schools, colleges, universities, governments, supreme courts, shopping malls, stores, restaurants, public transportations, parks, public squares, sports, Hollywood, mainstream media, social media, homes, etc.!

And Jesus is being rejected and evicted in the hearts of men, women, and children. And even you that is reading this book, you may have despised, hated, insulted, blasphemed, cursed, mocked, dishonored, disrespected, evicted, and rejected Jesus in your heart. But the amazing thing is that He still loves you. Yes indeed, something good came out of Nazareth, and that something good is Jesus Christ, the Savior of the world!

Therefore, all humans, it doesn't matter their race, or skin color, or creed, or religion, or ethnicity, or nationality, or gender, or age, or education, or status, or fetus, or abilities, or disabilities, born or unborn, and in all stages of their development in life, should all be treated equally with love, respect, dignity, equity, and justice, because ALL LIVES MATTER to God! For God Himself has said, *"Behold, all souls are Mine! As the soul of the father, so also the soul of the son is Mine!"* (Ezekiel 18:4 NKJV)

Did you hear that? God claims ownership of ALL SOULS! Why? Because He created all men equal in His own image and likeness for His own glory! Therefore, ALL LIVES MATTER to God and ALL SOULS belong to God! From conception to resurrection, from the womb to the tomb, from the cradle to the grave, and from birth to death, ALL SOULS belong to God and ALL LIVES MATTER to God!

All Black lives, all White lives, all Brown lives, all Blue lives, all Red lives, all elderly lives, and all babies' lives belong to God, and ALL LIVES MATTER to God! Therefore, no man, or woman, or boy, or girl, or child, or the unborn should ever be prejudiced or discriminated or segregated or differentiated or biased against because of the color of their skin, or race, or sex, or gender, or creed, or religion! Neither should any race or person ever assert or assume themselves as superior to their other fellow human beings because God never created superiors or inferiors, but He created equals!

This is that original Equality Act of God for the entire human race. Therefore, let every man, woman, child, and race, discover their true identity of who they truly and really are in God alone the Creator. God has never changed and His original Equality Act for the human race has never changed. For God Himself has said of Himself, *"For I AM the LORD, and I change not!"* (Malachi 3:6) It is man that has changed, but God has not, and will never change!

And the reason why Jesus came to the world is to restore back the original Equality Act of God in people's lives and to the entire human race. It is sin and the devil that has destroyed and distorted the original Equality Act of God.

But Jesus came to deliver us from the bondage to sin and to the devil, and to restore us back to the original Equality Act of God. Jesus came to restore back our destroyed and distorted racial identity which was created and made in the image and likeness of God, and not in the image and likeness of the devil or any man or culture.

Therefore, if you are struggling from any form of identity crisis, you can rediscover and recover your true identity in Jesus Christ alone, who is the physical expression and manifestation of God. Racism and all racial and societal identity-crisis are as a result of our stolen and distorted original identity which was made in the image and likeness of God. And the feeling of racial superiority, inferiority or inadequacy are all distorted identity crises. And that is why Jesus came to rectify all identity crisis and to restore back our true created and God-given self-identity, self-worth, and self-dignity.

This is why the Bible says, *"For God sent not His Son into the world to condemn the world; but that the world through Him might be saved."* (John 3:17 KJV) The Bible also says that there is no condemnation to all those who have discovered and recovered their stolen and distorted racial identities in Christ Jesus. They have been redeemed, healed, restored, and freed. For he or she that the Son sets free is free, indeed. For it is for freedom that Christ came to set us free! Would you therefore like to rediscover and recover your true created God-given identity today? All you have to do is to ask Jesus to come into your life and restore back your true identity and the image and likeness of God in your life.

We should never treat people based on their race, or skin color, or tribe, or ethnicity, or nationality, or sex, or age, or status, or fetus in society. But rather, we should treat them based on their intrinsic value, dignity, and inalienable rights as human beings created in the image and likeness of God.

This should be the racial and societal prism through which we must perceive all peoples and accord them equal dignity and treatment, just as we would have them treat us. This is the universal "Golden Rule" set forth by our Lord Jesus Christ in the original Equality Act of God. Therefore, we should never treat people because of their relationships, friendships, associations, or fraternities in society, but rather we should treat them because of who and whose they are: our fellow human beings made in the very image and likeness of God. And if we cannot afford them with anything else in this world, at least let us accord them with love, dignity, equity, and respect!

Therefore, there is no one race that is superior or inferior to another, but all races are equal! Therefore, let not the Whites, or Blacks, or Hispanics, or Asians, or Europeans, or Russians, or Arabs, or Africans, or Jews, or Australians, or Indians, or Chinese, or any other race ever think themselves to be superior or inferior to the other races. The Bible says that no man should ever think of themselves more highly or superior to the others.

Men may try to change and to redefine the original Equality Act of God, and to reclassify the human race. But no matter what men may do, the original Equality Act of God for the entire human race remains the same as it was in the beginning. It is immutable, immortal, and eternal. And one day, we all shall stand before God the Almighty Creator to give account on what we have done with the original Equality Act of God, and how we have treated our fellow human beings who have been created in the image and likeness of God. ALL SOULS BELONG TO GOD AND ALL LIVES MATTER TO GOD! THIS IS THAT ORIGINAL EQUALITY ACT OF GOD, AND IT WAS VERY GOOD!

CHAPTER FOUR

How The Different Races And Languages Came About And The Importance Of Words In Our Communication And Race Relations

L anguages are very powerful tools of communication and relationships. But it is not so much the language that we speak
that is important or that matters. All languages are important.
But what is most important are the words that we speak. This is
what matters the most. In fact, regarding the importance of the
words that we speak, here is what the Bible says, *"Death and
life are in the power of the tongue, and those who love it will eat
its fruit."* (Proverbs 18:21, NKJV) This is a concise summary
of the power of the tongue. Now, we must understand that the
tongue by itself is not powerful: it's only an organic organ that
God has placed in the mouth. What makes the tongue powerful
are the words spoken through the organ of the tongue.

The tongue is like a keyboard or an organ or a piano. An
organ or a keyboard or a piano does not play music by itself.
Someone has to turn it on and touch the different keys to produce either some life-giving or some death-giving music. And
so, it is with the tongue. The tongue is the organ or keyboard

or piano in our mouth by which we speak life-giving or death-giving words to their recipients.

Therefore, our words are extremely important in our everyday communication and race relations. Very sadly though, words have become the latest weapons of mass media and social media destruction, distortion, misinformation, disinformation, racial slurs, political vitriolic, hate speeches, defamation, manipulation, psychological warfare, and control.

Therefore, I believe that in order for us to better understand the race issues and our race relations, I think it is important that we understand the complexities and the dynamics involved in God's mysterious and intricate design of all the different races and languages of the world and the importance of words in our everyday communication.

Understanding the origin of all the different races and languages and the importance of the words that we speak will help in the fight against racism, hatred, discrimination, xenophobia, prejudice, and all other injustices. In this chapter, we are going to discuss how all the different races and languages came about, and the importance of words in our everyday speech, communication and in our race relations.

And it all began, "In the Beginning," when God created the heavens and the earth, and made man in His own image and likeness, blessed, and commanded them to *"Be fruitful and multiply; fill the earth and subdue it; have dominion over the fish of the sea, over the birds of the air, and over every living thing that moves on the earth."* (Genesis 1:28, NKJV)

As we have seen from the above scriptural passage, Adam and Eve were given specific commands to be fruitful, multiply, populate and dominate the earth with their own humankind. And the Bible says that everything that God made was very good. This means there was perfect harmony between man and his environment.

How Sin Disrupted and Affected the Whole of Creation

But then something catastrophic happened that would have a devastating effect on the entire human race and the whole of creation: Adam and Eve sinned against God, and their sin disrupted and affected the whole of creation. This means that the whole of creation has been unwillingly subjected under the curse of sin and has been groaning and rumbling ever since in pain. The Apostle Paul writing about this, said,

"Yet what we suffer now is nothing compared to the glory He will reveal to us later. For all creation is waiting eagerly for that future day when God will reveal who His children really are. Against its will, all creation was subjected to God's curse. But with eager hope, the creation looks forward to the day when it will join God's children in glorious freedom from death and decay.

For we know that all creation has been groaning as in the pains of childbirth right up to the present time. And we believers also groan, even though we have the Holy Spirit within us as a foretaste of future glory, for we long for our bodies to be released from sin and suffering. We, too, wait with eager hope for the day when God will give us our full rights as His adopted children, including the new bodies He has promised us. We were given this hope when we were saved." (Romans 8:18-24, NLT)

This has been the plight and blight of the human race and the whole of creation ever since the fall of man. And like a pregnant woman in intense birth pangs, the whole of creation: the earth, the heavens, the planets, the seas, the weather, the plants, the animals, mankind, you and I, are all groaning under the heavy burden of the curse of sin.

The Noah Flood

The Bible tells us that when men began to multiply on the face of the earth and daughters were born unto them, some of Satan's fallen angels saw the daughters of men that they were very beautiful, and so they took some of them to wives. This was contrary to their original creative nature. Angels were created holy and never permitted to have any sexual intercourse of whatever sort. But in their fallen, sinful, and depraved state, these fallen angels left their first estate and lusted after the daughters of men. And this was the beginning of all sexual perversions and immoralities, and it was a deliberate act by Satan to further corrupt the pure Adamic race of the coming Savior into the world.

The Bible says, *"Now it came to pass, when men began to multiply on the face of the earth, and daughters were born to them, that the sons of God saw the daughters of men, that they were beautiful; and they took wives for themselves of all whom they chose. "Then the LORD saw that the wickedness of man was great in the earth, and that every intent of the thoughts of his heart was only evil continually. And the LORD was sorry that He had made man on the earth, and He was grieved in His heart. So, the LORD said, "I will destroy man whom I have created from the face of the earth, both man and beast, creeping thing and birds of the air, for I am sorry that I have made them." But Noah found grace in the eyes of the LORD.*

The earth also was corrupt before God, and the earth was filled with violence. So, God looked upon the earth, and indeed it was corrupt; for all flesh had corrupted their way on the earth. *And God said to Noah, "The end of all flesh has come before Me, for the earth is filled with violence through them, and behold, I will destroy them with the earth. Make yourself an ark of gopherwood; make rooms in the ark, and cover it inside and outside with pitch...And behold, I Myself am bringing floodwaters on the earth, to destroy from under heaven all flesh in which is the breath of life; everything that is on the earth shall die..."* (Genesis 6:1-22, NKJV)

From the above scriptural account, we see how the first Adamic race became corrupted and wicked, but Noah found favor with God because he was just and perfect. Therefore, God told him to build an ark because He was going to destroy the earth and all living things with a flood. The flood did destroy the entire human race, and only Noah and his wife, his three sons, and their three wives: a total of eight souls survived.

After the flood, God gave to Noah the same original command that He gave to Adam to *"Be fruitful and increase in number and fill the earth...As for you, be fruitful and increase in number, multiply on the earth and increase upon it."* (Genesis 9:1-3, NIV)

And so, Noah and his family continued with God's original program for man to be fruitful, multiply, populate and dominate the earth. And it was through his three sons: Shem, Ham, and Japheth that men began to increase on the earth. It was also from these three sons of Noah that all the different races of people on earth came from.

The Tower of Babel and How the Different Races and Languages came About!

After the flood, the Bible says that the people began to increase in number and that they were all of one race and one language. They were given the same command to be fruitful, multiply, populate and dominate the earth, but they disobeyed and rebelled against God. In a direct and open rebellion and defiance, the people stopped migrating and decided to settle down and build a city and a tower for themselves. The Bible says that the people were led into this rebellion by Nimrod, one of the great-grand sons of Noah, who grew to become a mighty warrior and hunter on the earth.

The Bible says, *"Cush begot Nimrod; he began to be a mighty one on the earth. He was a mighty hunter before the LORD; therefore, it is said, "Like Nimrod the mighty hunter before the LORD. And the beginning of his kingdom was Babel...in the land of Shinar."* (Genesis 10:8-10, NKJV)

The name Nimrod itself had an ominous meaning. Its Hebrew origin, marad, means "to rebel," or "We will rebel." And rebel he did, and a rebel he became! He was said to have been a very violent and despotic tyrant. Josephus, the famous Jewish historian of antiquity, wrote this about Nimrod:

"Now it was Nimrod who excited them to such an affront and contempt of God. He was the grandson of Ham, the son of Noah, -a bold man, and of great strength of hand. He persuaded them not to ascribe it to God as if it was through his means they were happy, but to believe that it was their own courage which procured that happiness. He also gradually changed the government into tyranny,—seeing no other way of turning men from the fear of God, but to bring them into constant dependence upon his power. He also said he would be revenged on God, if He should have a mind to drown the world again; for that he would build a tower too high for the waters to be able to reach! And that he would avenge himself on God for destroying their forefathers! Now the multitude were very ready to follow the

determination of Nimrod, and to esteem it a piece of cowardice to submit to God."[12]

The Bible says that, *"At one time all the people of the world spoke the same language and used the same words. As the people migrated to the east, they found a plain in the land of Babylonia and settled there. They began saying to each other, "Let's make bricks and harden them with fire…" Then they said, "Come, let's build a great city for ourselves with a tower that reaches into the sky. This will make us famous and keep us from being scattered all over the world."* (Genesis 11:1-4, NLT)

So, from both Josephus' and the Bible's account, Nimrod was a rebel who led the multitude into rebellion against God. And we saw how that the tower of Babel was built as an open challenge and defiance to God. And no man or angel can openly or secretly challenge and defy God and go unpunished. Sin will always be punished unless it is repented of.

God's Divine Judgment

This was the height of man's rebellion, pride, arrogance and defiance, and God would not, and will not tolerate such! So, He came down and destroyed the tower, confused their language, and then scattered them abroad. The Bible says:

"But the LORD came down to look at the city and the tower the people were building. "Look!" He said, "The people are united, and they all speak the same language. After this, nothing they set out to do will be impossible for them! Come, let's go down and confuse the people with different languages. Then they won't be able to understand each other."

In that way, the LORD scattered them all over the world, and they stopped building the city. That is why the city was called Babel, because that is where the LORD confused the people with different languages. In this way He scattered them all over the world." (Genesis 11:5:9, NLT)

From the above passage, we see how God executed four divine judgments on the people:

First, He completely destroyed the tower of Babel to ground zero so that they were never able to rebuild it again; thus, breaking their very symbol of pride, arrogance, and power. The Tower of Babel represented a dictatorial, totalitarian, authoritarian and tyrannical form of government under their leader, Nimrod. Therefore, God would have to put a stop to man's first attempt of forming a one world government with a one world trade center and one world religion.

Secondly, God confused their language with incomprehensible babbling so that they were not able to understand each other anymore; thus, breaking their very art of communication, understanding and intelligence.

Now, I personally do not believe that by confusing the language of the people that God changed the original meanings of the words and names that Him and Adam gave to everything that He created. I believe they were still using the same words but in different forms and pronunciations. Linguistically speaking, this could have meant that they were still speaking the same words but with different pronunciations, vocabularies, and accents. For instance, the words man, woman, boy, girl, mother, father, food, water, etc., all have the same universal meanings but pronounced differently by all the different races and tribes in the world.

Thirdly, God scattered them abroad upon all the face of the earth so that they were never able to gather again as one group of people in one geographical location. This was the first forced mass migration of the entire human race upon the face of the earth enacted and enforced by God Himself; thus, breaking their power of unity and decentralizing their totalitarian and authoritarian one world government into the different governments and nations of the world.

Fourthly, after God had scattered and resettled them in the different parts of the world, He then went ahead and divided the whole earth into continents and islands with wide open oceans in between them; thus, enforcing His original mandate for man to be fruitful, multiply, populate and dominate the earth, and to teach all men in all ages that no matter man's rebellion, God's will, plans and purposes will and shall always be done here on earth as it is in heaven!

As to the division of the earth into the different continents and nations, God even predicted its fulfillment long before it happened by the giving of the prophetic name Peleg to one of Noah's great-grandsons from the lineage of Shem. And the meaning of the name, Peleg, is, "division." Here is the Biblical account of that:

"The sons of Shem were Elam, Asshur, Arphaxad, Lud, and Aram. The sons of Aram were Uz, Hul, Gether, and Mash. Arphaxad begot Salah, and Salah begot Eber. To Eber were born two sons: the name of one was Peleg, for in his days the earth was divided; and his brother's name was Joktan."

(Genesis 10:22-25, NKJV)

Interestingly, the division of the earth into continents has been scientifically proven to be true by geologists, geophysicists, paleontologists, and others, through their studies of continental drift, plate tectonics, fossil animals and plants, etc. One such notable scientist was Alfred Wegener, a German geophysicist and meteorologist, who was famous for postulating the theory of Continental Drift. Wegener believed that in the distant geologic age, the earth was once made up of one massive landmass that he called *"Pangea" or "Super-Continent,"* and that this supercontinent began to drift and split apart, forming the different continents of the world as we know them today.[13]

In fact, if you take the maps of the north-eastern continental seaboard of North America and the south-eastern continental seaboard of South America and you juxtapose them with the north-western and south-western continental seaboards of Africa, there will appear what looks like a perfect symmetry or match of those two continental landmasses, thus, proving the accuracy of both the biblical account and the scientific theories of continental drift and plate tectonics.

And so, we clearly see that the division of the human race into the different languages and continents was as a result of God's divine judgments against the Tower of Babel, which was the symbol of man's rebellion and defiance against God after the flood. According to Ethnologue, Languages of the World, it is estimated that there are currently about 7,117 languages spoken today in all the seven continents and the 193 or so countries of the world.[14]

The Importance of Languages and Words in Our Communication and Race Relations

Therefore, it doesn't really matter which language or dialect you speak. Your race or tribe or skin color does not define who you are. It is the words and language of your mouth that defines who you are. The Bible says that as a man thinks, so he is; for out of the abundance of the heart, the mouth speaks. And God has given us the different languages for two main reasons: Firstly, so that we can communicate and relate with each other in love and for building relationships, friendships, communities, bridges, and trust.

Secondly, so that we can communicate and relate with Him as our Creator and Heavenly Father at anytime, anywhere, and everywhere, 24/7-365!

This was God's original intent from the very beginning. God did not give the languages for racism, nor for hate speeches, cursing, slander, lying, gossiping, backbiting, filthy jokes, nor for hurting others!

It is sad that today one's language, dialect, accent, tribe, ethnicity, and nationality have all become weapons of racial and societal hatred, discrimination, and prejudice. One's accent or dialect alone could trigger off a set of emotional, mental, and psychological racial, tribal, and ethnic alarm systems with blinking red lights of unfounded suspicions, distrust, dislike, prejudice, discrimination, and hatred.

God has placed a very high premium and requirement on the language and words of our mouths. The Lord Jesus warned against the careless usage of the words and language of our mouths when He said,

"Make a tree good and its fruits will be good, or make a tree bad and its fruits will be bad, for a tree is recognized by its fruits. You brood of vipers, how can you who are evil say anything good? For out of the overflow of the heart the mouth speaks. The good man brings good things out of the good stored up in him, and the evil man brings evil things out of the evil stored up in him.

But I tell you that men will have to give account on the day of judgment for every careless word they have spoken. For by your words, you will be acquitted, and by your words you will be condemned." (Matthew 12:33-37, NIV)

Sadly indeed, today in our rapidly advancing digital age with many different mass media and social media platforms, languages and words have become the latest weapons of mass media, social media, and political destruction and distortion in our societies. Many are using languages and words for racial slurs, hate speeches, cursing, insults, gossip, backbiting, slander, mudslinging, cancel culture, character assassination, defamation, misinformation, disinformation, psychological warfare, manipulation, and control. This seems to have become the norm that has numbed the consciences of many with no conviction or remorse whatsoever!

The main-stream media and social media platforms have become the latest launching pads for short-range, medium-range, long-range and intercontinental ballistic missiles armed with lethal nuclear warheads of piercing, biting, bitter and hurting words! This is happening all over the world, but especially so in America. Words can inflict the deepest emotional, mental, and psychological wounds, hurts and pain even far greater than those of a bullet or a dagger. Words inappropriately and maliciously spoken are like a double-edged dagger that pierces and penetrates deep down inside the heart, affecting the spirit, soul, body, mind, bone, and marrow.

Words have caused wars between nations, races, tribes, families, husbands and wives, friends, neighbors, politicians, armies, etc. That is why the Bible warns about the usage of our tongue when it says:

"We all stumble in many ways. If anyone is never at fault in what he says, he is a perfect man, able to keep his whole body in check. When we put bits into the mouths of horses to make them obey us, we can turn the whole animal. Or take the ships as an example. Although they are so large and are driven by strong winds, they are steered by a very small rudder wherever the pilot wants to go.

Likewise, the tongue is a small part of the body, but it makes great boasts. Consider what a great forest is set on fire by a small spark. The tongue also is a fire, a world of evil among the parts of the body. It corrupts the whole person, sets the whole course of his life on fire, and is itself set on fire by hell.

All kinds of animals, birds, reptiles, and creatures of the sea are being tamed and have been tamed by man, but no man can tame the tongue. It is a restless evil, full of deadly poison. With the tongue we praise our Lord and Father, and with it we curse men, who have been made in God's likeness. Out of the same mouth come praise and cursing. My brother, this should not be. Can both fresh water and salt water flow from the same spring? My brothers, can a fig tree bear olive, or a grape-vine bear fig? Neither can a salt spring produce fresh water." (James 3:1-12, NIV)

What a perfect description of the power and danger of the human tongue! Therefore, my brothers and sisters and my fellow human beings, I enjoin you to employ your tongue into the proper industry for which God has created it for: and that is, for healthy communications, relationships, fellowships, friend-ships, and for building bridges and communities with love! Let us learn how to speak life-giving words and not death-giving words. Let us speak words that are uplifting, comforting, encouraging, complimentary, kind, helpful, peaceful, joyful, and loving. Let us speak words that build and not destroy. Let us speak words that bring healing and life, and not words that bring wounds, hurts and death. Many of our racial, societal, and political problems are caused by the wrong words spoken. Therefore, tame your tongue and shame the devil!

The Importance of Languages and Words in Our Relationship with God

The Bible tells us that the primary purpose for God creating man in His own image and likeness is for His glory and pleasure so that He can have an intimate love relationship with him: *"Thou art worthy, O Lord, to receive glory and honor and power; for Thou hast created all things, and for Thy pleasure they are and were created."* (Revelation 4:11, KJV)

From the very beginning God created man for an intimate love relationship, fellowship, communion, and communication. That was why He used to come down in the cool of the day to walk and to talk with Adam and Eve in the garden of Eden. (Genesis 3:8) And this is why God has given the different races different languages so that they can communicate and talk with Him directly in their own languages and mother tongues anytime, anywhere, and everywhere in the world, 24/7!

God speaks all the languages of the world, which itself is proof that He is the only true and All-Knowing God! For there is no other god in all the earth who speaks all the over 7,117 different languages of all the people in the world. None whatsoever! There may be other gods but made of wood, stone, iron, gold, silver, copper, and other created things. They have mouths but they cannot talk, eyes but they cannot see, ears but they cannot hear, nose but they cannot breathe, hands but they cannot touch, and feet but they cannot walk. Therefore, they are all dumb, blind, deaf, crippled, dead, useless, and hopeless gods!

But not so with our God, the Almighty Creator! He is the Living God, and you can talk to Him directly without any human mediator. He understands all the sounds, voices, accents, and languages of all the people, the birds, the animals, the plants, the planets, and of all creation! What an Awesome God we serve!

In fact, God has been talking to you in so many different ways and at so many different times through dreams and visions, through men and women of God, through the Bible, through your circumstances in life, through nature, through other people, through angels, through the Holy Spirit, and through your own very conscience. But over and above all, God has spoken to you through His Son Jesus Christ whom He has sent to speak to the whole wide world. There is no one person in all the world that God has not spoken to one way or the other. None whatsoever! Even right now as you are reading this book God is speaking to you. Therefore, today, do not harden your heart when you hear the voice of God speaking to you. (Hebrews 3:15) And let the God who speaks all the languages of the world be the only true God!

The Future Restoration and Reconciliation of All the Races

The Bible is the Book of Hope. Therefore, all hope is not lost in this chaotic and messy world! At the beginning of this chapter, we talked about how the whole of creation is groaning under the curse of sin, and eagerly awaiting its final redemption. The Bible has promised us that there is coming a future restoration and reconciliation of all the races, and of all things in the earth and in the heavens. The apostle John saw a vision of this and wrote,

"Now I saw a new heaven and a new earth, for the first heaven and the first earth had passed away. Also, there was no more sea. Then I, John, saw the holy city, New Jerusalem,

coming down out of heaven from God, prepared as a bride adorned for her husband.

And I heard a loud voice from heaven saying, "Behold, the tabernacle of God is with men, and He will dwell with them, and they shall be His people. God Himself will be with them and be their God. And God will wipe away every tear from their eyes; there shall be no more death, nor sorrow, nor crying. There shall be no more pain, for the former things have passed away." (Revelation 21:1-4, NKJV)

"After these things I looked, and behold, a great multitude which no man could number, of all nations, tribes, peoples, and tongues, standing before the throne and before the Lamb, clothed with white robes, and palm branches in their hands, and crying out with a loud voice, saying, "Salvation belong to our God who sits on the throne, and to the Lamb." (Revelation 7:9-10, NKJV)

What a comforting picture of that coming future restoration of racial reconciliation, peace and unity of the human race from every nation, tongue, tribe, ethnicity, nationality, and people, and the renovation of the new heavens and the new earth where there will be no more sin, no more devil, no evil, no more injustice, no more racism, no more hatred, no more envy, no more jealousy, no more politics, no more pain, nor more sickness, no more COVID-19, no more death, no more debts, no more bills, no more suffering, and no more weeping.

It will be a new kingdom and a new heaven and a new earth overflowing with the abundance of God's love, joy, peace, and everlasting happiness and blissfulness.

However, this promise is only for those who have fled from the sinful "Tower of Babel" of this present world to the saving Cross of Jesus Christ at Calvary's Hill! The Tower of Babel represents divine judgment because of sin, but the

Cross represents divine justice because of love. The Tower of Babel represents the confusing and scattering of the human race, but the Cross represents the gathering and reconciling of all the scattered lost sheep of the human race. The Tower of Babel represents man's pride and was built for self-exaltation, but the Cross represents Christ's self-abasement and self-sacrifice and was built to draw all men to God. Jesus said,

"If I be lifted up from the earth, I will draw all men unto Me!" (John 12:32)

Knowing these things therefore, let us put aside all our racial, facial, political and linguistical differences, and let us use the languages that God has given us to communicate and to relate with one another in love and to build bridges of loving relationships, friendships, fellowships, and communities. Therefore, if racism and all other evils and injustices and inhumanities are to be defeated, we must first experience God's love, and then we must begin to speak the Love Language and spread the Language of Love to all people on planet earth. Let us learn how to live a 24/7-365 Love! For God so loved the world!

CHAPTER FIVE

The Commonalities Of The Human Race

Just as there is equality of the human race, so also there are commonalities of the human race which not only reaffirm the equality of all men but also confirm our common origin. In this chapter, we are going to look at some of these commonalities to prove that we are not only created equal, but that we all do share the same human origin and ancestry. And these are facts that have been proven to be true biblically, scientifically, anthropologically, and sociologically. So, let's take a walk down our common ancestral tree and bloodline of the human race.

1.   We All Have the Same Common Creator: GOD

In spite of all the diversity of the different races, colors, ethnicities, tribes, nationalities, languages, and cultures, we all have one common Creator and Maker: God. The Bible gives this beautiful story of our creation: *"Then God said, 'Let Us make man in Our image, according to Our likeness; let them have dominion over the fish of the sea, over the birds of the air, and over the cattle, over all the earth and over every creeping thing that creeps on the earth.' So, God created man in His own image, in the image of God He created him; male and female He created them."* (Genesis 1:26-27 NKJV)

Furthermore, David, the psalmist, said this about our creation:

"You made all the delicate, inner parts of my body and knit me together in my mother's womb. Thank You for making me so wonderfully complex! Your workmanship is marvelous – how well I know it. You watched me as I was being formed in utter seclusion, as I was woven together in the dark of the womb. You saw me before I was born. Every day of my life was recorded in Your book. Every moment was laid out before a single day had passed." (Psalm 139:13-16 NLT)

What a most beautiful and wonderful story of our common creation! This means that you and I are a wonderful handiwork of God and not a scientific product of evolution or cloning or a Big Bang Theory. The human race is not a product of a Darwinian theory of evolution. We are created and not evolved. We are made and not cloned. You and I are children of God created in the image and likeness of God, conceived, and intricately formed in our mother's beautiful and mysterious womb!

Therefore, we all have one common God and Creator. The apostle Paul wrote and said, *"For this reason I bow my knees to the Father of our Lord Jesus Christ, from whom the whole family in heaven and earth is named."* (Ephesians 3:14-15 NKJV)

Do you now see how the entire human race is one big family of God? Therefore, we are all brothers and sisters, regardless of our race, skin color, ethnicity, nationality, tribe, language, or culture. We are a wonderful community of one big global family. If we know this truth, and embrace this truth, and act upon this truth, then we will grow to love, appreciate, respect, help, and treat one another as brothers and sisters and as neighbors. This will stem out racism and hatred and injustices and inhumanities in our societies.

So next time you come across someone, treat them with love and respect. God created us in love, with love, for love, and to love. Love is God's DNA, and we were created to love, therefore, let us love one another as brothers and sisters and as neighbors. It is only this love that conquers the world and all the hatred, racism, injustices, inhumanities, and evils in the world. Love knows no race nor skin color. Love loves all and love conquers all!

2. We All Are Made of the Same Common Material: Dust

There is no doubt that the color of one's skin has become a race problem. But the Bible clearly tells us that we are all dust, regardless of one's skin color. When God made the first man, Adam, the Bible says that He formed him out of the dust of the earth: *"And the LORD God formed man of the dust of the ground and breathed into his nostrils the breath of life; and man became a living being."* (Genesis 2:7 NKJV)

From the above account, it is important for us to observe that when God created man, He did not say, "Come and let us make man in our own color," but rather, He formed man out of the dust of the ground and breathed into his nostrils the breath of life. The Bible never told us that Adam and Eve were Black, or White, or Brown, or Pink, or Green, or Yellow. The name Adam itself in Hebrew, Adamah, means "earth," or "soil."

Recently, someone sent me a video clip of the late Bishop Benson Idahosa, one of Africa's greatest generals of God. In that video clip, he was preaching somewhere, and he shared the story about how he grew up struggling with his skin color as a Black African and the way Blacks have been mistreated. He said he went before God in prayer asking Him why did He make him Black? In response, he said God told him that He never knew that he was Black. Shocked by that answer, he asked God what exactly He meant by that? And he said God told him that when He created man, He never created him black, or white, or brown, or dark, but that He created man in His own image and likeness. He said that answer from God forever changed his perspective about race and about his skin color because he discovered then that his true identity is in Christ Jesus alone.

And that is the truth about our true identity and who we are. Every man, woman, and child bear in them the image and likeness of God. It doesn't matter whether your skin color is black, white, red, brown, dark, or otherwise, we are all made of dust. And not only are we made of dust, but to dust we shall return. God said to Adam:

"Because you listened to your wife and ate from the tree about which I commanded you, you must not eat of it,' Cursed is the ground because of you; through painful toil you will eat of it all the days of your life. It will produce thorns and thistles for you, and you will eat the plants of the field. By the sweat of your brow, you will eat your food until you return to the ground, since from it you were taken; for dust you are and to dust you will return." (Genesis 3:17-19 NIV)

Did you hear that? Dust we are, and to dust we shall return. Therefore, dust is our true skin color. And if you ever want to get your exact original skin color, which is dust, then I invite you to collect samples of all the different soil types in the world, such as loamy, sandy, clay, etc.; and collect samples of all the different rock types such as volcanic, igneous, granite, sedimentary, metamorphic, etc.; and collect all the different samples of minerals, such as potassium, magnesium, calcium, etc. And after you have collected all these different samples, take them to a laboratory and put all of them in a crushing or blending machine. And don't forget to add the right amount of water as your body is made up of an average of about 60% water. And the color of that mixture of soils, rocks, minerals, and water is your skin color: Dust!

In fact, you and I are nothing, but a speck of dust quarried and chiseled out of the earth by the hand of God. You and I are clay molded and fashioned by the great Potter. We are all earthy and are human arts of pottery that rusts, rots, wears, and tears away with time and age. We are all earthen vessels that crack, break away, and fall apart. Your life is precious and fragile, therefore handle it with great care because in the end when your life expires here on earth, your body will return back to the dust from which it was formed, and your spirit and soul will return back into the hands of God, your Maker.

This is why God said that ALL SOULS BELONG TO HIM! Therefore, ALL LIVES MATTER TO GOD! All Black lives, White lives, Red lives, Brown lives, and all babies' lives belong to God and matter to God!

Since the fall of Adam, man has become increasingly dissatisfied with almost everything about himself: his image, his race, his skin color, his nose, his eyes, his lips, his fingers, his toes, his nails, his hair, his shape, his belly, his height, his weight, his size, etc. That is why billions of dollars are being spent every year just in fitness and cosmetics alone. Have you ever wondered why some Blacks are using skin-lightening cream and bleach just to lighten their skin complexion, and why some Whites are burning or tanning under the sun or saunas just to tan or darkened their skin complexion? I find that very interesting. But no matter what your skin color is, we are all made of dust.

So, racism is not a skin problem but a sin problem. Therefore, get rid of sin in your life that is the root cause of racism and hatred, and keep your skin color and your race intact!

3. We All Have the Same Common Ancestors: Adam & Eve

The Bible says that we all have the same common ancestors and bloodline. Adam and Eve are our first human ancestors and parents. This means that all races of people descended from Adam and Eve and not from apes or monkeys. When God created the plants and the animals, He commanded them to produce after their own kinds: apes giving birth to apes, monkeys giving birth to monkeys, humans giving birth to humans, etc. This means plants producing their own plant-kind, animals producing their own animal-kind, and humans producing their own mankind.

When God created Adam and Eve, He gave them a command to procreate and bring forth children after their own kind: mankind: "Then God blessed them, and God said to them, *"Be fruitful and multiply; fill the earth and subdue it."* (Genesis 1:28 NKJV) God commanded them to procreate and bring forth offspring after their own kind, that is, children that look just like them, bearing the same common human DNA.

So, Adam and Eve became the progenitors of the human race. Therefore, it doesn't really matter whether you are African American, Caucasian, Hispanic, Native Indian, Asian, Jew, Arab, Aboriginals, Pygmies, Eskimos, or whatever race or ethnicity or nationality you are; we are all of the same common human ancestors.

4. We All Have the Same Common Blood Color: Red

As members of the same human race, we all do have the same common Adamic bloodline and blood color, which is red. Have you ever seen any black, or white, or brown, or green, or pink, or yellow blood? No! It's only red! This proves that we are all members of the same ancestral bloodline and lifeline. It doesn't matter which blood type or blood group you belong to we all have the same red color of blood. The Bible says this about our common blood line:

"God, who made the world and everything in it, since He is LORD of heaven and earth, does not dwell in temples made with hands. Nor is He worshiped with men's hands, as though He needed anything, since He gives to all life, breath, and all things. And He has made from one blood every nation of men to dwell on all the face of the earth and has determined their pre-appointed times and the boundaries of their dwellings... for in Him we live and move and have our being, for we are all His offspring. Therefore, since we are the offspring of God, we ought not to think that the Divine Nature is like gold or silver or stone, something shaped by art and man's devising." (Acts 17:24-29 NKJV)

And so, we see here that God has made from one blood, Adam, every nation of men to dwell on the face of the earth. The whole human race is one family, and the whole wide world is our family: black, white, dark, light, brown, yellow, red, pink, blue, we are all of one bloodline and blood color. We must therefore endeavor to love one another and to treat one another with love, respect, and dignity, and not hate or degrade one another.

But the greatest blood in the whole wide world is the blood of Jesus Christ, who came to donate His blood on the Cross to a fallen and sinful human race. Our common bloodline of the human race has been contaminated and poisoned by sin. We all carry that poisoned blood in us that eventually leads to eternal death. And that is why Jesus came to donate His blood to the entire human race on the Cross at Calvary.

His blood is the only pure and holy blood without sin. Therefore, the entire human race needs this supernatural blood transfusion from Jesus' veins in order to get rid of sin in our lives and to receive eternal life. Have you received your own supernatural blood transfusion from Jesus' veins yet? His blood purges from all sins of racism and hatred, and all injustices and inhumanities.

5.   We All Have the Same Common Enemy: Satan

As members of the same common human race, we all have the same common enemy, the devil, who is also called Satan. As our common enemy, Satan is the one who tempted Adam and Eve and made them to sin and fall. The devil is the embodiment of sin and of all evil and wickedness in the world. He is our common enemy number one, and he is the one responsible for sowing the seeds of racism, hatred, strife, discord, conflicts, division, discrimination, and acts of violence.

The Bible says, *"Woe to the inhabitants of the earth and of the seas! For the devil is come down unto you, having great wrath, because he knows that he hath but a short time."* (Revelation 12:12 KJV) In fact, the Bible even warns us about the devil when it says, *"Be sober, be vigilant; because your adversary the devil walks about like a roaring lion, seeking whom he may devour. Resist him."* (1 Peter 5:8-9 NKJV)

The Lord Jesus said that the main mission of the devil on earth is to steal, to kill, and to destroy the lives of men, women, and children, but that He has come to give life, and life more abundantly: "The thief does not come except to steal, and to kill, and to destroy. I have come that they may have life, and that they may have it more abundantly." (John 10:10 NKJV)

The Bible also says, *"For we are not fighting against flesh-and-blood enemies, but against evil rulers and authorities of the unseen world, against mighty powers in this dark world, and against evil spirits in the heavenly places."* (Ephesians 6:12 NLT) These are our real common enemies: Satan and his demon spirits.

From the above scriptural passages, we have seen how we all as a human race have the same common enemy, the devil. This means therefore that the Blackman is not the Whiteman's enemy, neither is the Whiteman the Blackman's enemy, nor the Latinos, nor the Asians, nor the Africans, nor the Arabs, nor the Jews, nor the Russians, nor the Indians, nor the Chinese, nor any other race are our enemies. Our parents, children, family members, neighbors, friends, are not our real enemies. Our real common enemy is Satan, the devil. And he is the one responsible for all the problems and troubles in our nation and in the world. And this is the enemy we all should be fighting and not against each another!

6. We All Have the Same Common Universal Problem: Sin

As members of the same human race, we all have the same common sin problem. Sin is a common universal problem affecting the entire human race. Since we are all one family of the same common ancestors therefore, we also have inherited the same sin problem from our first parents Adam and Eve. Sin is the common inheritance of the human race. The Bible says that it was through one man, Adam, that sin entered the world and infected the entire human race: *"Therefore, just as through one mam sin entered the world, and death through sin, and thus death spread to all men, because all sinned."* (Romans 5:12 NKJV)

The Bible also says, "For there is no difference; for all have sinned and fall short of the glory of God." (Romans 3:23 NKJV) Sin is the universal cancer that has infected and affected the entire human race. It is far more deadly than COVID-19 or any other virus. Sin is not racist either. There is no such thing as black sin, or white sin, or pink sin, or brown sin. Sin is sin, and we all have sinned and fall short of the glory of God.

We eat sin, we drink sin, we smoke sin, we inject sin, we think sin, we imagine sin, we invent sin, we talk sin, we sing sin, we walk sin, we watch sin, we listen to sin, we act sin, and we commit sin every day and night, 24/7! All the problems in the world are as a result of sin. Therefore, racism is not a skin or race problem but a sin and a heart problem. Sin is the universal cancer of the human race, and the only cure for it is the blood of Jesus Christ!

7. We All Have the Same Common End: Death

As members of the same human race, we all have the same common end, which is death and the grave. Because of sin, the entire human race has come under the penalty of death and therefore we all are destined to die. God said to Adam, *"Of every tree of the garden you may freely eat; but of the tree of the knowledge of good and evil you shall not eat, for in the day that you eat of it you shall surely die."* (Genesis 2:16-17 NKJV) The Bible also says, *"For the wages of sin is death, but the gift of God is eternal life in Christ Jesus our LORD."* (Romans 6:23,

NKJV) The Bible also says that for it is appointed unto men to die once, but after that, the judgment. (Hebrews 9:27)

Since we all have sinned, and since the wages of sin is death, and since it is appointed for all men to die once and after that judgment, therefore, all men must die. Whether we like it or not, we are all going to die one day at a time. Death is inevitable and inescapable, and death levels all men. We all must die and return to dust; for dust we are and to dust we shall return, dust to dust, and ashes to ashes!

And remember that death is not racist either. It comes for all: Black, White, Red, Brown, old, young, man, woman, child, rich, poor. Death will show up at anytime, anywhere, anyplace, and most times, at a time least expected. Therefore, the question is not whether you are going to die or not, but whether you are ready for death.

The grave is not racist either. Its standard measurement is six-feet deep. The grave will be your eternal six-feet social distancing from the world and from the rest of humanity, and hell and the lake of fire shall be your eternal distancing from God and from all your loved ones! Are you prepared for death?

Are you prepared to stand before a holy, just, and righteous God? You must answer and settle this eternal question before death strikes.

8. We All Have the Same Common Eternal Destiny: Heaven or Hell

As members of the same human race, we all have the same common eternal destiny: heaven or hell. Heaven for all those who have accepted Jesus Christ and have walked in love, and hell for all those who have rejected Jesus Christ and have walked in sin and hatred. Writing about the vision that he saw concerning the eternal destiny of the human race, the apostle John said:

"Then I saw a great white throne and Him who sat on it, from whose face the earth and the heaven fled away. And there was found no place for them. And I saw the dead, small and great, standing before God, and books were opened. And another book was opened. And the dead were judged according to their works, by the things which were written in the books.

The sea gave up the dead who were in it, and Death and Hades delivered up the dead who were in them. And they were judged, each one according to his works. Then Death and Hades were cast into the lake of fire. This is the second death. And anyone not found written in the Book of Life was cast into the lake of fire." (Revelation 20:11-15 NKJV)

This is a very frightening apocalyptic vision that the apostle John saw of the coming judgment and eternal destiny of the human race. Not only must we all die, but after death, we all are going to stand before God to be judged for all the things that we have done here on earth, whether they be good or bad.

Are you prepared to stand before The White judgment Throne of Jesus Christ, the righteous Judge of all the earth on that day? Do you know where you will spend eternity after you die? You must answer and settle these questions in your life before it is too late.

9.   We All Have the Same Common Savior: JESUS CHRIST

As members of the same fallen and sinful human race, we all have the same common Savior, Jesus Christ, who came to die on the Cross for the sins of the whole wide world. The Bible says, *"For God so loved the world that He gave His only begotten Son, that whosoever believes in Him, should not perish, but have everlasting life."* (John 3:16 KJV) The Bible also says that, *"Neither is there salvation in any other: for there is none other name under heaven given among men whereby we must be saved."* (Acts 4:12 KJV) The Lord Jesus Himself has said, *"I Am the way, the truth, and the life, no one comes to the Father except through Me."* (John 14:6 NKJV)

Since we all have the same common sin problem, therefore, we all also have the same common solution to our sin problem. And that common solution is Jesus Christ, the Savior of the world. Have you made Jesus your Savior yet? He is the only way, and there is no other way. Jesus is the only one without sin and the only one who came down from heaven to die for the sins of the world. No other man has ever come down from heaven, nor has died for the sins of the world. None, but Jesus alone! And His blood and His death and His resurrection is the only One that God has approved for the salvation of mankind and for the forgiveness of sin. Outside of Jesus there is no other way!

All of the above commonalities point to just one thing: that there is only one race of people in the world called the human race. Therefore, the next time you come across someone who doesn't look like you, talk like you, or dress like you, remember that person is your fellow human being and is your brother and your sister of another father and mother of the same human race from another part of the world!

Love them, be kind to them, and be respectful and helpful to them! Show them some love and some little kindness. Give them compliments of love, for love breaks down all racial and social barriers. So, go on and love your neighbor as yourself!

And remember this: Never be nasty or rude to a complete stranger! He or she could be an angel in disguise. The Bible encourages us to be kind to strangers, for by so doing, we could be entertaining angels: *"Keep on loving each other as brothers and sisters. Don't forget to show hospitality to strangers, for some who have done this have entertained angels without realizing it."* (Hebrews 13:1-2 NLT)

Could you imagine you being nasty or rude to a man or a woman or a child who could have been an angel of the LORD in disguise? That is why we need to be very careful how we treat other people. What if on that day standing before God you see that man, or woman, or child, or angel whom you have mistreated standing before you? Could you imagine the guilt? Therefore, let us love at all times, all day long, all week long, all month long, and all year round!

CHAPTER SIX

Why The Blacks Are Not Yet Free: Tracing The Root Causes Of Racial Tensions And Civil Unrest In America

I am a firm believer in the principle that you cannot cure a disease or solve a problem without first knowing the pathogen or virus or bacterium causing that disease or problem, otherwise, one will end up with the wrong diagnosis, the wrong prescription, and the wrong medication which could complicate and make matters worse. And so it is with the disease of racism and hatred which has become like a cancerous wound in our nation and in the world as a whole. In this chapter, we are going to trace the root causes of the ongoing racial, social, societal, and political tensions and civil unrest in America and the reasons why the Blacks are not yet free.

In my own little study and observation and by the divine revelation given me by the Holy Spirit concerning this cancerous disease of racism and the racial tensions in America, I have been able to identify about six main reasons that I strongly believe are the root causes for the continuing racial, social, and political tensions and civil unrest in America, and that have held the Blacks in bondage.

And these six main issues are slavery, the Jim Crow laws of racial segregation, systemic and institutional racism, the welfare system, the culture of drugs and gun violence, and the massive breakdown of the Black African American family.

These are the six main root causes and evil instruments of racial injustice that are causing deep-seated generational wounds, hurts, pain, anger, hatred, bitterness, resentments, unforgiveness, revenge, and killings in America.

Now, I used the word main, because I strongly believe that there are some people and movements that have hijacked this genuine cry for racial justice and equality of the Black African Americans and have made it into a political race card and for their own personal agendas and ulterior motives. And we are seeing all of that being played out hypocritically.

And it is my fervent prayer that the eyes of our African American brothers and sisters will be wide opened to see the light and to know the truth that will set them totally free. It is my fervent prayer that the eyes of racial, political, cultural, societal, and spiritual blindness will be opened, and every cataract that has blurred our vision in the past be totally removed so that we can regain our complete 20-20 vision and the right perspective and the right action and reaction to the race, social, and political issues and injustices in America and the world.

And I say this with a great burden and passion with weeping in my heart because it breaks my heart to see what is happening in our nation and in the world. And when I look at the whole history of the Black race, my heart throbs with pain deep down inside me.

That is why I am making this awakening call to all our Black, White, Hispanic, Native Indian, Jewish, African, Asian brothers and sisters and to all our other brothers and sisters of the different races in America and in the world to let our spirits and consciences be awakened to the truth, and be enlightened by the truth, and be set free by the truth! And that light and truth is Jesus Christ, who is the only way, the truth, and the life! He is the Lamb of God, and not a political elephant or donkey!

For only Jesus can save America and the world and not a political party or donkey or elephant! Jesus alone has come as the redeeming Lamb of God, slain on the Cross to emancipate us from slavery to sin, greed, selfishness, hatred, racism, injustices, inhumanities, wickedness, and from all bondages and strongholds of the devil, and to set us totally free! Therefore, *"Behold! The Lamb of God who takes away the sins of '**America**' and the world!"* (John 1:29 NKJV, emphasis)

For far too long we have been deceived, lied to, blinded, and muzzled, but now is the hour of awakening and enlightening! God is bringing a spiritual, moral, racial, societal, cultural, and political awakening and enlightenment! Therefore, let none of us be taken for granted or for a free ride anymore as political donkeys or elephants transporting politicians on our already whipped and bruised backs to the corridors of power in Washington, DC, and to their state capitols, governors' mansions, and mayoral offices and edifices where they dismount and send us back home empty handed with empty promises!

Let there be no more politically free rides! But let conscience arise! Let truth arise! Let justice arise! Let freedom arise! Let love arise! And let the people *"Arise and shine, for their light is come, and the glory of the LORD is risen upon them. For behold, darkness has covered **America** and the earth, and gross darkness the people; but the LORD shall arise upon His people, and His glory shall be seen upon them, and the Gentiles,* *and kings, and their sons and daughters shall come running to the brightness of their light!"* (Isaiah 60:1-3, emphasis)

I guess you can sense the righteous indignation and passion inside me. And this is because I hate racism and all forms of injustices and evils and wickedness and inhumanities being perpetrated against all our children, women, men, and against all our fellow human beings who have been created in the image and likeness of our God! They are all our fellow human beings and not "human pigs" or "guinea pigs" to be racially, socially, culturally, politically, and scientifically experimented and tested on! I HATE INJUSTICE IN ANY FORM!

Let us now take a look at each of these six main evil instruments of oppression and injustices that have continued to hold the Blacks in America in perpetual bondage and fanning the flames of racial, social, and political tensions and civil unrest in America.

I.   The Evil Instrument of Slavery

Freedom is an inalienable, creative, divine right for all men, women, and children who have been created in the image and likeness of God. This means that all men, women, and children are created and born free. And since all men are created and born free, therefore all men and all unborn babies have the freedom and right to life, the freedom and right to live, the freedom and right to breathe, the freedom and right to exist, and the freedom and right to justice, equality, and pursuit of happiness!

These golden principles have been meticulously crafted and enshrined in the article of the Declaration of Independence, which states that, *"All Men are created equal, and that they are endowed by their Creator with certain unalienable Rights among which are Life, Liberty, and pursuit of Happiness!"*

If that is the case, which I believe is the case, then slavery in America was therefore an act of total violation and an aberration from the very said July 4, 1776 article of the Declaration of Independence. We see therefore that from its very inception slavery was an ungodly, unjust, unconstitutional, undemocratic, inhumane, cruel, barbaric, devilish, hellish, and a diabolical act of racial injustice, discrimination, inequality, indignity, demoralization, degradation, dehumanization, suppression, repression, depression, and oppression of the Blacks and other races of people not only in America, but anywhere else in the world!

It was a high crime against humanity and against God who created all men equal and free. Slavery was harsh, cruel, brutal, and fatal! It was an existential threat against the Black race in America. Even though America is called the land of the free and of the brave, yet still, the Black slaves were not free and brave. Their freedom and bravery were muzzled by the fiery and brazen chains of brutal and cruel oppression and human degradation and indignity!

Slavery was so repulsive and so immoral a sin that even President Abraham Lincoln recognized and acknowledged its divine consequences. In fact, he even said that the bloodiest Civil War on American soil was the divine displeasure and judgment of God for the evil of slavery; a judgment in which he said,

"Fondly do we hope – fervently do we pray – that this mighty scourge of war may speedily pass away. Yet, if God wills that it continues until all the wealth piled by the bondman's two hundred and fifty years of unrequited toil shall be sunk and until every drop of blood drawn with the lash shall be paid by another drawn with the sword as was said three thousand years

ago so still it must be said 'the judgments of the Lord are true and righteous altogether."[15]

But thank God that there was hope for freedom and bravery at last! For on January 1, 1863, the same President Abraham Lincoln issued the Emancipation Proclamation, declaring that all slaves in the Southern states that are rebelling against the Union are forever free! And in December of 1865, by the end of the Civil War, the United States Constitution was amended to free all slaves living in any part of the United States. That Thirteenth Amendment stated that,

"Neither slavery nor involuntary servitude, except as a punishment for crime whereof the party shall have been duly convicted, shall exist within the United States, or any place subject to their jurisdiction." This completed the work that the Emancipation Proclamation had begun – ending all slavery in the United States.[16]

It was on that day that the old Negro spiritual song of the freed slaves could be heard arising from the dungeons of slavery to the pinnacles of freedom: "Free at last, free at last, Great GOD Almighty, I'm free at last!" And this was re-echoed in the late Rev. Dr. Martin Luther King's Jr.'s famous speech of, "I Have a Dream."

Now you may say or think that slavery ended over one hundred and fifty years ago, and it's got nothing to do with the continuing racial, social, and political tensions and civil unrest in America. Yes, it does, and this is how: When the LORD gave me the dream of this young African American man who was angry and raging and was full of bitterness, resentment, revenge, murder, and unforgiveness, the LORD also showed me the inside of this young Black man's heart how he was badly broken and deeply wounded, hurt, and bruised on the inside.

And the LORD said to me that what I saw in that young Black man's heart was a representation of the deep wounds, hurts, pain, offence, anger, bitterness, resentment, brokenness, unforgiveness that the majority of the Black African Americans have been carrying up to this point. He showed me how the cruelty of slavery has left deep emotional, mental, psychological, and generational wounds, hurts, pain, and scars on the Blacks in America.

The LORD also showed me that when the Black slaves were freed, that they came out of slavery badly broken and deeply wounded, bruised, shattered, and scarred emotionally, mentally, psychologically, physically, economically, politically, and racially. And the LORD showed me that the only thing that they came out with that was not broken in them was their faith in God. Their faith was the only thing that was unbroken in them; all else was broken!

And the LORD said to me that they've never been totally healed and set free because immediately after their slavery was ended, they were subjected to another evil instrument of oppression under the Jim Crow laws of racial segregation and discrimination.

And God said to me that these deep-seated wounds and hurts and pain and scars and anger and bitterness and resentments have become generational strongholds that have been passed onto their children, and which can only be broken by the conquering and redeeming power of the love of God.

And these things that the LORD showed me, I have personally encountered them with almost every Black African American that I have come into contact with. In one of those encounters, I have literally heard a Black father telling these things to his little girl, who became very upset and told her dad to stop telling her those things. My wife has also had similar encounters. I have also had conversations with quite a number of people both Blacks and Whites who have confirmed this to me.

And God wants to bring healing, restoration, reconciliation, peace, unity, and freedom not only to our African American brothers and sisters but also to all the other races and people in America and in the world. And until then, the Blacks are not yet free!

ii. The Evil Instrument of the Jim Crow Laws of Racial Segregation

The second evil instrument of oppression that has been used to deepen the wounds, scars, hurts, pain, and sufferings of the African Americans was the Jim Crow laws of racial segregation and discrimination that began in the 1870s and existed until the 1960s. And to me, the Jim Crow laws of racial segregation and discrimination were as evil as slavery itself, if not worse.

Like the Orwellian maxim that said, "All animals are equal, but some animals are more equal than others," so were the Jim Crow laws of racial segregation that acknowledged the equality of the White and Black races but then denied their integration, preferring racial segregation with "For Whites Only" signs and "For Blacks Only" signs. That was not equality, but another evil weapon of racial injustice and discrimination, inequality, suppression, repression, oppression, and depression of the Black race, who have just been freed from the shackles of slavery and were broken, bruised, crushed, wounded, weak, and dispirited!

For the newly freed slaves, the Jim Crow laws of racial segregation and discrimination were like jumping from the frying pan into the fire. When they lost the Civil War, which was over slavery, the Southern slave states went ahead to enact and implement the Jim Crow laws of racial segregation in order to disenfranchise and remove all political and economic gains made by Blacks during the Reconstruction period.[17] It was apartheid America!

In fact, to me, the Jim Crow laws were even more vicious than slavery itself. And the reason why I say that is because if by the time the slaves were set free and they would have been given equal and fair chances of opportunities and the freedom to compete and to advance themselves politically, economically, educationally, scientifically, technologically, and socially, I believe the African Americans would not have been in this kind of economic, financial, social, educational, political, and racial quagmire in which they find themselves, and the wheels of our nation's chariots would not have been bogged down in the middle of the Red Sea drowned by perennial racial, social, and political tensions and unrest.

Things would have been completely different, and we would not be talking about racial injustices and racial inequalities and unrest by now. The Jim Crow Laws of racial segregation were like Pharaoh's army coming after the newly freed Israelite slaves.

It was through the Jim Crow laws that the evil instruments of racial segregation, discrimination, prejudice, profiling, injustices, inequalities, and police brutality were all implemented and enforced. They were laws meant to deprive, strangulate, retardate, and stagnate the Blacks politically, economically, educationally, intellectually, scientifically, technologically, socially, and racially.

The Jim Crow laws of racial segregation that read for "Whites Only" were an assertion of the ideology of White supremacy and Black inferiority. And it was from these same Jim Crow laws of racial segregation that the White supremacist group, the Ku Klux Klan (KKK) was born in the same Southern former slave states. While "Blacks Only" schools and other institutions were underfunded and malnourished, the "Whites Only" schools and other institutions were well funded and well-nourished.

It was an evil system of classification and stratification of the American society. And that was the beginning of systemic and institutional racism in America. And this has further deepened the wounds, scars, hurts, pain, sufferings, anger, bitterness, resentments, and distrust deep down inside the Black African Americans.

The LORD also showed me how this ideology of White superiority and supremacy has also become a generational stronghold in the minds of our White brothers and sisters that can only be broken by the same conquering and redeeming power of the love of God, and which I strongly believe God is going to do. Until then, the Blacks are not yet free!

iii. The Evil Instrument of Systemic or Institutional Racism

The third evil instrument of oppression that has further deepen the wounds, scars, hurts, pain, anger, bitterness, and resentments of the African Americans is systemic and institutional racism that is deeply embedded in our society and institutions that continue to discriminate against Blacks, especially in our criminal justice system, employment, housing, health care, politics, education, the economy, etc. Yes indeed, slavery was abolished over a century and a half ago, and the Jim Crow laws of racial segregation were ended in the early 1960s, and yet still the evil legacy of systemic and institutional racism, racial discrimination, racial injustices, racial profiling, racial inequality, and police brutality continue to persist in our culture today, both covertly and overtly.

The civil rights movements of the early sixties were a response to these systemic and institutional racism and racial injustices, discrimination, and inequalities against the Black race in America. Or else, why is it that after 100 years of the emancipation of the Black slaves in 1863, that in 1963, on August 28, the late Rev. Dr. Martin Luther King, Jr. would lead a march to Washington, DC, calling for economic, social, educational, political rights and freedom and to end racism with his iconic speech of, "I Have a Dream?" A dream for the abolition of racism and for racial justice, equality, love, peace, harmony, and for racial reconciliation and prosperity. Listen to his speech:

"I am happy to join with you today in what will go down in history as the greatest demonstration for freedom in the history of our nation. Five score years ago, a great American, in whose symbolic shadow we stand today, signed the Emancipation Proclamation. This momentous decree came as a great beacon light of hope to millions of Negro slaves, who had been seared in the long night of their captivity.

But one hundred years later, the Negro still is not free. One hundred years later, the life of the Negro is still sadly crippled by the manacles of segregation and the chains of discrimination. One hundred years later, the Negro lives on a lonely island of poverty in the midst of a vast ocean of material prosperity. One hundred years later, the Negro is still languished in the corner of American society and finds himself an exile in his own land."[18]

Yes indeed, the Civil Rights Act of 1964 was a landmark act that supposedly ended discrimination based on race, color, religion, sex, or national origin, and yet still the evil legacy of systemic and institutional racism, racial injustice, racial profiling, racial discrimination, racial inequality, and police brutality continue to persist in our culture today, overtly, and covertly. The civil rights movement led especially by people like Rosa Parks, the Rev. Dr. Martin Luther King, Jr., and many others, was a great thrust and success that brought about some great changes in the lives of African Americans and in terms of our race relations in America.

The great "I Have a Dream" vision of the late Rev. Dr. Martin Luther King, Jr., has made some great strides, but it is yet to be fully realized because the evil tentacles of systemic and institutional racism continue to persist covertly and overtly.

What we have seen over the decades is that racism seems to be metamorphosing and evolving from one form of oppression to the other, like a hydra's head. And until these heads of this demonic hydra of systemic and institutional racism, racial discrimination, racial inequalities, and racial injustices are spiritually, socially, politically, and institutionally decapitated and its body dismembered and cast into the bottomless pit of hell! Until then, the Blacks are not yet free!

iv. The Welfare System

Now I know this is going to sound controversial, nevertheless, I am willing to take the bull by its horns. For to me, even the introduction of the welfare system to assist the poor disadvantaged Blacks and others may have been either well or ill or mixed intentioned. I don't know. The only thing I know is that if, as they say, that the end justifies the means, or if, as the Lord Jesus said, that wisdom is justified by her children, then certainly whatever the political or humanitarian intentions behind the introduction of the welfare system seemed to have neither justified the means, nor has wisdom been justified by her children!

And this is because so far, the welfare system has not proven to be an economically, financially, socially, politically, and racially viable program for the Blacks since its introduction. On the contrary, the welfare system has proven to become an economically, financially, socially, racially, and politically dependable program that doesn't bring economic and financial freedom, independence, advancement, and prosperity for the Black African Americans. You just have to take a look at the statistics and see the gap between the Blacks who live off this welfare system and their White counterparts and others who are gainfully employed and own houses, properties, businesses, etc.

The old English proverb that says, "Give a man a fish and you feed him for a day; teach a man to fish and you feed him for a lifetime," holds so true. It speaks of a proverbial economic, financial, social, political freedom and independence, advancement, and prosperity.

Now, let me make myself very clear here: I am not totally against the welfare system itself. We have vulnerable people in our society that need some form of government support and assistance, such as the elderly, the poor, the disabled, the unemployed, etc. That is moral responsibility. However, when the system itself has become politicized and culturized to keep the vast majority of Blacks in government handouts, food stamps, etc., then that becomes a problem, and is tantamount to another form of economic, financial, political, and societal slavery.

The welfare system, to some extent is a disincentive to hard work, to economic and financial freedom, to free enterprise and ownership, and to achieving the American Dream and the full realization of the "I Have A Dream" vision of the late Rev.

King, Jr. It leads to poverty, dependency, and bondage, and not to prosperity, independence, and freedom!

It has even led to some sort of a blind political patronage and bondage. And by that, I mean, any party or politician that advocates for the welfare system is the party and politician that many of those who depend on it will vote for. Of course, that's human nature. But to me, this is blind political patronage and bondage! The welfare system has become like a political and psychological stronghold to many: something almost like a spell. But what the Blacks desperately need is not sympathy or empathy but healing, freedom, justice, equality, and empowerment!

Like their White counterparts and other races, what the Blacks desperately need is economic, financial, and political freedom, private ownership, and entrepreneurship! They need financial, economic, educational, scientific, technological, and political leverage to compete! And until they are free from the welfare system and government handouts and food stamps, until then, the Blacks are not yet free!

v. The Culture of Drugs and Gun Violence in the Black Communities

Like I have already said at the beginning of this chapter that the physical chains of slavery may have been broken off the backs of the Black slaves, but then they came out of the cruelty of slavery badly and deeply broken, crushed, bruised, wounded, and hurting emotionally, mentally, psychologically, and intellectually.

And from the shackles of slavery to the manacles of the Jim Crow laws of racial segregation with its educational, political, economic, social, and racial discrimination, deprivations, injustices, and inequalities. And from there to the tentacles of systemic and institutional racism and discrimination. And from there to being locked into an economically and financially disadvantageous welfare system.

All of these societal ills and disadvantages combined have in turn plunged the Blacks into further societal and circumstantial bondages such as drugs, alcohol, crime, gun violence, and mass incarcerations. It is an already vulnerable people, and the enemy is preying on their vulnerability by offering them with drugs, alcohol, and guns. The Black-on-Black gun violence and death rates in our communities are outrageous!

Most of the Black communities and neighborhoods are plagued by dangerous drugs and substance abuse and alcohol and are rife in gun violence and crimes with mass incarcerations of hundreds and thousands of young and prospective Black men and women all across America. The precious lives and destinies and talents and gifts of these young prospective Black men and women are being wasted in the jail yards and graveyards of our nation!

I have lived in different neighborhoods and communities in America, but I have found out that it is mostly the Black neighborhoods that are rife in crime, drugs, alcohol, and gun violence. And I have also found out that all of these neighborhoods are replete with liquor stores, drugs, and crack houses. And I often wonder why is that? Is it by design or by default? I don't know. All I know is that all of these societal ills have further put the Blacks in bondage. And until our Black communities and neighborhoods are set free from these endemic societal problems; until then the Blacks are not yet free!

vi. The Destruction of the Black Family

This is the most destructive attack that the enemy has launched against the Blacks in America: the destruction of the Black family. The Bible says that if the foundations are destroyed what would the righteous do? One of the greatest contributing factors to the problems we are facing in our Black communities and the nation as a whole is the massive breakdown of the family unit.

The family is a divine institution ordained by God and it is the solid foundation upon which all other institutions for progress, development and advancement are built. It is true that the typical Black African American family heritage was built upon these godly principles, standards, and disciplines with a high sense of spirituality, morality, love, and community. However, it seems as if those godly principles, standards, and disciplines have been gradually eroded and corroded over the years to the degradation and disintegration of the Black African American family.

And once the institution of the family is broken, then the results will be broken families, broken homes, broken children, broken parents, broken neighborhoods, broken communities, broken schools, broken society, and a broken nation with high rates of teenage pregnancy, abortions, father-lessness, single parenting, joblessness, homelessness, drugs and alcohol abuse, gangs, gun violence, lawlessness, crimes, incarcerations, etc.! The statistics are out there for all to see and the evidence is clear. For instance, just take a look at the high abortion rate among the Blacks in America: it is the highest among all other races of people. This in itself carries with it the potential of a racial, socio-economic, and political "suicide" that is dwindling the Black population and significantly diminishing their Black voting power and leverage.

A Clarion Call!

The Blacks must arise and reclaim back their proud ancestral family and godly heritage that was once the strong biblical foundation of the African American family! Let the Blacks arise and reclaim back their lives, their children, their homes, their families, their neighborhoods, and their communities!

Let the Blacks arise and reclaim back their spiritual, moral, entrepreneurial, economic, political, educational, innovative, inventive, technological, academic, intellectual, and scientific brilliance and resilience! Let the Blacks arise to the spirit of diligence, excellence, competence, and competition! Let the Blacks arise and take charge of their divine destinies and of their prosperity, and posterity!

Let us raise our children as ministers, priests, royals, doctors, lawyers, judges, presidents, senators, governors, congressmen, mayors, teachers, professors, nurses, businessmen, scientists, astronauts, pilots, farmers, policemen, soldiers, marines, firefighters, innovators, inventors, investors, husbands, wives, fathers, mothers, families, and as leaders!

Let us raise them in love, dignity, virtue, excellence, and as patriots, victors, achievers, overcomers, and more than conquerors! These things must be taught, instilled, and inculcated in our children as they grow up in the home. The Bible says to train up a child in the way he should go, and when he is old, he will not depart from it! (Proverbs 22:6) Let us school our children well in spirituality, morality, integrity, dignity, discipline, diligence, and excellence before they are brainwashed and indoctrinated by society! Until then, the Blacks are not yet free!

But There Is Hope for Healing, Restoration, Reconciliation and Freedom!

These are the six main issues and evil instruments of racial injustices and oppression that have been affecting the Blacks in America for over two centuries now, and that are the main root causes for the continuing racial, social, and political tensions and civil unrest in America. What we have seen here is the subtle metamorphosis and evolving of this hydra of racism from one form to another, modernizing the instruments used along the way. And for the Blacks, it has been like jumping from the frying pan into the fire of pain kind of a scenario.

And so, for over four hundred years since slavery started in America, the Blacks have been carrying these generational wounds, scars, hurts, pain, anger, bitterness, resentments, offenses and unforgiveness, as I was shown in the dream. And God said they've never been totally healed and set free, but that He wants to bring healing, restoration, reconciliation, freedom, peace, and unity not only to the Blacks, but also to the Whites and to all the other races and colors of people in America.

The Bible says that *"A brother offended is harder to win than a strong city. And contentions are like the bars of a castle."* (Proverbs 18:19 NKJV) Our nation is right now broken, wounded, hurting, divided, and offended, but God wants to bring healing, restoration, freedom, reconciliation, peace, and unity through the power of His love that is in Christ Jesus. God is going to bring a revival of love that is going to come with forgiveness, healing, salvation, deliverance, reconciliation, miracles, signs and wonders, joy, peace, freedom, and blessings!

Again, speaking prophetically, the late Rev. Dr. Martin Luther King, Jr. did warn the Black African Americans not to drink from the cup of bitterness and hatred in their struggle for racial justice and freedom. He said:

"But there is something that I must say to my people, who stand on the warm threshold which leads into the palace of justice: in the process of gaining our rightful place, we must not be guilty of wrongful deed. Let us not seek to satisfy our thirst for freedom by drinking from the cup of bitterness and hatred. We must forever conduct our struggle on the high plane of dignity and discipline. We must not allow our creative protest to degenerate into physical violence. Again, and again, we must rise to the majestic heights of meeting physical force with soul force."[19]

The late Dr. Martin Luther King, Jr, would not have said that if he himself had not foreseen this: the hatred and bitterness. What this means is that you cannot fight injustice with injustice, and neither can you fight racism and hatred with hatred, but you fight racism and hatred with love.

All the street protests, rioting, burning, looting, shootings, killings, toppling down historical statues, defunding the police, etc., is not the answer. People are calling to reform the police, but the truth is, it is not just the police that needs reform, but our politicians, our government, our congress, The White House, our supreme court, our justice system, our families, our homes, our schools, our colleges, our universities, our prisons, our workplaces, our institutions, the protesters, the rioters, and America as a whole need reform.

In fact, you cannot reform institutions when the heart of man remains spiritually and morally deformed by sin, racism, hatred, bitterness, resentment, anger, revenge, and unforgiveness. It is the heart that is in desperate need of transformation and reformation. Before kingdoms can change, man must change first, and from within. Therefore, before our communities and nation can change man must change first from within the heart.

God is going to send us a revival of love that is going to break off the chains and fetters and shackles of these generational curses and strongholds of slavery, racism, hatred, anger, bitterness, resentments, unforgiveness, and of all other racial, societal, economic, educational, and political bondages and injustices. And God is going to bring healing, deliverance, salvation, restoration, reconciliation, justice, freedom peace, unity, love, joy, blessings, breakthroughs, miracles, signs, and wonders. This is the only answer for our racial, societal, political, and national healing and reconciliation in America and the world. Therefore, God is saying to the "Pharaohs" of this world to "Let My people go!"

CHAPTER SEVEN

There Is A New Breed Of" I Have A Dream" Generation Rising Up!

There is a new breed of "I Have a Dream" generation of children rising up! Yes! I see a new breed generation of children of both Millennials and Generation-Z rising up in America and in the nations of the world who care less about racism and hatred and the color of one's skin or race. All they care about is love! All they care about is loving, appreciating, honoring, respecting, supporting, caring for one another, and looking after each other. It is a generation of children that only cares to love their neighbors as themselves. It is a generation whose love knows no racial boundaries and will cross and crisscross every racial line and ethnicity and nationality.

It is not a pedigree generation, but a new breed generation arising out of the burnt ashes of the flames of slavery and oppression, racial segregation, institutional racism, societal discrimination, inequalities, injustices, inhumanities, and hatred!

They are arising out of the poisonous and infectious miry clay of political quagmire of divisiveness, polarization, vitriols, and brinkmanship!

They are made up of children of the descendants of freed slaves, and children of the descendants of former slave masters and slave owners, and children of the descendants of immigrants from every race, ethnicity, and skin color!

This new breed generation is the generation that is desperately yearning for the full realization of the late Rev. Dr. Martin Luther King, Jr.'s "I Have a Dream" prophetic vision, whereby Blacks, Whites, Indians, Hispanics, Jews, Africans, Asians, Europeans, and all the children of the other races and colors of people can live together in love, peace, harmony, and dignity as brothers and sisters and as neighbors of the same human race and as true Americans! They can hear that distant voice and sound and echo of:

"Let us not wallow in the valley of despair. I say to you today, my friends: so even though we face the difficulties of today and tomorrow, I still have a dream. It is a dream deeply rooted in the American dream.

I have a dream that one day this nation will rise up and live out the true meaning of its creed – we hold these truths to be self-evident that all men are created equal.

I have a dream that one day on the hills of Georgia the sons of former slaves and the sons of former slave owners will be able to sit down together at the table of brotherhood.

I have a dream that one day the state of Mississippi, a state sweltering with the heat of injustice, sweltering with the heat of oppression, will be transformed into an oasis of freedom and justice.

I have a dream that my four little children will one day live in a nation where they will not be judged by the color of their skin but by the content of their character.

I have a dream today!

I have a dream that one day, down in Alabama, with its vicious racists, with its governor having his lips dripping with the words of interposition and nullification; one day right there in Alabama little black boys and black girls will be able to join hands with little white boys and white girls as sisters and brothers.

I have a dream today!

I have a dream that one day every valley shall be exalted, and every hill and mountain shall be made low, the rough places will be made plain, and the crooked places will be made straight and the glory of the Lord shall be revealed and all flesh shall see it together.

This is our hope. This is the faith that I will go back to the South with. With this faith we will be able to hew out of the mountain of despair a stone of hope.

With this faith we will be able to transform the jangling discords of our nation into a beautiful symphony of brotherhood. With this faith we will be able to work together, to pray together, to struggle together, to go to jail together, to stand up for freedom together, knowing that we will be free one day.

This will be the day, this will be the day when all of God's children will be able to sing with new meaning: 'My country 'tis of thee, sweet land of liberty, of thee I sing. Land where my fathers died, land of the Pilgrim's pride, from every mountainside, let freedom ring!' And if America must become a great nation, this must become true."[20]

This is that dream and hope that this new breed of "I Have a Dream" generation is desperately longing to be fully realized in their lives and in their time! They are disgusted and tired with all that they see taking place around them. They want to love one another regardless of their race, color, tribe, ethnicity, nationality, religion, creed, or their social, educational, economic, or political status or fetus in society.!

They want to relate, share, support, work, play, eat, laugh, and live together free with no racial or societal barriers! This is God's original intent and purpose for the entire human race since the beginning of times for all men to dwell together in love, peace, joy, unity, harmony, and happiness.

And it is still God's plan and purpose even now and in the coming future millennial reign of our Lord and Savior Jesus Christ. And in that time, not only will all the redeemed from every nation and every tongue and every race be gathered and live together in eternal love, joy, peace, and happiness, but that even all of creation will enter an endless age of eternal peace and harmony. The Bible says for:

"In that day the wolf and the lamb will live together: the leopard will lie down with the baby goat. The calf and the year-ling will be safe with the lion, and a little child will lead them all. The cow will graze near the bear. The curb and the calf will lie down together. The lion will eat hay like a cow. The baby will play safely near the hole of a cobra. Yes, a little child will put its hand in a nest of deadly snakes without harm. Nothing will hurt or destroy in all My holy mountain, for as the waters fill the sea, so the earth will be filled with people who know the LORD." (Isaiah 11:6-9 NLT)

This is how it's going to be like when the Lord Jesus shall come again the second time to rid this earth of all sin and evils, and to establish His eternal kingdom of love, peace, joy, truth, justice, and righteousness!

What God Showed Me

I used to drive for Uber in the Washington DC and DMV metropolitan area of Maryland and Virginia. One day, I picked up this elderly Black African American man in his late sixties or early seventies with a little girl about 10 years old or so, whom I thought was his granddaughter, but it turned out to be she was his daughter. The moment they got into the car; he went into a tirade against the Whites; complaining about almost every-thing racially prejudiced and discriminated against the Blacks in America, beginning from the time of slavery.

As I listened to him, I could sense that there was hatred, anger, bitterness, resentment, unforgiveness, pain, and hurt coming out of him. And as he was going on like that, suddenly, the little girl said to him in distress that he should stop telling her these stories and that she doesn't want to hear or listen to them anymore.

I could tell that the little girl was evidently upset and trau-matized emotionally, mentally, and psychologically. I myself was in utter shock. And so, I said to the dad that what his daughter was telling him is the truth. I told him that he should be teaching his daughter about love, forgiveness, virtue, values, patriotism, etc. I told him to go past this history of slavery, racism, and hatred. But he insisted that it is his duty as a father to pass on this history to his children.

After I dropped them off, I began to ponder on these things and on the racial problems in America. It was then that God began to give me an in-depth knowledge and understanding of how deep-rooted the stronghold of racism and hatred in America is. God showed me that the little girl is a representa-tion of a new breed generation of children that is rising up who do not care about racism, race, and the skin color of a person. And that all they care about is loving and caring for one another.

God is about to bring the full realization of the late Dr. Martin Luther King Jr.'s "I Have a Dream" prophetic vision. And this is that generation that will see the fulfillment and full realization of that. It has already begun, but it has not been fully realized yet, and God wants to bring that to full realization.

And that is why He is raising up this new breed generation out of those burnt ashes to break the final shackles and chains of racism, hatred, bitterness, resentments, and unforgiveness, and to bring healing, restoration, and reconciliation.

It is a new breed generation that is crying and desperately yearning for the full realization of the article of the Declaration of Independence that states, *"WE hold these Truths to be self-evident, that all Men are created equal, that they are endowed by their Creator with certain unalienable Rights, that among these are Life, Liberty, and the Pursuit of Happiness."*[21]

It is a new breed generation that believes in the Equality Act of God and the commonalities of the human race, and not in the superiority or inferiority of the races!

It is a new breed generation that yearns to see all races and colors of people to be treated equally and fairly with love, justice, respect, dignity, freedom, liberty, and the pursuit of happiness!

It is a new breed generation that hates to see all the street protests, rioting, burnings, looting, shootings, killings, lawlessness, and anarchy, and are tired of being fed with daily contaminated and unhealthy fake and toxic news! They are crying for genuine love, peace, calm, unity, and reconciliation. They just want to love everyone regardless of their race or skin color. They want to be their brothers and sisters and neighbors and promised keepers! They are yearning for the full realization of the American dream for everyone!

A Clarion Call!

Therefore, here is my clarion call to all parents, fathers, mothers, families, relatives, guardians, teachers, professors, pastors, priests, rabbis, politicians, journalists, etc., let us stop indoctrinating and brainwashing our children with the poison of racism and hatred, and let us teach them love. Let us teach them patriotism and not racism or terrorism or extremism. Let us teach them virtues and values and not violence and vices. Let us teach them forgiveness and not bitterness, resentment, and revenge.

Let us teach them principles, law, and order and not rebellion and lawlessness. Let us teach them dignity, respect, and honor and not indignity, disrespect, and dishonor. Let us teach them about the sacredness and sanctity of life, the institution of marriage, and of the family as the foundation of society and civilization.

Over and above all, let us teach them about God and His amazing love, joy, peace, justice, mercy, freedom, and of His saving grace toward all mankind. Let us train up our children in the ways of God at home so that when they grow old, they will not depart from it. Let us teach them godly values and not gun violence.

Let us teach them love for God, love for neighbors, love for country, and love for self. Let us inculcate these things in them in the home before they are indoctrinated and brainwashed in the schools, colleges, universities, and by the mainstream and social media. Let us reclaim back our children, our families, and our homes!

Just like the late Rev. Dr. Martin Luther King, Jr., said that we would not be satisfied until justice rolls down like waters and righteousness like a mighty stream, so also I urge that we should not give our eyes rest until tears run down like a river, day and night, pouring out our hearts like water before the face of the Lord, lifting our hands toward heaven with weeping and mourning and groaning and travailing for the precious souls of our dear children that are hungering, famishing, languishing, and being destroyed in every street corner of our societies!

Like the prophets of old, let us cry out, *"O wall of the daughter of Zion, let tears run down like a river day and night; Give yourself no relief; Give your eyes no rest. Arise, cry out in the night; At the beginning of the watches; Pour out your heart like water before the face of the LORD. Lift your hands toward Him for the life of your young children who faint for hunger at the head of every street."* (Lamentations 2:18-19 NKJV)

Not only should we not be satisfied until justice and freedom run down as waters and righteousness and love as a mighty ocean; but we should also not give ourselves rest nor give God rest for the precious souls of our children until revival breaks out from heaven above, and until God pours out His Spirit upon us and upon our children with a new awakening and a new dawn and a new realization of the "I Have A Dream" prophecy! This is how God is going to do it and to bring it about! For this is the only answer! (Joel 2:12-32; Acts 2:1-21)

CHAPTER EIGHT

A Cry For Freedom: What Is True Freedom?

One of the greatest cries and thirsting of the soul of man is for freedom! It is one of the cries and yearning of every man, woman, and child. The world is crying for freedom, but there is no true freedom because all men are born slaves to sin. And this means that every man, woman, and child ever born into this world is born a slave to sin. The entire human race has been subjected to this universal slavery to sin when Adam and Eve sinned. And since all men are born slaves to sin, therefore no man is ever truly free without Christ because true freedom is found in Christ Jesus alone! Sin enslaves all men, but love sets all men free. There is no freedom in sin, but there is freedom in love!

America is called the land of the free, but is America truly free? When President Abraham Lincoln issued the "Emancipation Proclamation," declaring that all Black slaves in the states rebelling against the Union are "forever free," were those Black slaves forever free? The answer as to whether America is truly the land of the free and whether the Black slaves were forever truly free is, "No!" Both America and the freed slaves are not truly free. As we have seen, there is not only a violation of people's freedom and rights in America, but there is still racism, racial injustices, discrimination, and inequalities. Therefore, America and the freed slaves and the whole wide world for that matter, are not truly free. The entire human race is not free but are slaves!

The Universal Slavery to Sin of the Entire Human Race

There is another kind of slavery in America and in the world that is not physical but spiritual. It is a universal slavery that has bound Blacks, Whites, Browns, Reds, Hispanics, Asians, Africans, Europeans, Australians, Russians, Jews, Indians, Chinese, Arabs, and all other races of people all over the world. It is a universal slavery that has bound all men, women, teenagers, children, old, young, rich, poor, kings and paupers alike. It is a universal slavery that has been going on for over six thousand years and is even more sinister, cruel, brutal, destructive, deadly, and damnable in nature. This is the slavery to Sin, and with this kind of slavery, the entire human race are the slaves, while the Devil is the slave owner and slave master, and his demons and evil spirits are his cruel and harsh taskmasters, and the whole wide world is the devil's plantation of sin and slavery.

All other forms of slavery, racism, segregations, apartheid, racial injustices, inhumanities, and all other forms of oppressions, suppressions and repressions are all byproducts of this universal slavery to sin. The whole wide world is the devil's plantation of sin and slavery. And millions and billions of the precious souls of men, women, teenagers, and children are all bound by this slavery to sin.

What the "Emancipation Proclamation" did was to set the Black slaves free politically and physically from corporeal slavery in the Whiteman's plantations. What the African

National Congress (ANC) did in South Africa was to end the cruel apartheid system of racial segregation against Black South Africans. What the wars of independence and liberation did in Africa, Asia, and South America were to end colonial rule from Britain and other European powers. What the Revolutionary War did in America was to gain independence from colonial Britain.

And what every other fight or struggle for freedom has done in the world is to break loose the chains of political, economic, social, religious, and racial oppressions, suppressions, and repressions over the oppressed. But what all of these movements of emancipation, liberation, revolution, and independence have not been able to do and cannot do is to set people free from the spiritual, emotional, mental, psychological, and moral bondages and slavery to sin and to the devil!

This means that even though people may be physically, politically, democratically, economically, technologically, scientifically, intellectually, socially, and racially free, yet still they are not spiritually, morally, emotionally, mentally, and psychologically free. They are still slaves to all kinds of sins and evils. They are still slaves to anger, bitterness, resentments, malice, grudges, and unforgiveness. They are still slaves to hurts, wounds, shame, guilt, and condemnation.

They are still slaves to hatred, racism, prejudice, and discrimination. They are still slaves to alcohol, drugs, cocaine, and smoking. They are still slaves to all kinds of sexual perversions, immoralities, pornography, prostitution, adultery, fornication, pedophilia, rape, sex trafficking, gambling, and addictions.

They are still slaves to witchcraft, idolatry, the occult, and satanism. They are still slaves to lustfulness, greed, envy, selfishness, jealousy, covetousness, lying, stealing, slander, backbiting and gossip. They are still slaves to fear, anxiety, depression, and suicide. They are still slaves to money, wealth, riches, material possessions, power, fame, popularity, pride, and arrogance. They are still slaves to their own bellies, appetites, carnal desires, gluttony, indulgences, debauchery, and pleasures.

And this type of slavery does not discriminate in that all men, women, children, old, young, rich, poor, kings, queens, princes, princesses, presidents, prime ministers, governors, senators, congressmen, Whites, Blacks, Browns, Reds, Hispanics, Asians, Africans, Europeans, Indians, Chinese, Jews, Arabs, Russians, and all other races of people are all bound, chained, and shackled in fetters by sin and by the devil!

It is a universal slavery of all mankind in the devil's plantation of sin in which you have demons and evil spirits trafficking the earth as harsh taskmasters lashing and lynching men, women, and children all over the world.

It is no longer a "Trans-Atlantic Slave Trade," but a "Trans-Global Slave Trade" of all mankind in which millions and billions of poor, precious souls of men, women, and children are being cheaply auctioned into slavery to sin and bondage by the devil! And there is no man born of a woman that can deliver the human race from this kind of slavery to sin and to the devil because all men have sinned, and a sinner cannot save another sinner! Therefore, America and the rest of the world would need another different kind of "Emancipation Proclamation" from this kind of slavery to sin.

And that is why over two thousand years ago, even long before President Abraham Lincoln signed that "Emancipation Proclamation" that ended slavery in America; and even long before the abolition of the Atlantic Slave Trade, there walked a "Man of Destiny" on Planet Earth by the name of Jesus Christ of Nazareth, who came down from heaven to declare a universal

"Emancipation Proclamation" of true freedom and liberty and justice to all mankind!

The Bible says that *"the whole world lieth in wickedness."* (1 John 5:19 KJV) The Bible also says that, *"For all have sinned, and come short of the glory of God."* (Romans 3:23 KJV)

Did you hear that? Not only does the whole wide world lies in wickedness, but that all men have sinned and have fallen short of the glory of God. And this means that if the whole wide world lies in wickedness, then the whole wide world has become the devil's plantation of sin and slavery, and if all men have sinned and fallen short of the glory of God, then all men are sinners and are slaves to sin!

The Apostle Paul describes the nature of this kind of spiritual and moral slavery when he wrote to the Christians in Rome, saying,

"Don't you realize that you become the slave of whatever you choose to obey? You can be a slave to sin, which leads to death, or you can choose to obey God, which leads to righteous living. Thank God! Once you were slaves of sin, but now you wholeheartedly obey this teaching we have given you. Now you are free from your slavery to sin, and you have become slaves to righteous living.

Because of the wickedness of your human nature, I am using the illustration of slavery to help you understand all this. Previously, you let yourselves be slaves to impurity and lawlessness, which led ever deeper into sin. Now you must give yourselves to be slaves to righteous living so that you will become holy.

When you were slaves to sin, you were free from the obligation to do right. And what was the result? You are now ashamed of the things you used to do, things that end in eternal doom. But now you are free from the power of sin and have become

slaves of God. Now you do those things that lead to holiness and result in eternal life. For the wages of sin is death, but the free gift of God is eternal life through Christ Jesus our Lord." (Romans 6"16-23, NLT)

This kind of slavery to sin leads to both spiritual, physical, and eternal death and damns the soul to hell. It is a universal slavery that began over six thousand years ago in the Garden of Eden when our first parents Adam and Eve sinned and became slaves to sin and to the devil. And there is no other man born of a woman that can save mankind from this kind of slavery except Jesus Christ, the Savior of the world.

The Bible says that there is salvation in no other name: for there is no other name under heaven given among men whereby we must be saved, except the name of Jesus. (Acts 4:12) The Bible also says that Jesus Christ is the only Savior of the whole world. (John 4:42) And that is why when Jesus began His earthly ministry, His first universal "Emancipation Proclamation" of true freedom and liberty was, *"The Spirit of the LORD is upon Me, Because He has anointed Me To preach the gospel to the poor; He has sent Me to heal the brokenhearted, to proclaim liberty to the captives and recovery of sight to the blind, to set at liberty those who are oppressed; To proclaim the acceptable year of the LORD."* (Luke 4:18-19 NKJV)

In that "Emancipation Proclamation" was included freedom, liberty, justice, righteousness, truth, equality, forgiveness, redemption, justification, salvation, sanctification, deliverance, healing, reconciliation, restoration, love, joy, peace, provision, protection, safety, assurance, hope, and eternal life for all men, women, and children! It is freedom and liberty for all and to all!

Jesus came to proclaim true freedom and liberty and release for the captives to sin, and to set at liberty all those who are oppressed; to open blind eyes and deaf ears; to heal the brokenhearted and all those who have been bruised by sin; to heal the sick, raise the dead, cleanse the lepers, cast out devils. He came to destroy the power of sin and death and of the devil and to announce the abolition of this "Trans-Global Slave Trade" and human trafficking and to free the captives from the devil's plantation of sin and slavery. He came to announce the arrival of God's true freedom and liberty and the forgiveness of sins and salvation and eternal life to all mankind.

Jesus said to the Jews, *"You are My disciples if you remain faithful to My teachings. And you will know the truth, and the truth will set you free." "But we are descendants of Abraham,"* they said. *"We have never been slaves to anyone. What do You mean, "You will be set free?" Jesus replied, "I tell you the truth, everyone who sins is a slave of sin...So if the Son sets you free, you are truly free."* (John 8:31-36 NLT)

In the above scriptural passage, Jesus made it very clear that anyone who commits sin is a slave to sin and that whoever the Son of God sets free is free indeed. This is that true freedom and liberty. Therefore, we clearly see here that true freedom and liberty from the bondage to sin and the devil and from racism, injustices, hatred, and from all other evils and addictions is found in Christ Jesus alone.

The Bible says, *"It is for freedom that Christ has set us free. Stand firm, then, and do not let yourselves be burdened again by a yoke of slavery."* (Galatians 5:1 NIV)

It is said of John Newton that he was an English sailor who later owned his own slave ship and traded in slaves, especially in West Africa. As a slave trader who shackled his slaves in chains, little did he know that he himself was a slave to a greater evil and that his own soul was chained in slavery to sin and the devil, until the day he encountered Jesus in the middle of a raging storm at sea. Terrified by the ferocity of the storm, and faced with the danger of imminent death, the torture of the horrors of his sins, and the fear of the terrors of hell, he cried out to God for mercy. That night, Jesus broke his chains of slavery to sin and freed him from his slave owner, the devil. For the first time in his miserable life, he breathed in the fresh life-giving breath of true freedom and liberty and was totally set free!

And it was after this divine encounter with Jesus that he went on to pen down one of the greatest hymns of all times: "Amazing Grace, How Sweet Thou Art, That Saved a Wretch Like Me." Like the prodigal son, he considered himself once blind, but now can see, and once lost, but now have been found. He went on to be ordained and became a very successful preacher, even to the final years of his death.

Jesus became his new slave owner who took away his heavy load of sin and gave him His yoke that is light and easy to carry. For Jesus has said, *"Come to Me, all you who are weary and carry heavy burdens, and I will give you rest. Take My yoke upon you. Let Me teach you, because I am humble and gentle at heart, and you will find rest for your souls. For My yoke is easy to bear, and the burden I give you is light."* (Matthew 11:28-30, NLT)

Like John Newton, it is because of this same heavy burden of sin that you are carrying that Jesus is inviting you to come to Him so that He can take it away from you and give you rest! Would you do that right now?

What Is True Freedom?

In the world today there is a global cry for freedom from human rights organizations, women's groups, Black Lives Matter, United Nations, governments, politicians, civil right activists, and from men, women, and children all over the world.

They are demanding freedom of choice, freedom of lifestyle, freedom of sex, freedom of dress, freedom of gender, freedom of speech, freedom of everything under the sun.

The cry for freedom and for free choice are in their highest demand ever. But the question is, what is true freedom? Because not all freedom is true freedom. As we have seen from scriptures that there is bondage and slavery in man's own choice of freedom without God. We saw that right from the very beginning when Adam and Eve exercised their own freedom, independence, and free choice apart from God.

What is true freedom then? As we have seen, Jesus' universal "Emancipation Proclamation" of true freedom and liberty is a supernatural proclamation of freedom and liberty from bondage to sin and from the devil's plantation of sin. It is freedom from all unrighteousness, ungodliness, wickedness, injustice, inhumanity, and racism, hatred, anger, bitterness, resentment, malice, unforgiveness, revenge, envy, jealousy, sexual perversions, immoralities, adultery, fornication, rape, pornography, prostitution, lustfulness, sex trafficking, and human trafficking and from all evil.

It is freedom from all selfishness, self-ambition, pride, greed, lying, stealing, slander, backbiting, gossip, dishonesty, corruption, gun violence, terrorism, crimes, murder, abortion, alcohol, drugs, smoking, gambling, addictions, idolatry, witchcraft, the occult, satanism, voodooism, juju, ancestral worship, and idol worship.

It is freedom from all fear, worry, anxiety, depression, oppression, unworthiness, hopelessness, and from all mental and emotional breakdowns and suicidal thoughts.

True freedom is living and experiencing Jesus' universal "Emancipation Proclamation" of freedom, liberty, justice, righteousness, truth, mercy, grace, forgiveness, salvation, redemption, deliverance, healing, blessings, provision, protection, safety, security, love, peace, joy, happiness, kindness, honor, racial equality, brotherly love, reconciliation, eternal hope, and eternal life!

This is that universal "Emancipation Proclamation" of true freedom and liberty that Jesus came to proclaim to the whole wide world! Man is not free until there is a supernatural emancipation of the spirit, soul, body and mind from the bondage and slavery to sin and to the devil. And no man or woman or child is ever free without Christ!

Even those who claim to have achieved the "American Dream" and have it all in life, many of them are in bondage to sin and to the devil. They are in bondage to all kinds of drug, alcohol, sex, pornographic, prescription, and antidepressants addictions. Yes, they may have it all, but deep down inside them their souls are empty, void, and devoid of love, joy, peace, satisfaction, happiness, and hope.

Deep down inside them is a dark chasm and empty void filled with nothing but broken-hearts, hurts, pain, betrayals, disappointments, discouragements, unhappiness, sadness, anger, hatred, bitterness, unforgiveness, malice, grudges, resentments, fear, anxiety, worries, guilt, regret, shame, accusations, condemnation, torments, helplessness, hopelessness, suicidal thoughts.

They are haunted by their past and their acts. Their own very souls have become "ghost-haunted" and "guilt-hounded!" And they try to fill that empty void with drugs, alcohol, sex, money, fame, riches, and with all kinds of pleasures.

But they forget to realize that the soul of man is an empty hole filled with nothing but emptiness without Christ. The implosion and explosion of sin in man has caused a deep spiritual crater and chasm in the soul of man. It is like the very bottomless pit of hell itself which cannot be filled or be satisfied by anything in this world that is man-made, but by Christ alone!

Jesus is the fullness of the Godhead and we are complete in Him alone! (Colossians 2:9-10) In Christ alone we live, and move, and have our being! (Acts 17:28) Only Jesus can fill that chasm, that void, that emptiness, that hole, and that bottomless pit of hell in the soul of man. In Him alone is true freedom and liberty! The Bible says that where the Spirit of the LORD is, there is freedom and liberty! (2 Corinthians 3:17)

And it is only through this universal "Emancipation Proclamation" of true freedom and liberty that Jesus came to proclaim that America and the world will be set free from the power of sin and the devil. It was on the Cross that Jesus destroyed the power of sin and of death and of the devil. And it was on the Cross that He has purchased our true freedom and liberty and redemption and remission, and has broken all the chains, fetters, shackles, yokes, and bondages of sin, death, and of the devil. Therefore, true freedom is freedom from all sins, all evils, and all devils! It means that sin does not reign in your mortal body anymore and has no control over you any-more. The Bible gives a brilliant description of what that true freedom means when it says:

"Well then, should we keep on sinning so that God can show us more and more of His wonderful grace? Of course not! Since we have died to sin, how can we continue to live in it? Or have you forgotten that when we were joined with Christ Jesus in baptism, we joined Him in His death? For we died and were buried with Christ by baptism. And just as Christ was raised from the dead by the glorious power of the Father, now we also may live new lives.

Since we have been united with Him in His death, we will also be raised to life as He was. We know that our old sinful selves were crucified with Christ so that sin might lose its power in our lives. We are no longer slaves to sin. For when we died with Christ, we were set free from the power of sin. And since we died with Christ, we know we will also live with Him. We are sure of this because Christ was raised from the dead, and He will never die again. Death no longer has any power over Him. When He died, He died once to break the power of sin. But now that He lives, He lives for the glory of God. So, you also should consider yourselves to be dead to the power of sin and alive to God through Christ Jesus.

Do not let sin control the way you live; do not give in to sinful desires. Do not let any part of your body become an instrument of evil to serve sin. Instead, give yourselves completely to God, for you were dead, but now you have new life. So, use your whole body as an instrument to do what is right for the glory of God. Sin is no longer your master, for you no longer live under the requirements of the law. Instead, you live under the freedom of God's grace." (Romans 6:1-14 NLT)

The above scriptural passage clearly shows the absolute freedom and liberty from sin's power. It describes how Christ has destroyed the power of sin and of death and of Satan by His death on the Cross. Jesus did not only come to forgive sin, but He also came to destroy the power of sin and its sting of death, and the power of the devil. He had the victory not only over Satan but also over sin and death, the grave and hell.

This means that not only are those who believe in Him and have received Him as Lord and Savior in their lives are forgiven of their sins, but even more so, the power of sin and death and of Satan have been destroyed in them. Therefore, sin has no control over them anymore because they are no longer slaves to sin and to the devil. In other words, they've been set free from the devil's plantation of sin and slavery. And this means that sin doesn't dwell in them anymore, sin doesn't tell them what to do anymore, sin doesn't have power over them anymore, sin doesn't control them anymore, and they are no longer slaves to sin anymore!

True freedom means that sin has lost its power over them, death has lost its sting over them, the grave has lost its victory over them, hell has lost its torment over them, Satan has lost his battle over them, men have lost their control over them, and the world has lost its influence over them! This is what true freedom is, and it is found in Christ alone!

This true freedom means having a pure heart of love that is free from all sin and guile; and having a pure conscience that is free from all guilt, condemnation, and accusation; and having a free spirit that is free from any bondage of oppression and depression; and having a body that is free from all harmful drugs, substance abuse, immoralities, perversions, and addictions.

It is living a life of purity and holiness that is full of love, compassion, joy, peace, kindness, goodness, justice, truth, righteousness, patience, integrity, faithfulness, humility, meekness, tenderness, gentleness, temperance, mercy, forgiveness, respect, dignity, hope, and happiness! This is that true freedom and liberty that Jesus came to proclaim.

This true freedom for those who have made Christ as their Lord and Savior means that they were once slaves to sin and in the devil's plantation of slavery and bondage, but now they've been snatched out of the jaws of hell and from the claws of the devil! They've been bought and redeemed with the precious blood of Jesus Christ, the redeeming Lamb of God! This means that they were not bought with corruptible things like silver and gold, even as the Bible declares:

"For you know that God paid a ransom to save you from the empty life you inherited from your ancestors. And the ransom He paid was not mere gold or silver. It was the precious blood of Christ, the sinless, spotless Lamb of God. God chose Him as your ransom long before the world began, but He has now revealed Him to you in these last days." (1Peter 1:18-20, NLT)

This means that they were bought and not auctioned! Therefore, neither the devil, nor the world, nor any man can put a price tag on them anymore because they've been totally sold-out, totally bought-out, and totally lived-out for Christ! They are in this world, but they are not of this world. This world and all its offers of pleasures and treasures has become an anathema to them. This is that true freedom in Christ!

It means: *"So now there is no condemnation for those who belong to Christ Jesus. And because you belong to Him, the power of the life-giving Spirit has freed you from the power of sin that leads to death."* (Romans 8:1-2, NLT) It means: *"Therefore, if any man be in Christ, he is a new creation; old things have passed away; behold, all things have become new."* (2 Corinthians 5:17 NKJV)

This is what true freedom and liberty in Christ means. For whosoever the Son of God sets free, is free indeed! For it is for freedom that Christ came to set us free! And where the Spirit of the LORD is, there is freedom and liberty, righteousness, justice, peace, joy, and love in the Holy Ghost! For where there is love, there is freedom and justice also. And Jesus is All! This is that true freedom and liberty. And this is the only truth that can set you free, and Jesus is the only way, the truth, and the life. He is the true freedom and liberty and the answer for America and for the world and for your life today, tomorrow, and forever!

To All Those Crying for True Freedom and Liberty

There are those of you who find themselves bound as slaves to all kinds of sins and bondage and to the devil: slaves to alcohol, drunkenness, drugs, sexual perversions, immoralities, pornography, prostitution, addictions, demonic oppression, witchcraft, the occult, to money, riches, power, and material possessions. And there are those of you who are slaves to guilt, shame, condemnation, unworthiness, hopelessness, and suicidal thoughts.

And if that is you, I have good news for you: Jesus wants to set you totally free! No matter your condition in life, no matter who you are, no matter what you have done, and no matter where you are, Jesus loves you and He wants to set you free from whatever bondage you are in. All you have to do is to surrender your tired life to Him and let Him take control. He will come in and destroy the power of sin and death and of the devil in your life. He will come in and break every chain and shackle and fetters in your life. He will come in and destroy every yoke and bondage, and stronghold, and generational curses and addictions in your life, and He will set you totally free!

Jesus will come in and forgive you all your sins, wash you in His blood, heal you, deliver you, save you, and set you totally free. He will make you whole and fill you with His love, joy, peace, hope, and with the Holy Spirit. And then, you will become a brand new-born again child of God, and your life will never be the same again. This is that freedom that Jesus wants to bring into your life! And that is why Jesus is inviting you to, *"Come now, let's settle this," says the LORD. "Though your sins are like scarlet, I will make them as white as snow. Though they are red like crimson, I will make them as white as wool."* (Isaiah 1:18 NLT)

The blood of Jesus Christ is the only power that can break sin's power and set you totally free from the devil's plantation of sin and slavery! Therefore, it is not the color of your skin that needs changing but the color of your heart that has been stained and tainted by sin. And only the blood of Jesus Christ is able to change your heart. No matter the condition of your heart, the blood of Jesus Christ is able to wash, cleanse and make you as white as snow and as white as wool!

Jesus wants to bring freedom, liberty, and release in your life from all slavery and bondages to sin and to the devil, and to set you totally free because whosoever the Son of God sets free is free indeed. It is for freedom that Christ came to set us free; therefore, receive your true freedom and liberty and release today. Receive your emancipation right now! And remember: True freedom Is freedom from all sin, guilt, condemnation, bondages, addictions, the Devil, Judgment, Hell, and from Eternal Death and Separation from God!

CHAPTER NINE

A Cry For Justice: What Is True Justice?

There is a cry for justice arising from the four corners of the earth. But we must understand that all sins and injustices and inhumanities are as a result of breaking the two greatest commandments of not loving God and our neighbors as ourselves. When asked which is the greatest commandment in the Bible, Jesus answered and said, *"The first, of all the commandments is: 'Hear, O Israel, the LORD our God, the LORD, is One. And you shall Love the LORD your God with all your heart, with all your soul, with all your mind, and with all your strength.' This is the first commandment. And the second, like it, is this: 'You shall Love your neighbor as yourself.' There is no other commandment greater than these."* (Mark 12:28-33, NKJV)

From the above scriptural passage, Jesus made it very clear that the greatest commandment in the Bible is first to love God, and second to love your neighbor as yourself. Therefore, love is the supreme law of God and the entire Bible is based on this supreme law of God's love. Therefore, not to love is injustice itself, because love is justice. In fact, there is no law in love because there is no sin or evil or wickedness or hatred or racism or injustice or inequality in love.

The Bible says that the law was given because of transgression and was therefore made for sinners, *"We know that the law is good when used correctly. For the law was not intended for people who do what is right. It is for people who are lawless and rebellious, who are ungodly and sinful, who consider nothing sacred and defile what is holy, who kill their father or mother or commit other murders..."* (1 Timothy 1:8-11 NLT)

As we can see from the above passage, the law was not made for the just but for the unjust. All those who are just practice justice, and all those who are unjust practice injustice. All those who love God and their fellow human beings practice justice, and all those who do not love God and their fellow human beings practice injustice. All sin is injustice, and all injustice is sin!

Following the tragic death of George Floyd, there was a national and a global outcry over police brutality, racial injustice, discrimination, and inequalities which led to mass protests and rioting with protesters demanding justice, equality, defunding the police, and judicial reform. And most of these were legitimate demands. But as we watch the protests turn into rioting, looting, burning of businesses, destruction of historical statues and monuments, burning of our national flag, forced occupation of state capitol buildings, shootings, killings of innocent lives, mayhem, anarchy, and lawlessness; then we must ask ourselves the question: what is true justice and what is injustice?

It is very important that we ask these burning questions as one cannot fight injustice with injustice, but rather, we fight injustice with justice. Neither can we fight evil with evil, but we fight evil with good. Neither can we fight hatred with hatred, but we fight hatred with love. Neither can we fight darkness with darkness, but we fight darkness with light. Neither can we fight lie with lie, but we fight lie with truth.

Therefore, if we are to truly fight racism and racial injustices and all other societal injustices and inhumanities, then we must understand what true justice is from a God perspective and not from the world's, nor man's perspective or opinion. And we do this for two main good reasons: First, because as Sovereign Creator of the universe, God is the only one that is just and is the source of all true justice, and dispenses true justice, and demands true justice for all. He is the Law Giver. He said, *"I will make justice the measuring line and righteousness the plumb line."* (Isaiah 28:17 NIV) The Bible also says, *"He is the Rock, His work is perfect' For all His ways are justice, a God of truth and without injustice; righteous and upright is He."* (Deuteronomy 32:4 NKJV)

Secondly, because we cannot trust the world's, nor men's opinion on what is true justice because all men are sinners and are unjust, who have perverted the justice of God, calling good evil and evil good, even as the Bible said:

"Woe to those who call evil good, and good evil; Who put darkness for light, and light for darkness; Who put bitter for sweet, and sweet for bitter! Woe to those who are wise in their own eyes, and prudent in their own sight! Woe to them who justify the wicked for a bribe and takes away justice from the righteous man! Therefore, as the fire devours the stubble, And the flame consumes the chaff, So, their root will be as rottenness, and their blossom will ascend like dust; Because they have rejected the law of the LORD of hosts, and despised the word of the Holy One of Israel." (Isaiah 5:20-24 NKJV)

The above scripture shows God's estimation of the world's corrupt justice system. Therefore, since God is just and is the source of all justice, and since He dispenses justice to all, and commands justice for all, and demands justice from all, and judges all injustice, then we should try to understand what is the meaning of true justice from God's own standpoint.

A Cry for Justice from Heaven!

Since the fall of mankind there has been a cry for justice coming from both heaven and earth. When Adam and Eve sinned against God, there was a cry for justice coming from heaven to the earth for the just punishment for sin and for the just banishment of the sinner. And when Cain slew his brother Abel, there was a cry for justice arising from the earth to heaven for the just punishment for sin and for the just banishment of the sinner.

In the case of Adam and Eve, God commanded them, saying, *"Of every tree of the garden you may freely eat, but of the tree of the knowledge of good and evil you shall not eat, for in the day that you eat of it you shall surely die."* (Genesis 2:16-17 NKJV) For the wages of sin is death. Adam and Eve ate of the forbidden tree and they sinned against God, and they incurred the death penalty as punishment for their sin and banishment from the Garden of Eden: *"So He drove out the man; and He placed cherubim at the east of the garden of Eden, and a flaming sword which turned every way, to guard the way to the tree of life."* (Genesis 3:24 NKJV)

In the case of Cain, God said to him, *"Where is Abel thy brother? And he said, I know not: Am I my brother's keeper? And He said, "What hast thou done? For the voice of thy brother's blood crieth unto Me from the ground."* (Genesis 4:10 KJV) Like Adam and Eve, Cain sinned by murdering the innocent blood of his brother Abel and there was also a call for his punishment and banishment:

"And Cain said to the LORD, 'My punishment is greater than I can bear! Surely You have driven me out this day from the face of the ground; I shall be hidden from Your face; I shall be a fugitive and a vagabond on the earth, and it will happen that anyone who finds me will kill me.'" (Genesis 4:13-14 NKJV)

From the above passages, we see that there was a call for justice from both heaven and earth because acts of injustices and of unrighteousness have been committed. God is a God of justice and He will judge sin and punish the sinner unless he repents. However, God's justice is intricately and divinely interwoven with His love. In fact, we must understand that because God is love, therefore everything that He does is out of love. The foundation of His throne is love and justice and truth.

In the first classic case between "God versus Man," Adam and Eve stood accused of high treason by rebelling and sinning against God and mortgaging the earth to the devil. They were found guilty and sentenced to death by hell fire because the penalty for sin is death. And since that day, man became a sinner on death row, awaiting God's final judgment. Let's say, man was put on probation pending his final judgment and depending on his repentance for his sins.

However, while heaven and earth were both demanding swift justice and retribution for sin and the sinner, there was a divine intervention that took place in heaven: Love intervened on behalf of the sinner and became his defense attorney. Justice has justly prosecuted the sinner and demanded just punishment for sin and banishment of the sinner to hell fire! But then Love defended the sinner, demanding forgiveness for sin and salvation for the sinner!

Love convened an extraordinary plenary meeting in heaven in which God the Father, God the Holy Spirit, Love, Mercy, Truth, Righteousness, Justice and Peace were all in attendance to deliberate the case of the accused: Man. It was a holy convocation convened and chaired by Love, who made a very convincing presentation and a passionate plea to All Present on behalf of the accused: Man. In that meeting, it was established that God cannot break His own righteous law as set forth in The Eternal Constitution of Heaven, or else, the foundation of His Throne, and the Scepter of His Righteous Judgments would have been compromised. Therefore, the accused must die for his sin.

It was just then that Love offered to take upon Himself the sins of man, and to die in man's behalf on the Cross. And to that "Breaking News," God the Father and God the Holy Spirit were well pleased and satisfied. And Mercy and Truth hugged each other, and Righteousness and Peace kissed each other. The Bible said that, *"Mercy and truth are met together; Righteousness and peace have kissed each other. Truth shall spring out of the earth; And righteousness shall look down from heaven."* (Psalm 85:10-11 KJV)

And so, while justice said, "Yes!" Love said, "Wait a Minute!" And to accomplish this "Master Plan of Salvation," Love decided to come down from heaven to earth and announced to the whole wide world, *"For God so loved the world that He gave His only begotten Son, that whosoever believes in Him should not perish but have eternal life!"* (John 3:16 NKJV)

Thus, God tempered His justice with His love. And so, God stayed His imminent judgment pending man's repentance and acquittal of his sins through the blood of His Son Jesus Christ. Therefore, in Christ alone God's justice and love are met as demonstrated on the Cross. His death on the Cross was a culmination of both God's love and justice on behalf of a fallen and sinful mankind. Therefore, true love and justice are found in

Christ alone. On the Cross, Jesus became the epitome of gross injustice and inhumanity!

And God, who is the only holy and righteous and just God has declared that all men have sinned and have become unrighteous and unjust, *"As it is written: 'There is no one righteous, not even one; there is no one who understands, no one who seeks God. All have turned away, they have together become worthless; there is no one who does good, not even one.' Their throats are open graves, their tongues practice deceit. The poison of vipers is on their lips. Their mouths are full of cursing and bitterness. Their feet are swift to shed blood; ruin and misery mark their ways, and the way of peace they do not know. There is no fear of God before their eyes. There is no difference, for all have sinned and fall short of the glory of God."* (Romans 3:10-18, 23 NIV)

This is God's divine verdict of the human race. Not only have we all sinned and fallen short of the glory of God, but there is none righteous; no, not one of us is righteous before God. The Bible says that in the sight of God there is no man living that is justified (Psalm 143:2) because we are all as unclean things, and all our righteousness are as filthy rags in the eyes of God! (Isaiah 64:6) The Bible also says that the whole world is guilty before God! (Romans 3:19) The Supreme Court of Heaven has passed a guilty verdict on the whole wide world. And that means that every man, woman, child, you, and I are guilty before God!

A Synopsis of What Is True Justice!

God is the only One that is just, righteous, holy, and perfect. And because His Kingdom is a Kingdom of righteousness; and because the foundation of His Throne is truth; and because

His Scepter is a scepter of righteousness; and because He rules and judges in justice, righteousness, and truth; and because He hates injustice and wickedness; and because all His laws and commandments are just and righteous and equity, that is why He is demanding justice, righteousness, truth, and equity in the earth from all men!

In His Book of Laws, which is the Bible, He has given mankind His righteous and just laws on how we should live and conduct our lives and how we should treat one another. Here is a synopsis of what is His true justice:

"You must not pass along false rumors. You must not cooperate with evil people by lying on the witness stand. You must not follow the crowd in doing wrong. When you are called to testify in a dispute, do not slant your testimony in favor of a person just because that person is poor. In a lawsuit, you must not deny justice to the poor. Be sure never to charge anyone falsely with evil.

Never sentence an innocent or blameless person to death, for I never declare a guilty person to be innocent. Take no bribes. You must not oppress foreigners. Pay close attention to all My instructions. You must not call on the name of any other god. Do not even speak of their names." (Exodus 23:1-11 NLT)

"Do not steal. Do not deceive or cheat one another. Do not defraud or rob your neighbor...Do not twist justice in legal matters by favoring the poor or being partial to the rich and powerful. Always judge people fairly. Do not spread scandalous gossip among your people. Do not stand idle by when your neighbor's life is threatened. I Am the LORD. Do not nurse hatred in your heart for any of your relatives...Do not seek revenge or bear a grudge against a fellow Israelite but love your neighbor as yourself. I Am the LORD. You must obey all My decrees." (Leviticus 19:11-19 NLT)

"Do not practice fortune-telling or witchcraft. Do not defile your daughter by making her a prostitute, or the land will be filled with prostitution and wickedness. Do not defile yourselves by turning to mediums or to those who consult the spirits of the dead. I Am the LORD your God. Stand up in the presence of the elderly and show respect for the aged. Fear your God. I Am the LORD.

Do not take advantage of foreigners who live among you in your land. Treat them like native-born Israelites and love them as you love yourself. Do not use dishonest standards when measuring length, weight, or volume. Your scales and weights must be accurate. I Am the LORD your God who brought you out of the land of Egypt. You must be careful to keep all of My decrees and regulations by putting them into practice. I Am the LORD!" (Leviticus 19:26-37 NLT)

"Love your enemies! Do good to those who hate you. Bless those who curse you. Pray for those who hurt you…Do to others as you would like them to do to you. You must be compassionate, just as your Father is compassionate. Do not judge others, and you will not be judged. Do not condemn others, or it will all come back against you. Forgive others, and you will be forgiven." (Luke 6:27-38 NLT)

This is an all-inclusive true racial, social, societal, political, governmental, economic, moral, ethical, legislative, and judicial justice! And Love is the pendulum of true justice around which all the commandments and righteous judgments of God revolve. All the laws and commandments, decrees, statutes, and instructions in both the Old and New Testaments are summed up in just two words: LOVE and JUSTICE! And this is what God demands of all men, because where there is love and justice, there would be no sin or injustice or inhumanity or racism or evil.

And God's jurisprudence and jurisdiction is universal, eternal, and binding, and includes all areas of spiritual, moral, ethical, family, marital, sexual, dietary, social, societal, economic, political, governmental, judicial, legislative, executive, educational, scientific, technological, natural, and physical laws. This is true justice from the only Law Giver! God is Law, and without Him there is lawlessness, anarchy, and chaos!

A Cry for Justice from the Earth!

The Bible says that the whole world lies in wickedness, and there is a tidal wave of hatred, racism, violence, terrorism, killings, lawlessness, evil, wickedness, corruption, unrighteousness, ungodliness, sexual perversions and immoralities, sex trafficking, human trafficking, organ trafficking, child rape and molestation, abortion, injustices, and inhumanities battering the earth and engulfing the human race!

The Bible further says that darkness has covered the earth and gross darkness the people! (Isaiah 60:1-3) And in the midst of this rising tidal waves of wickedness in the earth, there is a universal cry for justice arising from every nation and from the ends of the earth. And it is a cry that began with the voice of the innocent blood of Abel.

The Bible says, *"Now Cain talked with Abel his brother; and it came to pass, when they were in the field, that Cain rose up against Abel his brother and killed him. Then the LORD said to Cain, 'Where is Abel your brother?' He said, 'I don't know. Am I my brother's keeper?' And He said, 'What have you done? The voice of your brother's blood cries out to Me from the ground. So now you are cursed from the earth, which has opened its mouth to receive your brother's blood from your hand.'"* (Genesis 4:8-11 NKJV)

From the above passage, we see how Cain was the first murderer in the world by killing his baby brother Abel. He thought that no one saw him, but God saw him and told Cain that the voice of his brother's blood is crying out to Him out of the ground from which it has been shed. The Bible says that the life of all flesh is in the blood. (Leviticus 17:14) That is why God is against the shedding of another man's blood because it is taking away that person's life that God has given to them.

And from the blood of Abel to the blood of all those who have been unlawfully murdered, including the voiceless voices of all the millions and billions of unborn babies being killed in their mothers' wombs in America and all over the world are rising from the ends of the earth to heaven crying for justice!

The voices of all the oppressed, the poor and needy, hungry, thirsty, naked, orphans, fatherless, motherless, the homeless, rejected, neglected, dejected, despised, destitute, are all crying out for justice! The voices of all those who have been physically, emotionally, and mentally abused; the voices of all the women, elderly, boys, and girls who have been raped, sexually abused, and molested; the voices of the victims of sex-trafficking, human-trafficking, and human slavery are all crying for justice!

The voices of all those who suffer from racial injustices, racial inequalities, racial discrimination, and prejudices are crying for justice. The voices of all those who are being persecuted and martyred; the voices of all those who are being racially, politically, economically, socially, educationally, and religiously oppressed and deprived; and the voices of injustice and of crimes against humanity are all crying from the ends of the earth to heaven for justice!

From every continent, every nation, every city, every town, every village, every community, every neighborhood, every household, every building, every prison, every hospital, every courtroom, every street corner, and from everywhere and anywhere, the voices of the oppressed are crying for justice! And the Bible says, *"This poor man cried, and the LORD heard him, and saved him out of all his troubles."* (Psalm 34:6 KJV) And God has heard their cry!

So, we see here that we need more than just racial, social, economic, political, judicial, legislative reform, or any other reform. As important and as necessary as these are, none of these can change the heart of man.

What America and the world desperately need is a spiritual and moral transformation and reformation and renewal of the heart and mind. Only this can bring about true racial, societal, economic, political, and governmental justice in America and in the world. There will be no healing, reconciliation, peace, and unity without this true justice from above!

What Is Injustice?

Not to love is injustice because love is justice! Again, we cannot define injustice from the world's, or man's perspective but from God's own perspective for the same reasons as stated at the beginning of this chapter. Injustice in God's justice system goes beyond racial, social, societal, cultural, economic, political, governmental, and religious injustices, discrimination, and inequalities. It goes beyond what we perceive as injustice and unfairness.

In the eyes of God, injustice means any act of sin and unrighteousness committed against God and against others.

This means that any act of injustice is sin, and any act of sin is injustice. Therefore, any act of sin or injustice that we commit against any man, woman, or child is an act of sin and injustice committed directly against God. It is a terrible sin and crime in the eyes of God when we commit sins of injustice and inhumanity against our fellow human beings who have been created in the image and likeness of God!

It is a high crime to mistreat our fellow human beings. It is a direct attack on God and a slap in His face! Well, you may ask how is it a direct attack on God and a slap in His face? Here is an example: When Saul of Tarsus was persecuting the early Christians in Jerusalem and beyond, the Lord Jesus Christ appeared to him on the road to Damascus and said to him, *"Saul, Saul, why are you persecuting Me?" And he said, "Who are You, Lord?" Then the Lord said, "I Am Jesus, whom you are persecuting."* (Acts 9:4-5, NKJV)

Now, Saul was not physically persecuting the Lord Jesus, but the Christian believers. And Jesus saw it as a direct attack on Him. And so also it is when we commit any act of injustice and inhumanity against our fellow human beings. It is an attack on God Himself because you are touching and mistreating one of His creatures made in His image and likeness.

There is no loving parent who will sit by and watch their child being abused and mistreated unjustly and that will not fight back to defend that child from their attacker. They will intervene and fight back! If you then as an earthly father or mother can justly defend your child, how much more will God our heavenly Father and Creator not defend His children whom He has created in His very own image and likeness! Surely, He will!

And since God is holy, righteous, and just, He has therefore promised to judge all sins and injustices and inhumanities committed against Him and against other people if those who commit them do not repent and practice love and justice in the earth.

God will judge all sins of racism, hatred, discrimination, murder, envy, jealousy, gossip, backbiting, slander, lying, stealing, greed, cheating, dishonesty, terrorism, lawlessness, idolatry, witchcraft, unforgiveness, drugs, drunkenness, fornication, adultery, pedophilia, pornography, prostitution, rape, sexual perversions and immoralities, sex trafficking, human trafficking, slavery, racial injustices, social injustices, political injustices, religious injustices, and all other sins of unrighteousness, injustices, and inhumanities!

God is just and righteous and dispenses justice to all. Therefore, all sins of unrighteousness and injustices and inhumanities are being weighed in His divine scales and balances of justice and judgment. All the works of men are measured and weighed in the divine scales and balances of God, be they good or bad. His scales and balances are just and perfect and fitted with equity. For God is no respecter of persons. Blacks, Whites, Browns, Reds, etc., and all sinners will be judged justly and equitably.

The pendulum of divine justice is swinging, and there is coming a day when each man's scales and balances will be full, and will be summoned by the Supreme Court of Heaven to stand trial before the only righteous and just God, just like He did with Belshazzar, of whom it is written:

"Then Daniel answered, and said before the king...But you his son Belshazzar, have not humbled your heart, although you knew all this. And you have lifted yourself up against the LORD of heaven. They have brought the vessels of His house before you, and you and your wives and your concubines, have drunk wine from them.

And you have praised the gods of silver and gold, bronze and iron, wood and stone, which do not see or hear or know;

and the God who holds your breath in His hand and owns all your ways, you have not glorified.

Then the fingers of the hand were sent from Him, and this writing was written. And this is the inscription that was written: MENE, MENE, TEKEL, UPHARSIN: This is the interpretation of each word. MENE: God has numbered your kingdom and finished it; TEKEL: You have been weighed in the balances and found wanting; PERES: Your kingdom has been divided and given to the Medes and Persians." (Daniel 5:17-30 NKJV)

As we have seen, there is coming a day of each man's own handwriting on the wall. On that day, you will not be standing before the United States Supreme Court or any earthly judge or court system, but before the Supreme Court of Heaven and before the Supreme Judge of the whole earth!

All earthly judges and court systems are tainted with corruption and erosion and corrosion of justice and equity, calling that which is good evil and that which is evil good. The world's scales of justice systems are unbalanced and swaying with prejudice, favoritism, personal opinions, public opinion, popular opinion, political patronages, political correctness, biases, bribery, and corruption; where the guilty go scot-free and the victims and poor are denied justice and victimized.

But not so with the Supreme Court of Heaven! Therefore, as the Scripture has said that all those of you that are crying for justice, are you not also unjust and unrighteous yourselves? All those of you that are crying against injustice and inhumanity, do you not also commit acts of injustice and of inhumanity yourselves? For when you hate, discriminate, mistreat others, gossip, backbite, envy, jealous, slander, lust, curse, swear, rape, commit sexual perversions and immoralities, lie, steal, murder, molest children, cheat, etc., are you not unjust and committing injustice yourselves?

The Bible says, *"You may think you can condemn such people, but you are just as bad, and you have no excuse! When you say they are wicked and should be punished, you are condemning yourself, for you who judge others do these very same things. And we know that God, in His justice, will punish anyone who does such things. Since you judge others for doing these things, why do you think you can avoid God's judgment when you do the same things? Don't you see how wonderfully kind, tolerant, and patient God is with you? Does this mean nothing to you? Can't you see that His kindness is intended to turn you from your sin?"* (Romans 2:1-4 NLT)

That's it! You who cry injustice, are you not unjust yourselves? You who accuse and judge others, are you not guilty yourselves? For how can you say to your brother there is a speck in your eyes when there is a plank lodging in your own eyes blinding you? (Matthew 7:1-5)

Fighting injustice with injustice is injustice itself. But fighting injustice with true justice will lead to the truth that will set people free. Jesus said that a tree is known by its fruit. A good tree brings forth good fruit, and a bad tree bad fruit. By their fruit ye shall know them! (Matthew 7:16-20) And so also is the heart of man: a good heart produces good things, and a bad heart produces bad things. For out of the abundance of the heart, the mouth speaks! (Matthew 12:33-37) A fountain does not send forth from the same place sweet and bitter waters, or yield both salt water and fresh water. No! (James 3:11-12)

Therefore, true justice is loving God and obeying all His commandments, and loving your neighbor as yourself, and doing to others what you would have others do unto you! For there is no true justice without love and truth. Justice dispensed without love and truth is injustice and a miscarriage of true justice!

To All Those Crying for True Justice!

"Unfortunately, all of us have suffered injustice one way or the other!" Those were the exact words I was told when my kids were unjustly snatched away from me, and when in righteous anger, I thumbed the table and cried aloud, "I hate injustice!" I was very upset, heartbroken, wounded, and hurting. It was one of those traumatizing moments for me and for my kids, and I will never forget that day.

And like me and many others, there are those of you who might have suffered some terrible and horrible injustices in your life. Whoever you are, wherever you are, and whatever you may be going through in life, there is hope and justice for you. Jesus sees and knows and feels your every pain and hurt, and He wants to come into your life and set things straight, and right all the wrongs in your life. He wants to bring justice into your life and to justify you with His blood and make you just as if nothing ever happened to you.

That is why He is right now asking you to, *"Come to me, all you who are weary and carry heavy burdens, and I will give you rest. Take my yoke upon you. Let me teach you, because I am humble and gentle at heart, and you will find rest for your souls. For my yoke is easy to bear, and the burden I give you is light."* (Matthew 11:28-30 NLT)

Jesus has already paid the full price for all our sins and injustices and inhumanities on the Cross. He that knew no sin was made sin for us; the Just for the unjust! The Innocent for the guilty! If you want to experience true justice in your life, then you must invite Jesus into your life. He will come and justify you with His blood and nullify all your sins and fill you with His true justice and peace. True justice is found in His blood alone. It is His blood that justifies. (Romans 5:9)

Would you therefore let Him in? Let Justice, Truth, Love, Mercy, Peace and Freedom come in. Jesus is Justice, Truth, Love, Mercy, Peace and Freedom. He is the only way, the truth, and the life. If you let Him into your life, Jesus will come in and justify you with His blood of all injustices, and He will heal and restore you. His truth will set you totally free, and He will clothe you with His amazing love.

The Bible says that we are already condemned by sin, and therefore there is no true freedom without true justification. Without His justification, your sins will never be forgiven you, and you will never find true justice, true freedom, true love, true joy, and true peace in your life, both here in this world and after you die. Because without His justification, you will die in your sins and be lost in hell forever. That is why the Bible says that there is no condemnation for those who are in Christ Jesus, who have been justified by His blood. (Romans 8:1-2)

This is that true justice that Christ came to give to the whole world! Will you accept Him and be justified, or will you reject Him and be condemned? The choice is yours. And I pray that you will accept Him and be justified by Him, because true justice is to be justified and be acquitted by the blood of Jesus Christ from all sins!

CHAPTER TEN

A Cry For Love: What Is True Love?

The greatest cry of all cries of the human soul is the cry for true love, and the greatest need of all needs of the human race is the need for true love! It is the cry and highest desire and need of every child, every woman, every man, every wife, every husband, and every person. The cry for true love is even far greater than the cry for freedom and justice. Why? Because it is love that conquers the world and the hearts of all men, and because where there is true love, there will also be true freedom and true justice. Freedom and justice can be exercised without true love, but true love cannot be exercised without freedom and justice!

Freedom and justice are legal terms, but love is not. Love is relational and is a Person. The reason why we have all this hatred, racism, evil, wickedness, injustices and inhumanities in the world is because there is no true love. And the reason why there is no true love in the world today is because men do not have the love of God in them to be able to love their neighbors as themselves. There is no true love because men have rejected the true love from God, which is Jesus Christ whom He has sent to the world to manifest and to demonstrate His love to the whole wide world!

And as we have already seen, the central theme and message in this book is about love, but which or whose love? I ask that question simply because it is not everything that the world calls love that is true love. In fact, the word love is not just the most beautiful and the most frequently used vocabulary in the world, but it is also the most misunderstood, the most misinterpreted, the most misused, the most mismanaged, the most misapplied, the most misappropriated, and the most abused thing in the world today!

Over the centuries, the concept and meaning of true love has been defined and redefined by men to gratify and to satisfy their own pleasures to the point that the world has lost the originality and purity and creative purpose and intent of God's love. Today, what the world calls love is not love but lust. God is love and the devil is lust! Lust is perverted love, and that's the kind of love that the world is promoting. Therefore, not all that is called love is true love, just as not all that glitters is gold!

In this chapter, we are going to talk about what is true love and the cry for true love. There is true love and there is fake love. The devil has photocopied, reproduced, and duplicated counterfeits to everything "good" that God has created, and love is the most photocopied, most reproduced, most duplicated, and most counterfeited of all!

If we say that love conquers the world and the hearts of all men; and if we say that love is the antidote and panacea for all evils and devils; and if we say that love is the answer for racial and societal healing and reconciliation, then we need to know what this kind of a true love really is, and how we can experience it in our own lives and apply it in all our relationships, friendships, fellowships, communications, communities and in our race relations

Of all the different definitions and interpretations of the word love, the truest and simplest and supreme of them all is this: that, "LOVE IS GOD AND GOD IS LOVE!" This means that love is a Person and is Divine, and that Divine Person is God. He is Love and Love is Him. This is exactly what the Bible says, *"Beloved, let us love one another, for love is of God; and everyone who loves is born of God and knows God. He who does not love does not know God, for God is love...And we have known and believed the love that God has for us. God is love, and he who abides in love abides in God, and God in him."* (1 John 4:7-8, 16 NKJV)

This is an active and interactive relational love between God the Creator and His creation. This means that the very divine essence and nature and attribute of God is love. God is not only love, but in Him is love, and of Him is love, and with Him is love, and by Him is love, and through Him is love, and from Him is love!

He self-exists in love, self-manifests in love, and self-reveals Himself in love. He lives love, breathes love, thinks love, speaks love, and acts love. Everything that He is and that He does is love. He is the very origin and originator of love, and without Him, there is no love! To simply put it in a common parlance, God's divine DNA is LOVE!

And because God is love, therefore, everything that He created was out of love. The creation of man is the highest pinnacle of His love, and the sending forth of His Son Jesus Christ to die for the sins of the world is the highest demonstration of His love toward mankind. Man is the apex and highest quality product of all of God's creation. He created all things out of love, but when it came to the creation of man, He said, "Come, let Us make man in our own image and likeness," and that image and likeness is His love and His divine nature. Therefore, man was not only created out of love, but with love, in love, for love, to love, and to be loved! Man was created with the very divine nature of God, so that if God is love, then man must also be love, and if God is holy, man also must be holy, and if God is just, man also must be just, like Father, like son! And because God is divine, holy, pure, perfect, blameless, and harmless, therefore, His love also is divine, holy, pure, perfect, blameless, and harmless.

It is love that gave the laws and commandments, "Thou shalt love the LORD your God with all thine heart," 'Thou shalt love thy neighbor as thyself," "Thou shalt not kill," "Thou shalt not steal," "Thou shalt not lie," "Thou shalt not commit adultery," "Thou shalt not covet," "Thou shalt not hate," "Thou shalt love thine enemies," etc.! Love is sinless because God is sinless! There is no evil in love. O, the supremacy, and purity of this love!

Love Is a Divine, Creative and Inalienable Right for All Men!

The American Constitution states, "We must hold these truths to be self-evident, that all men are created equal, and that they are endowed by their Creator with certain unalienable Rights, that among these are Life, Liberty and the pursuit of Happiness." And to that, I would like to add this, that, "We hold these truths to be self-evident, that love is a divine, creative, and inalienable right for every man, woman, and child made in the image and likeness of God and are therefore entitled to love and to be loved!"

Love is not a human right or a constitutional right or a societal privilege, but rather, it is a divine, creative, and inalienable right. Love is a God-Right, and not a human right! This was God's original intent and purpose, and that has never changed. This is why the Bible says: *"Blessed be the God and Father of our Lord Jesus Christ, who has blessed us with every spiritual blessing in the heavenly places in Christ, just as He chose us in Him before the foundation of the world, that we should be holy and without blame before Him in love, having predestinated us to adoption as sons by Jesus Christ to Himself, according to the good pleasure of His will, to the praise of the glory of His grace, by which He made us accepted in the Beloved."* (Ephesians 1:5-6 NKJV)

The Divine Nature, Ingredients, Qualities and Characteristics of This Kind of a True God-Love!

Since God is Love and Love is God, let us therefore take a look at some of the divine nature, ingredients, qualities and characteristics of this kind of a true God-Love. In Paul's love letter to the Corinthian Christians, he wrote:

"If I speak in the tongues of men and of angels, but have not love, I am only a resounding gong or a clanging cymbal. If I have the gift of prophecy and can fathom all mysteries and all knowledge, and if I have a faith that can move mountains, but have not love, I am nothing. If I give all I possess to the poor and surrender my body to the flames, but have not love, I gain nothing.

Love is patient, love is kind. It does not envy, it does not boast, it is not proud. It is not rude, it is not self-seeking, it is not easily angered, it keeps no record of wrongs. Love does not delight in evil but rejoices with the truth. It always protects, always trusts, always hopes, always perseveres. Love never fails...And now these three remain: faith, hope and love. But the greatest of these is love!" (1 Corinthians 13:1-13 NIV)

Wow! This is absolutely, mind-blowing and mind-boggling!

This is hard to comprehend with our own finite human mind. From the above passage, the Bible is telling us that first of all,

True Love is Patient. This means there is no impatience or intolerance in this kind of a true God-Love, but rather there is patience, tolerance, and long-suffering. And how we desperately need this today in a world that is becoming increasingly impatient, intolerant, and impenitent!

True Love is Kind. This means there is no unkindness, cruelty, ill-treatment, mistreatment, brutality, molestation, injury, abuse, or injustice in this kind of a true God-Love, but rather there is kindness, goodness, courtesy, mercy, graciousness, compassion, sympathy, and empathy.

True Love does not Envy. This means there is no envy, jealousy, malice, bitterness, resentment, lustfulness, covetousness, and hatred in this kind of a true God-Love, but rather there is benevolence, goodwill, contentment, satisfaction, appreciation, rejoicing, and compliment.

True Love is not Boastful. This means there is no bragging or boasting of one's self-importance or self-achievements in this kind of a true God-Love, but rather there is meekness, gentleness, lowliness, and quietness of spirit.

True Love is not Proud. This means there is no arrogance, pomposity, superiority, supremacy, self-importance, flamboyancy, imposition, or presumption in this kind of a true God-Love, but rather there is humility, meekness, gentleness, quietness, calmness, and simplicity of spirit.

True Love is not Rude. This means that this kind of a true God-Love is not rude, impolite, offensive, indecent, abusive, vulgar, insulting, obscene, and disrespectful, but rather it is respectful, polite, descent, honorable, kind, nice, and it dignifies.

True Love is not Selfish. This means there is no selfishness, no self-interest, no self-motive, no greediness, no self-loving, and no self-seeking in this kind of a true God-Love, but rather, it is sacrificial, selfless, and unselfish. Any love that puts "self" first before God and before others is selfish and is all about me, mine, myself, and I!

True Love is not easily Angered. This means that this kind of a true God-Love is not easily provoked, enraged, offended, mad, resentful, retaliate, and revengeful, but rather, it is self-control, self-restraint, peaceful, calm, serene, tranquil, pacific and temperance.

True Love Keeps no Records of Wrongs. This means that this kind of a true God-Love has no ledger book where to record every wrong done, and no storage house where to store up all those records of wrongs, offenses, resentments, bitterness, malice, hurts, unforgiveness, and of all the bad things that have been done, but rather it keeps record of only what is right, good, just, pure, kind, honorable, lovely, virtuous, praiseworthy, and it extends mercy and forgiveness for every wrong suffered. (Philippians 4:8)

True Love does not Delight in Evil. This means that this kind of a true God-Love does not participate or take pleasure or delights in doing anything that is sinful, evil, devilish, wicked, unrighteous, ungodly, immoral, perverse, corrupt, injustice, inhumane, or in anything spiritually, morally, or ethically wrong. It does not follow the advice of the wicked, nor stand together in agreement with sinners, nor join with those who mock God, but rather it delights in the laws of God and meditates on them day and night, and it delights and rejoices in what is just, righteous, holy, pure, loving, kind, true, honest, virtuous, excellent, and in all that is good and pleasing to God!

True Love Rejoices with the Truth. This means that this kind of a true God-Love hates lying, deceit, dishonesty, insincerity, unfaithfulness, hypocrisy, and falsehood, and it rejoices with what is true, just, right, genuine, sincere, faithful, honorable, honest and integrity.

True Love always Protects. This means that this kind of a true God-Love does not assault, insult, injure, betray, harm, shame, disgrace, molest, abuse, neglect, expose, endanger, and make vulnerable, but rather it defends, contends, protects, guards, guides, shields, preserves, secures, watches over, and lays down its own life for others!

True Love always Trusts. This means that there is no betrayal, conspiracy, treachery, distrust, mistrust, suspicion, doubt, unbelief, disloyalty, infidelity, insecurity, or unfaithfulness in this kind of a true God-Love, but rather there is faith, trust, confidence, integrity, fidelity, reliance, assurance, transparency, and accountability.

True Love always Hopes. This means that there is no despair, despondency, uncertainty, emptiness, faithlessness, unbelief, meaninglessness, helplessness, and hopelessness in this kind of a true God-Love, but rather there is hope, faith, belief, promise, prospect, possibility, opportunity, expectation, anticipation, aspiration, destiny, fulfillment, and a future.

True Love always Perseveres. This means that there is no quitting, no giving up, no giving in, no retreat, and no surrender in this kind of a true God-Love, but rather there is endurance, perseverance, persistence, importunity, resilience, tenacity, determination, and purpose.

True Love never Fails. This means that there is no failure, or disappointment, or loss, or deficit, or defeat in this kind of a true God-Love, but rather there is success, profit, victory, and triumph. This kind of a true God-Love is always conquering, victorious, triumphing, and overcoming!

The Bible says that there are three things that will last forever: faith, hope, and love. But the greatest of them all is love.

These then are the divine nature, ingredients, qualities, and characteristics of this kind of a true God-love. And this is that superiority and supremacy of this kind of a true God-Love that conquers the world and the hearts of all men!

It is that superiority and supremacy of this kind of a true God-Love that conquers the devil and all evils and disarms all its enemies! All other man-invented love will fail, but this kind of a true God-Love never fails and never falters and never alters! It is unchangeable, immutable, immortal, and eternal!

No wonder this same Apostle Paul in his other letter to the Christians in Ephesus, prayed diligently for them to be able to grasp and to understand the divine magnitude, altitude, latitude, longitude, and depth of this kind of a true God-Love when he wrote and said, *"And I pray that you, being rooted and established in love, may have power, together with all the saints, to grasp how wide and long and high and deep is the love of Christ, and to know this love that surpasses knowledge – that you may be filled to the measure of all the fullness of God!"* (Ephesians 3:17-19 NIV)

Do you now see the divine magnitude, altitude, latitude, longitude, and depth of this kind of a true God-Love that surpasses all human knowledge and understanding and blows away our minds and imagination? This stands in stark contradiction to what the world calls love and is contrary to the fallen and sinful nature of man, which is to hate, envy, unforgiveness, and revenge.

This is not just "Amazing Grace, How Sweet Thou Art," but this is also "Amazing Love, How Precious Thou Art!" And that is why this kind of a true God-Love is divine and not human. It is supernatural and not natural. It is heavenly and not earthly. It is celestial and not terrestrial. It is immutable and not mutable. It is immortal and not mortal. It is eternal and not temporal. And it is God's and not man's!

From the above scriptural passages, we now see that there is no sin, no evil, no wickedness, no injustice, no unrighteousness, no inhumanity, no hatred, no racism, no inequality, no discrimination, no segregation, no prejudice, no supremacy, no superiority, no inferiority in this kind of a true God-Love! There is no violence, no brutality, no hatred, no bitterness, no resentments, no malice, no grudges, no unforgiveness, no revenge, no killing, no terrorism, and no violence in this kind of a true God-Love!

There is no betrayal, no treachery, no dishonesty, no cheating, no lying, no stealing, no gossip, no backbiting, no slander, no false accusation, no false witness, no condemnation, no character assassination, no pull him or her down (P.H.D.), no mudslinging, no name-calling, no political correctness, no vitriolic, and no cancel culture in this kind of a true God-Love!

There is no abuse, no molestation, no rejection, no disrespect, no indignity, no dishonor, no shame, no cursing, no envy, no jealousy, no lust, no covetousness, no adultery, no fornication, no prostitution, no rape, no pornography, no pedophilia, no sexual perversion, no immorality, no lawlessness in this kind of true God-Love!

There is no rebellion, no disobedience, no rioting, no burning, no looting, no anarchy, no selfishness, no self-centeredness, no greed, no wrongdoing, no pride, no arrogance, no boastfulness, no unworthiness, no condemnation, no guilt, and no hopelessness in this kind of a true God-Love!

There is no fear in this kind of a true God-Love because perfect love casts out fear, and because fear involves torment. But he who fears has not been made perfect in love. (1 John 4:18, NKJV)

This kind of a true God-Love is holy, pure, perfect, just, righteous, innocent, blameless, and harmless. It is the perfection of love. If all men would have this same kind of a true God-Love, there would have been less or no evil and wickedness in the world. The world would have been a far better place to live in love, peace, harmony, justice, equality, and freedom. But I'm afraid that is not the case!

This is that kind of a true God-Love that conquers the world and the hearts of all men! This is that kind of a true God-Love that conquers the devil and all evils and disarms all its enemies! And this is that all-powerful, all-conquering, all-victorious, all-triumphing, all-overcoming, all-consuming, all-redeeming, all-saving, all-healing, all-reconciling, all-liberating, and all-eternal life-giving Love of God that is in Christ Jesus, Savior of the world, and that is the answer for all our racial, social, political, and societal problems in America and in the world!

The Bible commands us to owe no man nothing but to love because love does no evil to its neighbor: *"Owe no one anything except to love one another, for he who loves another has fulfilled the law. For the commandments, 'You shall not commit adultery,' 'You shall not murder,' 'You shall not steal,' 'You shall not bear false witness,' 'You shall not covet,' and if there is any other commandment, are all summed up in this saying, namely, 'You shall love your neighbor as yourself.' Love does no harm to a neighbor therefore love is the fulfillment of the law."* (Romans 13:8-10 NKJV)

"Repay no evil for evil. Have regard for good things in the sight of all men. If it is possible, as much as depends on you, live

peaceably with all men. Beloved, do not avenge yourselves, but rather, give place to wrath; for it is written, 'Vengeance is Mine. I will repay,' says the Lord. Therefore, if your enemy is hungry, feed him; If he is thirsty, give him a drink; For in so doing you will heap coals of fire on his head. Do not be overcome by evil but overcome evil with good!" (Romans 12:17-21, NKJV)

What an amazing love is this that owes no man nothing but love itself? What an amazing love is this that does not repay evil for evil, but good for evil? What an amazing love is this that does not commit adultery, rape, murder, steal, lie, bear false witness, covet, or slander? What an amazing love is this that does not avenge, and is not racist, prejudiced, discriminates, unjust, and inhumane? What an amazing love is this that feeds its hungry enemies, gives drink to its thirsty enemies, clothes its naked enemies, forgives its enemies, and loves its enemies? This can only be the supernatural love of God and not of man nor of this world!

Love Is Heaven's Currency and Legal Tender for All our Relationships and Interactions!

Love is heaven's currency and legal tender for all of life's transactions, interactions, communications, friendships, and relationships! Therefore, when the Bible says that you should owe no man nothing but love, it really means that Love should be the motivation and umpire in your life and the currency and legal tender for all your life's transactions, interactions, communications, friendships, and relationships! This means that you cash-out Love from the treasury of your heart to all men freely! Love is never overdrawn or overdraft, therefore your heart must never be bankrupt of Love! There should always be sufficient funds of Love in your heart's bank account, and you should always maintain a constant demand and supply line of Love from your heart to the world!

The whole wide world is in great need of a true God-Love right now! But unfortunately, love seems to be in very low supply. The demand is very high, but the supply is very low. The economics of love has been worst impacted by the global pandemic of the cancer of sin and hatred that is gnawing away the hearts of men like a cankerworm! And the only way you can receive this kind of a true God-Love is by inviting Jesus Christ to come into your life and ask Him to fill you with His love.

Now, just as sin is a matter of the heart, so also is love a matter of the heart. A pure heart that is full of love is a heart that is free from sin and from all hatred and evils. Pure love must flow from a pure heart and not from a corrupt heart. The Bible says that a fountain cannot produce forth both fresh and bitter water at the same time. It is impossible! And the reason why we see all these evils and wickedness and injustices and inhumanities all over the world is because there is no more love in the hearts of men. Jesus said that one of the signs of the end times and of His coming is that sin and wickedness will increase in the world and will cause the love of many to grow cold.

The apostle Paul even went further to give a vivid description of the perilous times that we are living in right now when he wrote to Timothy and said:

"You should know this, Timothy, that in the last days there should be very difficult times. For people will love only themselves and their money. They will be boastful and proud, scoffing at God, disobedient to their parents, and ungrateful. They will consider nothing sacred. They will be unloving and unforgiving; they will slander others and have no self-control. They will be cruel and hate what is good. They will betray their friends, be reckless, be puffed up with pride, and love pleasure

*rather than God. They will act religious, but they will reject the power that could make them godly. Stay away from people like that!" (*2 Timothy 3:1-5 NLT)

What the above scriptural passage describes is the heart of man that has gone cold without love. Men have lost affection toward their fellow human beings, including their neighbors, and loved ones. And this is exactly what we see happening in America and all over the world: an exponential implosion and explosion of sin and wickedness and evil and hatred, violence, injustice, and inhumanities.

Love is the supreme law of God to man. Therefore, to love is divine, and to hate is sin. To love is Christ, and to hate is the devil. To love is freedom and justice, and not to love is bondage and injustice! The Bible makes it very clear that when you hate, lie, and murder, you are a child of the devil because the devil is a liar, a thief, a hater, a murderer, a racist, and a rapist from the beginning.

The Bible says, *"For you are the children of your father the devil, and you love to do the evil things he does. He was a murderer from the beginning. He has always hated the truth, because there is no truth in him. When he lies, it is consistent with his character; for he is a liar and the father of lies."* (John 8:44 NLT)

Love is the antidote and the panacea for all evil, hatred, racism, injustices, and inhumanities! This is that kind of a true God-Love that conquers the world and the hearts of all men; and that conquers the devil and all evils and disarms all its enemies; and that is the answer for racial, societal, political, and national healing and reconciliation, peace and unity in America and the world.

There is supernatural power in this kind of a true God-Love to love, to forgive, to save, to deliver, to heal, to reconcile, to justify, and to set free. It is medicinal, curative, therapeutic, and aesthetic. It is the antidote and panacea for all evils. The healing qualities and ingredients of this kind of a true God-Love are the most powerful, more than any pharmaceutical or man-made drugs. It comes at a zero-dollar cost and is 100% guaranteed with no side effects whatsoever! The only side effect and addiction to this kind of a true God-Love is loving God and others and doing good to all.

It contains all the A-Z essential spiritual, emotional, mental, psychological, and physical vitamins and minerals that your spirit, soul, body, and mind desperately need. It has got all the "alphas and omegas" of love that your body needs, and because Jesus is the Alpha and Omega, therefore He is the Alpha and Omega of love, the Beginning and the End of love, the First and the Last of love! No one else in the whole wide world can love you more than Jesus!

Because that in the beginning was Love, and Love was with God, and Love was God! The same was in the beginning with God! All things were made by Love, and without Love nothing was made that was made! In Love was life, and the life was the light of men. And the light of Love shines in the darkness of this world, and the darkness could not comprehend it. This is that true Love which is the true Life and Light of the world that gives life and light to all men! Love was in the world, and the world was made through Him, and the world did not know Him. Love came to His own, and His own did not receive Him. But as many as received Love to them He gave the right to become the children of God, to those who believe in His name, who were born, not of blood, nor of the will of the flesh, nor of the will of man, but of God! And Love became flesh and dwelt among us, and we beheld His glory, the glory as of the only begotten Son of the Father, full of grace and truth! (John

1:1- 14) This is that true Love! And is a Person! The Person of JESUS CHRIST!

To All Those Who Feel Unloved and Rejected and Are Crying for True Love!

Right now, there are millions or even billions of people in America and around the world who are feeling spiritually, emotionally, mentally, psychologically, maritally, relationally, physically, racially, politically, financially, economically, pandemically, and medically broken, crushed, shattered, wounded, bruised, abused, molested, raped, shamed, dishonored, rejected, depressed, oppressed, and hurting.

There are those of you that are filled with anger, rage, hatred, resentments, bitterness, malice, grudges, envy, jealousy, revenge, and unforgiveness.

And there are those of you that are filled with all kinds of fears, anxieties, perplexities, worries, uncertainties, insecurities, unworthiness, meaninglessness, helplessness, and hopelessness with suicidal thoughts. And there are those of you who may be feeling unloved, rejected, dejected, dumped, abandoned, and forsaken.

But no matter what racial, social, political, spiritual, emotional, mental, psychological, physical, marital, relational, financial, economic, and medical state of condition you find yourself in, there is hope for you: Jesus wants to heal and to restore you with His love and set you totally free. He is the Savior, Redeemer, Deliverer, Healer, and Restorer of broken hearts, broken souls, broken bodies, broken lives, broken marriages, broken homes, broken families, broken relationships, broken finances, broken health, broken promises, broken dreams, and broken hopes! God sees every injustice and inhumanity that has been committed against you. He sees how you have been hated, unloved and mistreated. He feels your hurts and pain!

And that is why the Lord Jesus is inviting you, saying, *"Come to Me, all of you who are weary and carry heavy burdens, and I will give you rest. Take My yoke upon you. Let Me teach you, because I Am humble and gentle at heart, and you will find rest for your souls. For My yoke is easy to bear, and the burden I give you is light."* (Matthew 11:28-30 NLT)

Jesus wants to heal, restore, and comfort you, and give you a crown of beauty instead of ashes, the oil of gladness instead of mourning, the garment of praise instead of the spirit of despair. He wants to turn your death into life, your darkness into light, your bondage into freedom, your injustice into justice, your racism into grace, your hate into love, your shame into honor, your brokenness into wholesomeness, your mourning into dancing, your bitterness into sweetness, your hopelessness into hope, and your pain into praise!

Will you therefore invite LOVE into your heart, your life, your home, your marriage, and into your every situation and circumstances in life? LOVE is right now standing outside at the front door of your heart and home, gently knocking, patiently waiting, and tenderly saying, *"Behold, I stand at the door and knock. If anyone hears My voice and opens the door, I will come into him and dine with him, and he with Me."* (Revelation 3:20, NKJV)

You do not have to worry about anything. All He is asking you to do is for you to open the door of your heart, your life, your home, your marriage, your family, and of your situation and circumstances in life so that He can come in and have supper with you. He has already prepared supper for the two of you. And that supper is made of His body that was broken for your healing on the Cross, and His blood that was shed for the forgiveness of your sins. Please STOP what you are doing right now and take a moment to listen attentively to His still small tender-loving and caring voice knocking on the door of your heart and invite Him in! Would you?

CHAPTER ELEVEN

There Is No Greater Love Than This!

John Three Sixteen, *"For God so loved the world that He gave His only begotten Son, that whoever believes in Him should not perish but have everlasting life,"* is the greatest verse in the entire Bible! It reveals the greatest love ever demonstrated by God toward mankind. This means that God loves all the races of people in the world. This means there is no man, or woman, or child, or sinner that is beyond God's love and redemption. Christ died for all, to save all!

Christ loved and died for all the races and colors of people in the world. He died for all the Blacks, the Whites, the Latinos, the Indians, the Africans, the Europeans, the Russians, the Jews, the Arabs, the Asians, the Chinese, the Australians, the Eskimos, the Pygmies, etc.! He died for all peoples from every nation, every tribe, and every tongue! He died for all the Christians, the Muslims, the Buddhists, the Hindus, the atheists, and for all the heathens!

It was on the Cross that Christ died for all the races and colors of people and for all sinners. The Cross is the divine convergence and confluence and influence of God's love and justice in His Son Jesus Christ for the sins of the world. This goes to show that the Cross of Jesus Christ is not racist, and His blood is not racist! Christ shed His blood for all sinners, and He donated His blood for all sinners! He is the universal blood donor to the human race and His blood type is universal for the saving of the souls of all men!

The Cross is the center-stage where that eternal lifesaving and life-giving blood donation took place over two thousand years ago. And that is where all sinners must go to receive their eternal life-saving blood transfusion! For all have sinned and fall short of the glory of God! Jesus said that if He be lifted up on the Cross, then He will draw all men and all sinners unto Himself. His blood is not racist, and His Cross is not racist!

John Three Sixteen also means that God loves all sinners, including you and me! In fact, I was a grand chief patron of the most wretched of sinners, but still God loved me and sent His only begotten Son to die for me on the Cross. If God so loved me to save a filthy, rotten, stinking, ugly, grand chief patron of a wretched sinner like me, then surely God loves all sinners to save them.

God loves the sinner but hates his sins. He does not love nor condone his sins, but He loves the sinner and hates his sins. His love for the sinner is the thesis of His love, His hatred of the sinner's sins is the antithesis of His love, and the Cross is the synthesis of both His love for the sinner and His hatred of his sins! My wife said it rightly when she said that "God is for souls!"

The Cross is where God's love and justice met and kissed each other over the plight of the poor helpless sinner and his sins, and over the poverty and impoverishment of his wretched soul! It was on the Cross that Christ died for all the races and colors of people and for all sinners. This goes to show that the Cross of Jesus Christ is not racist, and His blood is not racist!

Christ shed His blood for all sinners, and He died for all the races of people in the whole wide world!

John Three Sixteen means that God has loved you even before the foundations of the world. He has loved you even before you were ever conceived in your mother's womb.

He has loved you even before you were ever born. He has loved you even before you ever committed any sin. He has loved you even after you have committed so many sins. He has loved you even after you have rejected Him. And He has loved you even right now in your present sinful condition and circumstances in life. This means His relentless love keeps chasing after you everywhere and anywhere you go.

His love follows you to school, to college, to the mall, to work, to the bar, to the night club, to the strip club, to the brothel, to the crack house, to the drug house, to the hospital, to the prison, to the car, to the train, to the plane, to the house, to the kitchen, to the living room, to the bedroom, at night, in the day, and everywhere and anywhere else you go!

Day and night, night and day, 24/7, 365 days, His relentless love chases after you, and it will keep chasing after you until the day you die, and until the day you finally reject it! And this is because true love never loses hope and never gives up until it is rejected and trampled underfoot!

John Three Sixteen means that God did not spare His own Son, but gave Him up for us all, and how then shall He not also give us all things? (Hebrews 8:32)

John Three Sixteen also means there is no greater love than this, that Christ should lay down His own life for His friends! (John 15:13-17)

For those of you who may be thinking or saying that God does not love you, I say that's not true. It is a lie from the devil himself, who is a liar and the father of all lies. If God does not love you, He would never have created you in the first place. For how could God create something that He hates? And how could God hate something that He has created in His own image and likeness?

The Bible says that God is love, and in Him is no evil. God loves you purely because God is love, and because He loves you, God cannot help but to love you because love is what He is all about. He lives love, breathes love, eats love, drinks love, thinks love, feels love, speaks love, and acts love! If you are still doubting God's love for you, then let us take a look at the extremity and severity of His love for you as demonstrated through His Son Jesus Christ on the Cross. The Cross is the proof!

The Extremity of God's Love as Demonstrated through His Son Jesus Christ on the Cross for All Sinners!

John Three Sixteen shows the extremity and severity of God's love as demonstrated through His Son Jesus Christ on the Cross. The Cross is the epitome of the extremity and severity of God's love toward all mankind. Because you are extremely made in God's love, and because His love toward you is extreme and radical, therefore, He has to take the most extreme and most radical action in order to save you from slavery to sin, death, hell, and the devil!

John Three Sixteen is the most extreme and most radical of all verses in the Bible! It is the highest declaration of the extremity and radicality of God's love toward you. His love for you is so extreme and so radical that He was even willing to send His only begotten Son Jesus Christ to come and die for your sins and for the sins of the world.

Just as obedience to God did not prevent Abraham from withholding his only beloved son Isaac who was a type of Christ, but offered him up as a sacrifice unto God, so likewise did God's love for sinners did not prevent Him from withholding His only begotten Son Jesus Christ but offered Him up for us all as a sacrifice for the sins of the world!

Therefore, there is no greater love than this that Christ should empty Himself and lay aside everything in heaven and come down to the earth to save poor wretched sinners like you and me. The Bible describes this kenosis–this extreme and radical self-abasement and self-emptying of Christ in this way:

"You must have the same attitude that Christ Jesus had. Though He was God, He did not think of equality with God as something to cling to. Instead, He gave up His divine privileges; He took the humble position of a slave and was born as a human being. When He appeared in human form, he humbled himself in obedience to God and died a criminal's death on the cross." (Philippians 2:5-8 NLT)

The Bible also says that, *"Since the children have flesh and blood, He too shared in their humanity so that by His death He might destroy him who holds the power of death – that is, the devil – and free those who all their lives were held in slavery by their fear of death."* (Hebrews 2:14-15 NIV)

Only extreme, radical, and selfless love can do that! Earthly men, kings and rulers fight and kill to cling on to power, but not so with Jesus. He voluntarily stepped down and stepped out of His throne and relinquished His divine powers and privileges, emptied Himself, and became a servant in order to save sinners! By so doing, He identified Himself with sinners and became sin for us. What extreme, radical, and selfless love! Christ's death on the Cross is the most extreme and most radical demonstration of God's love to the world. And by this extreme and radical expression of His love for the world, this means that there is nothing more, nothing less, and nothing else that God can do for you and me other than what He has already done and accomplished in His Son Christ Jesus on the Cross! For there is no greater love than this!

In Christ alone is all the fullness of God's love, and in this love is all the fullness of redemption, salvation, forgiveness, mercy, grace, deliverance, healing, provision, protection, blessings, joy, peace, happiness, hope, abundant life, and eternal life. The Bible says, *"And this is the record, that God has given to us eternal life, and this life is in His Son. He that has the Son has life, and he that has not the Son of God has not life!"* (1 John 5:11-12 KJV)

The extremity and radicality of God's love toward mankind means that His love is boundless and seamless to reach the extreme-most and uttermost ends of the earth and the bottom-most depths of hell to save every man, every woman, and every child from the bondage of sin, and death, and hell, and from the devil's plantation of sin and slavery! No man, or woman or child is beyond God's boundless and seamless love and redemption! The image and trademark of God is on every man, woman, and child ever conceived and born into this world!

Therefore, there is no place in the entire universe where the extremity of God's love cannot reach. The heavens are His throne, the earth is His footstool, His outstretched arm reaches to the ends of the earth, His ears are attentive to the cry of all His creatures, and His eyes travel to and from the earth to save and to rescue. Therefore, there is no greater love than this, that God so loved the world, that He gave up His only begotten Son Jesus Christ to die for the sins of the whole wide world,

so that whoever believes in Him should not perish but have
everlasting life!

The Severity of God's Wrath and Fury and Punishment on His Son Jesus Christ on the Cross for the Sins of the Whole Wide World!

John Three Sixteen does not only show God's extreme love
for all sinners and for the whole wide world, but it also shows
the severity of God's wrath and fury and judgment against sin
on His Son Jesus Christ on the Cross. This means that God
would have to give up His only begotten Son to die for the
sins of the world. And to demonstrate that, the Bible says that
God did not spare His own Son, but gave Him up to die for us
all: *"He who did not spare His own Son, but delivered Him up
for us all, how shall He not with Him also give us all things?"*
(Romans 8:32 NKJV)

But what does it mean by God not sparing His own Son
but gave Him up for us all? This means that Christ was made
a substitute for our sins and must suffer the full penalty for our
sins. This means that the curse and death penalty for sin that
was upon Adam and the entire human race was put upon Jesus.
And when the Bible says that for the wages of sin is death, those
wages of sin and death came upon Jesus. Sin is an abomination and an abhorrence to God, and to demonstrate the severity
of His hatred and wrath and judgment and punishment for sin,
God therefore did not spare His own Son!

This means that God did not show any mercy or leniency
or clemency toward Jesus just because He was His Son. No!
Neither did God try to circumvent nor contravene His own
righteous laws and justice system in order to show leniency
on Christ. No! Neither did He introduce any 1st, or 2nd, or

3rd amendments to try and amend His own eternal laws as set forth in the Supreme Constitution of Heaven. No! *"For I Am the LORD, and I change not!" saith the LORD!* (Malachi 3:6, KJV) The constitutions and governments of this world may change, but God and His Word and His Kingdom and His Throne endure forever!

Neither did God try to mitigate nor lessen the severity of His punishment for sin just because Jesus was His only beloved Son. No! Neither did God try to dilute or adulterate the density and intensity of the mixture and contents of the cup of wrath and fury and of bitterness and sufferings which God Himself has prepared for His Son to drink as penalty for the sins of the world. No! The severity and intensity and density of God's cup of wrath and fury and of judgment and punishment for sin was not from concentrate. It was not concocted nor diluted nor adulterated. It was raw, organic, freshly squeezed, and hand-crafted by the very hand of God the Father Himself! God the Father made His Son to drink the full contents of the mixture of the cup of His wrath and fury and judgment and punishment for sin all by Himself, though not for Himself! He drank it all for you and me!

The contents of that cup of trembling were made of the mixture of all the ugliness, filthiness of all our sins, mingled with the penalty for sin, and the fury of the wrath, judgment, and fierce punishment of God for the sins of the whole world! O, what amazing love! What vicarious sacrifice for a wretched and ungrateful world! God made His own Son Jesus Christ drink the full contents and mixture of the cup of His wrath and fury against sin. He made Him drink it to the last drop, even unto the dregs!

The severity, fierceness, density and intensity of God's wrath and fury and judgment and punishment for sin upon

His Son was so bitter, so severe, and so fierce that even Jesus pleaded with the Father to take that cup of His wrath and fury away from him when He cried, *"O My Father, if it is possible, let this cup pass from Me; nevertheless, not as I will, but as You will."* (Matthew 26:36-46 NKJV)

The Bible even tells us that in His intense agony, Jesus' sweat became as drops of blood: *"And being in agony, He prayed more earnestly. Then His sweat became like great drops of blood falling down to the ground."* (Luke 22:44 NKJV)

The severity and intensity and density and bitterness and agony of this cup of wrath upon Jesus was so intense and tense that His blood capillaries and pores were so overstretched to the extreme that they ruptured, and His sweat became bloodied! What severe agony! What extreme love! Indeed, there is no greater love than this!

The Bible also says this of Christ's sufferings: *"Who, in the days of His flesh, when He had offered up prayers and supplications, with vehement cries and tears to Him who was able to save Him from death, and was heard because of His godly fear, though He was a Son, yet He learned obedience by the things which He suffered. And having been perfected, He became the author of eternal salvation to all who obey Him, called by God as High Priest according to the order of Melchizedek."* (Hebrews 5:7-10 NKJV)

What kind of extreme and radical love is this that can endure such severity and intensity of agony? Truly, there is no greater love than this! On the Cross, the severity and fierceness and fury of God's wrath and judgment against sin upon His Son was so intense and severe that Christ in His humanity, cried out an agonizing cry of separation from the Father: *"My God, My God, why has Thou forsaken Me?"* (Matthew 27:45-46, KJV)

Christ suffered the eternal separation from God for sin. It is sin that has separated man from God. On the Cross, Christ was separated that you and I may be reconciled back to the Father. He was rejected that you and I may be accepted in the Father. He was forsaken that you and I may be forgiven. He bled to death that you and I may have eternal life. O, what amazing love! What sacrifice! Truly there is no greater love than this!

On the Cross, when He cried, *"I thirst,"* and was offered wine mingled with myrrh for Him to drink to help deaden or lessen the agony of His sufferings, Jesus refused to drink it. *"Then they gave Him wine mingled with myrrh to drink, but He did not take it."* (Make 15:23 NKJV) Christ refused to be sedated, anesthetized, or tranquilized! He refused to be numbed! For it has already been predetermined by the determinate counsel of God that Christ should drink the full contents of this cup of trembling of the wrath of God for the sins of the world with no reduced cost!

Christ knew that in order for Him to be able to save mankind He must pay the full penalty for man's sins, or else His mission to save the world would have backfired and failed, and the entire human race would have been doomed and damned forever! It would have been mission unaccomplished! Knowing this therefore, Jesus refused to drink anything that would have numbed His body, His senses and His faculties to the pangs and agony of death and of the penalty and sufferings for sin for which He came to suffer on the Cross in order to save sinful mankind. Christ as a Son drank from the very hand of God the Father the severity and fierceness of the cup of His wrath and fury against sin. And He drank it all alone by Himself, though not for Himself, but for you and me!

Christ did not commit suicide on the Cross, but He died willingly for the sins of the world! Christ willing and voluntarily laid down His own life as a sacrifice for the sins of the world. He Himself walked willingly to the gallows carrying His own Cross to Golgotha! Jesus Himself said this of Himself:

"I am the good shepherd; and I know My sheep, and I Am known by My own. As the Father knows Me, even so I know the Father; and I lay down My life for the sheep. And other sheep I have which are not of this fold; them also I must bring, and they will hear My voice; and there will be one flock, and one shepherd. Therefore, My Father loves Me, because I lay down My life that I might take it again. No man takes it from Me, but I lay it down of Myself. I have power to lay it down, and I have power to take it again. This commandment I have received from My Father." (John 10:14-18, NKJV)

What greater love is there than this, that Christ should lay down His life for the sins of the world? Even as the hymn writer, William Walsham How, wrote and said, "It is a thing most wonderful, almost too wonderful to be, that God's own Son should come down from heaven and die to save a child like me."

It is indeed a most wonderful thing! A most incomprehensible thing! And a most amazing story ever told: That God Himself should step down from heaven to earth to die and to save a most wretched sinner like me and you! The Creator dying for His creation! For God was in Christ Jesus on the Cross, reconciling the world and all sinners unto Himself! (2 Corinthians 5:17-19) What baffling, unexplainable, indescribable, unimaginable, and incomprehensible love!

What a price to pay to save a rebellious human race and an ungrateful world! Truly, there is no greater love than this! How loving and tender are His words when He said, *"Greater love has no man than this, than to lay down one's life for his friends."* (John 15:13 NKJV) Indeed, there is no greater love than this that Christ should lay down His life for His friends.

Yes! He calls you and me His friend! What a drastic change and elevation in status from that of an enemy to that of a friend, and from that of a wretched sinner to that of a holy saint of Christ, and from that of a child of the devil to that of a child of God!

No wonder the apostle Paul by the inspiration of the Holy Spirit wrote and said, *"For scarcely for a righteous man will one die; yet perhaps for a good man someone would even dare to die. But God demonstrates His love toward us, in that while we were still sinners, Christ died for us!"* (Romans 5:7-8 NKJV) He even called Judas Iscariot who betrayed Him His friend. How tender and loving!

Therefore, God did not spare His own Son. On the Cross, Christ suffered the spiritual, mental, emotional, psychological, and physical horrors of sin and death. He suffered the terrors and tremors of hell and of eternal separation from God. God did not spare Him one bit, but He suffered every bit of the penalty for the wages of each sin you and I have ever committed. There is no sin that He has not already died and paid the price for.

God did not spare His own Son, but He administered the fullest justice and penalty for sin against His own Son. There was no plea bargain, no bail bond, no reduced sentence, no mitigating of His fury, and no tempering nor tampering of His justice with mercy! Christ has to face the fullest justice system of God, and to pay the fullest price for sin with no reduced cost. In Christ alone, God's justice was fully met, the price was fully paid, the sacrifice was fully pleasing, His wrath was fully appeased, His heart was fully satisfied, and the sinner was fully justified!

This was both a retributive justice of God on His Son Jesus Christ who was made the propitiation and atonement for the sins of the world, as well as a restorative justice on Christ who was made the victim and scapegoat for the sins of the world in order to reconcile man back to God. For God has made Him to be sin for us who knew no sin, so that we might be made the righteousness of God in Him!

Such was the severity of God's wrath and fury and judgment and punishment against sin that was upon Christ, in such that the very heavy-weighted divine "gavel" of God's righteous justice and judgment for sin came crushing down heavily upon Christ on the Cross, in so much so that the prophet Isaiah wrote and said of Christ, *"But He was wounded for our transgressions, He was bruised for our iniquities: the chastisement of our peace was upon Him; and with His stripes we are healed. Yet it pleased the LORD to bruise Him."* (Isaiah 53:5, KJV)

God did not spare Him an ounce of mercy, but He executed the fullest justice for sin and exacted the fullest punishment for sin! In Christ alone, God's fury and justice against sin was fully justified and fully satisfied! Christ became our propitiation, and He suffered and died in our stead: The Just for the unjust, the Righteous for the sinner, the Innocent for the guilty! This is what it means by God not sparing His own Son but delivered Him up for us all.

Indeed, there is no greater love than this! It was not only out of love that Christ came to die for you and me, but it was also out of holy jealousy. The Bible did not only say that God is love, but it also says that God is jealous. In fact, God describes Himself not only as a jealous God, but that His name is called Jealous: *"Do not worship any other god, for the LORD, whose name is Jealous, is a jealous God."* (Exodus 34:14 NIV)

So, we see that Christ's death on the Cross was driven by a combination of holy love and fiery jealousy for His fallen creation. For how can God sit by and allow the devil to destroy the human race which He has created in His own very image and likeness? Impossible! Love will not permit that! Man was created for God's glory and pleasure and therefore God was jealous for His creation!

And so, out of a holy and fervent love and fiery jealousy, Christ descended from heaven to deal an eternal blow to sin, to death, to the grave, to hell, and to the devil! It was out of strong love and cruel jealousy for mankind that Christ died a cruel death on a cruel cross as a criminal just to save you and me! The Bible says that *"Love is as strong as death, and jealousy as cruel as the grave!"* (Song of Songs 8:6)

The Bible says that the devil came down to the earth with great wrath to steal, to kill, and to destroy the human race, but that Jesus Christ came down from heaven to give life, and life more abundantly. Christ is jealous for you because He loves you. His fervent love and fiery jealousy for you led Him to die a cruel death on that rugged Cross at Calvary! True love begets holy jealousy, and where there is no true love, there is no jealousy. Christ genuinely loves you, and He is jealous and zealous for you! The Cross is the proof! Truly indeed, there is no greater love than this!

God's Relentless Love Is Chasing after You!

Such was the extremity and severity of God's love for you and me that He did not spare His own Son, but gave Him up for us all, that while we were yet sinners, Christ died for our sins. Therefore, only Christ alone is able to save to the uttermost all those who come to God by faith through Him, seeing that He now lives forever to make intercession for them. (Hebrews 7:25)

Therefore, there is no place in the heavens, nor in the earth, nor below the earth where His love cannot reach you. The extremity of His love can reach the extreme-most and uttermost places in the earth, and the bottom-most and lowest-most pit of hell just to save you! Therefore, there is no place in the whole universe where you can flee from God's love. The psalmist said,

"Where can I go from Your Spirit? Or where can I flee from Your presence? If I ascend into heaven, You are there; If I make my bed in hell, behold, You are there. If I take the wings of the morning, and dwell in the uttermost parts of the sea, even there Your hand shall lead me. If I say, "Surely the darkness shall fall on me," Even the night shall be light about me; Indeed, the darkness shall not hide from You, But the night shines as the day; The darkness and the light are both alike to You." (Psalm 139:7-12 NKJV)

His love fills the whole universe and the whole of creation and is chasing after you. Day and night, night and day, His extreme and relentless love is following you around wherever you go, pleading with you to receive Him. Even though you may be ignoring, snubbing, slighting, and even insulting and rejecting Him, His extreme and relentless love still keeps chasing after you like a deserted and rejected lover, pleading with you! Even though you may not have invited or welcomed Him inside your heart and inside your home, love is still standing outside at the door of your heart and of your home, gently knocking, patiently waiting, and tenderly saying, *"Behold, I stand at the door and knock. If anyone hears My voice and opens the door, I will come into him and dine with him, and he with Me."* (Revelation 3:20 NKJV)

Jesus Christ is your unseen lover, and the Holy Spirit is wooing you into His Love. His love for you is extreme and His punishment for you was severe. Right now, will you consider the extremity of His love for you and the severity of His punishment for you on the Cross and invite Him into your heart and home? Are you going to invite Him in or are you going to continue to leave Him standing outside in the frigid frost-biting cold? **Remember this: That in The Whole Wide World There Is No One Else That Can Love You More Than JESUS, For There Is No Greater Love Than His, And There Is No Greater Lover Than Him!**

CHAPTER TWELVE

It Is Love That Conquers The World And The Hearts Of All Men!

I t is an indisputable truth that it is Love that conquers the world and the hearts of all men, women, and children; and it is Love that conquers the devil and all evils and disarms all its enemies; and it is Love that is the antidote to racism and hatred and the panacea for all evils, injustices and inhumanities in the world; and it is Love that is the answer for all racial, societal, political and national healing, reconciliation, peace and unity in America and in the world!

The greatest weapon in the world is not the atomic or hydrogen or nuclear bomb. The greatest weapon in the world is Love, whose Commander-In-Chief is Jesus Christ! It is Love that conquered the world over two thousand years ago on the Cross at Calvary, and it is Love that continues to conquer the world today, and it is Love that will triumph in the end and will reign in power, justice, truth, righteousness, splendor, majesty, beauty, and glory! It is Love that conquers all!

By its very divine nature, this kind of a God-Love is the purest, perfect, gentle, innocent, blameless, and harmless, and yet it is the most powerful non-lethal weapon in the whole wide world that has conquered the world and the hearts of all men and has conquered all sins and evils and devils and has demolished and disarmed all its enemies without ever firing a shot!

I know this may sound ironic and paradoxical, but it is the truth. This kind of a God-Love has no lethal ammunitions, no nuclear weapons, no hydrogen bombs, no explosives, no guns, no tanks, no intercontinental ballistic missiles, and yet still it has conquered the greatest kings and emperors and their kingdoms and empires. It has conquered the greatest military leaders and their armies. It has conquered the greatest enemy of God and of man: Satan and all his demons and principalities and powers of darkness.

It has conquered sin and death and the grave and hell and has disarmed all its enemies. How is that possible, you may ask? Well, it is possible because the ammunitions of this kind of a true God-Love are spiritual and divine in nature and power, and they include salvation, deliverance, redemption, healing, kindness, goodness, compassion, tenderness, gentleness, meekness, humility, patience, long-suffering, mercy, grace, forgiveness, temperance, righteousness, justice, truth, wisdom, knowledge, understanding, purity, godliness, holiness, integrity, sincerity, honesty, joy, peace, hope, faithfulness, freedom, light, and life!

The Bible says that, *"If I speak in the tongues of men and of angels, but have not love, I am only a resounding gong or a clanging cymbal. If I have gift of prophecy and can fathom all mysteries and all knowledge, and if I have a faith that can move mountains, but have not love, I am nothing. If I give all I possess to the poor and surrender my body to the flames, but have not love, I gain nothing.*

Love is patient, love is kind. It does not envy, it does not boast, it is not proud. It is not rude, it is not self-seeking, it is not easily angered, it keeps no record of wrongs. Love does not delight in evil but rejoices with the truth. It always protects, always trusts, always hopes, always perseveres. Love never fails...And now these three remain: faith, hope and love. But the greatest of these is love." (1 Corinthians 13:1-13 NIV)

The Bible also says that the fruit of the Holy Spirit is love, joy, peace, patience, kindness, goodness, faithfulness, gentleness, and self-control. (Galatians 5:22-23) These are the non-lethal ammunitions of love. Let us now see how love has conquered Satan and all his powers of darkness; and how love has conquered sin and all evils; and how love has conquered the world and breaks and melts every heart of man, woman, and child on the Cross.

1. How Love Has Conquered Satan and His Powers of Darkness on the Cross

The greatest demonstration and accomplishment of this conquering and vanquishing power of this kind of a true God-Love was on the Cross at Calvary over two thousand years ago. It was on this one divine act of love of Jesus Christ being crucified on the Cross for the sins of the world that He was able to conquer, demolish, and disarm the devil and all his demonic powers and kingdom of darkness. It was on the Cross that God manifested the mystery of His hidden wisdom which He has hidden from the foundation of the world, and which no man nor the devil ever knew about. Of the mystery of this hidden wisdom of God, the apostle Paul wrote:

"Howbeit we speak wisdom among them that are perfect: yet not the wisdom of this world, nor of the princes of this world that come to nought: but we speak the wisdom of God in a mystery, even the hidden wisdom which was ordained before the

world unto our glory: which none of the princes of this world knew: for had they known it, they would not have crucified the LORD of glory." (1 Corinthians 2:6-8 KJV)

It was through the foolishness of the Cross that God unveiled this mystery of His hidden wisdom and unleashed the power of His love through His Son Jesus Christ that conquered Satan, demolished his kingdom of darkness, and disarmed all his principalities and powers. The Bible tells us that it was on the Cross that Jesus defeated Satan and then proceeded to dismantle and disarm him and all his principalities and powers and demons and rulers of darkness, making a public spectacle of them by triumphing over them openly on the Cross: *"Having disarmed principalities and powers, He made a public spectacle of them, triumphing over them in it."* (Colossians 2:15 NKJV)

So, on the Cross, we see the mighty conquering, vanquishing, and triumphing power of the love of God that has conquered the devil. The Bible says, *"But when people keep on sinning, it shows that they belong to the devil, who has been sinning since the beginning. But the Son of God came to destroy the works of the devil."* (1 John 3:8 NLT)

Writing about the coming final defeat of the devil, the apostle John said, *"Then I saw an angel coming down from heaven, having the key to the bottomless pit and a great chain in his hand. He laid hold of the dragon, that serpent of old, who is the Devil and Satan, and bound him for a thousand years, and he cast him into the bottomless pit, and shut him up, and set a seal on him, so that he should deceive the nations no more till the thousand years are finished...*

Now when the thousand years have expired, Satan will be released from his prison and will go out to deceive the nations which are in the four corners of the earth, Gog and Magog, to gather them together to battle, whose number is as the sand

*of the sea. They went out on the breadth of the earth and sur-
rounded the camp of the saints and the beloved city. And fire
came down from God out of heaven and devoured them. The
devil, who deceived them, was cast into the lake of fire and
brimstone where the beast and the false prophet are. And they
will be tormented day and night forever and ever!"* (Revelation
20:1-3, 7-10 NKJV)

As we have seen, the devil is already a defeated foe, and the
lake of fire will be his final eternal abode. So, the devil that you
see today prowling around like a roaring lion seeking whom
he may devour, is just a desperate wounded lion making his
last stand, for his days are already numbered, and he has been
weighed in the balances and found wanting. Like Belshazzar
in the Book of Daniel, God has already numbered Satan's
kingdom and finished it, and he has been weighed in the balances and is found wanting!

2. How Love Has Conquered Sin and All Evil on the Cross

It is on the Cross that Jesus conquered sin, death, and all
evil. The Bible says that, *"Because God's children are human
beings – made of flesh and blood – the Son also became flesh
and blood. For only as a human being could He die, and only
by dying could He break the power of the devil, who had the
power of death. Only in this way could He set free all who
have lived their lives as slaves to the fear of dying."* (Hebrews
2:14-15 NLT)

Sin is the root cause of all evils, injustices, racism, violence,
inhumanities, and of all wickedness in the world. And because
sin is found inside the heart and flesh of man, therefore Jesus
also has to become like man to be born of flesh and blood, so

that by so doing, He was able to destroy the power of sin and death and the devil inside the body of man. It was on the Cross that Jesus was able to destroy the power of sin and of death, the grave, hell, and the devil.

And it is because of this defeat of sin that the Bible says:

"Well then, should we keep on sinning so that God can show us more and more of His wonderful grace? Of course not! Since we have died to sin, how can we continue to live in it? Or have you forgotten that when we were joined with Christ Jesus in baptism, we joined Him in His death? For we died and were buried with Christ by baptism. And just as Christ was raised from the dead by the glorious power of the Father, now we also may live new lives.

Since we have been united with Him in His death, we will also be raised to life as He was. We know that our old sinful selves were crucified with Christ so that sin might lose its power in our lives. We are no longer slaves to sin. For when we died with Christ, we were set free from the power of sin. And since we died with Christ, we know we will also live with Him. We are sure of this because Christ was raised from the dead, and He will never die again. Death no longer has any power over Him. When He died, He died once to break the power of sin. But now that He lives, He lives for the glory of God. So, you also should consider yourselves to be dead to the power of sin and alive to God through Christ Jesus.

Do not let sin control the way you live; do not give in to sinful desires. Do not let any part of your body become an instrument of evil to serve sin. Instead, give yourselves completely to God, for you were dead, but now you have new life. So, use your whole body as an instrument to do what is right for the glory of God. Sin is no longer your master, for you no longer live under the requirements of the law. Instead, you live under the freedom of God's grace." (Romans 6:1-14 NLT)

The above passage clearly describes how Christ has destroyed the power of sin and death by His death on the Cross. Jesus did not only come to forgive sins, but to also destroy the power of sin and its sting of death. He has the victory not only over Satan but also over sin and death. This means that not only are those who believe in Him and have received Him as Lord and Savior in their lives are forgiven of their sins, but even more so, the power of sin and death and of Satan has been destroyed in them. Therefore, sin has no control over them anymore because they are no longer slaves to sin and to the devil. In other words, they have been set free from the devil's plantation of sin and slavery. And this means that sin does not dwell in them anymore, sin doesn't tell them what to do anymore, sin doesn't have power over them anymore, sin doesn't control them anymore, and they are no longer slaves to sin anymore!

Christ has not only forgiven and set them free from slavery to sin, but He has also given them divine power to overcome sin, temptation, and the devil. The Bible says that believers in Jesus Christ have overcome the devil by the blood of the Lamb and by the word of their testimony, not loving their own lives anymore even unto death. This simply means that believers in Christ now have divine power in them not only to resist, but to also overcome sin, temptation, and the devil just as He Himself overcame the devil and his temptations in the wilderness. (Luke 4:1-13) The power of sin, death, the grave, hell, and of the devil have all been broken and destroyed in the Christian's life!

What this means now for anyone who receives and believes in Jesus Christ as Lord and Savior is that sin has lost its power over them, death has lost its sting over them, the grave has lost its victory over them, hell has lost its torment over them, Satan has lost his battle over them, and the world has lost its influence over them! This is that victory and freedom to anyone whom the Son of God sets free and is free indeed!

The apostle Paul describing this conquering, vanquishing, victorious, triumphing and overcoming power of Christ's love in the Christian's life, wrote and said:

"What then shall we say to these things? If God is for us, who can be against us? He who did not spare His own Son, but delivered Him up for us all, how shall He not with Him also freely give us all things? Who shall bring a charge against God's elect? It is God who justifies. Who is he who condemns? It is Christ who died, and furthermore is also risen, who is even at the right hand of God, who also makes intercession for us. Who shall separate us from the love of Christ? Shall tribulation, or distress, or persecution, or famine, or nakedness, or peril, or sword? As it is written:

'For Your sake we are killed all day long; We are accounted as sheep for the slaughter.' Yet in all these things we are more than conquerors through Him who loved us. For I am persuaded that neither death nor life, nor angels nor principalities nor powers, nor things present nor things to come, nor height nor depth, nor any other created thing, shall be able to separate us from the love of God which is in Christ Jesus our LORD!" (Romans 8:31-39 NKJV)

This is that conquering, vanquishing, victorious, triumphing and overcoming power of Christ's love in a believer's life! Not only has Christ's love conquered the Christian believers, but He has also made them more than conquerors together with Himself as the Commander-In-Chief and mighty Conqueror of the world! Moreover, there is absolutely nothing in heaven, nor in the earth, nor below the earth, nor in hell, that will ever be able to separate those who have this kind of a true God-Love in them from Him!

3. How Love Has Conquered the World and the Hearts of all Men on the Cross!

It is this same mighty conquering, vanquishing, triumphing, victorious and overcoming power of Christ's love that has also conquered the world and the hearts of all men on the Cross. And for over two thousand years now, this same conquering and vanquishing power of Christ's love continues to conquer the hearts of men, women, and children all over the world. It continues to conquer, break, melt, and disarm the most hardened sinner and vilest criminal.

Christ fought evil with love because love is the only weapon that conquers all evils and disarms all its enemies without firing a shot. The bullets of love do not kill or maim, but rather, they bring salvation, deliverance, healing, restoration, reconciliation, joy, peace, happiness, justice, freedom, and liberty to all. It is love, that conquers the most vile and wicked heart. It is love, that breaks and melts and softens the most stubborn and stony heart.

It is love that extinguishes the flames of hell in a man's soul and cools off the inflamed and indignant soul. Love is the only balm of Gilead that heals and soothes the wounded and weary soul. Love is the healer of broken and hurting souls, the restorer of broken homes and marriages, and the refresher of the anguished and thirsty soul. Love is the greatest physician of the human soul, and love is the thirsting and yearning of every human soul!

It is love that continues to conquer and to disarm hardcore criminals, racists, rapists, terrorists, rebels, murderers, robbers, liars, drug addicts, alcoholics, drunkards, prostitutes, adulterers, fornicators, pedophiles, pornographers, sex perverts, idolaters, gangsters, atheists, animists, and the heathens!

It is love that continues to conquer Christians, Muslims, Buddhists, Hindus, kings, queens, princes, princesses, presidents, prime ministers, governors, senators, congressmen, mayors, politicians, businessmen, professors, celebrities, soldiers, the police, the homeless, orphans, widows, and the poor!

It is love that continues to conquer the oppressed, the depressed, the possessed, the sick, the brokenhearted, the wounded, the hurting, the bruised, the rejected, the helpless and the hopeless!

It is love that continues to conquer schools, colleges, hospitals, prisons, brothels, strip clubs, night clubs, gambling houses, bars, abortion clinics, crack houses, drug houses, communities, villages, towns, cities, nations, and the whole wide world!

It is love that continues to conquer husbands, wives, fathers, mothers, men, women, children, young and old from every nation, tongue, race, tribe, language, and people!

The great French revolutionary and military commander, Napoleon Bonaparte, was quoted as saying, *"Alexander, Caesar, Charlemagne, and myself founded empires, but what foundation did we rest the creations of our genius? Upon force. Jesus Christ founded an empire upon love, and at this hour millions of men would die for Him."*[22]

What a profound statement of truth coming from one of the world's greatest military commanders and leaders! It is true that all these great military leaders and their armies did try to conquer the world by force of war, bloodbath, violence, tyranny, and dictatorship, but they all failed. They and their armies are all dead and are in their graves. Their empires and kingdoms are vanquished forever! But Jesus Christ was crucified on the

Cross and on the third day He rose again from the grave triumphant, having the keys of hell and death with Him, and is alive forevermore! He said to John the apostle, *"Fear not; I am the first and the last: I am He that lives, and was dead; and behold, I am alive for evermore, Amen; and have the keys of hell and death."* (Revelation 1:17-18 KJV)

The Bible says that, *"The kingdoms of this world are become the kingdoms of our Lord and of His Christ; and He shall reign for ever and ever!"* (Revelation 11:15 KJV). The Bible also says that God has highly exalted Jesus Christ and has given Him a name which is above every other name, that at the name of Jesus every knee should bow, of those in heaven, and of those on earth, and of those under the earth, and that every tongue should confess that Jesus Christ is Lord, to the glory of God the Father! (Philippians 2:9-11)

It is true that Napoleon, Alexander, Caesar, Charlemagne, Hitler, Herod, Pharaoh, Lenin, Stalin, Mao, Idi Amin, and many other political, military, and religious leaders, past, present, and future, including the coming Antichrist, ruled their nations by force of power, tyranny, dictatorship, brutality, suppression, oppression, repression, wars, and bloodbath. They gave command to their armies, soldiers, and police to fight, shoot, and to kill.

But not so with King Jesus, Commander-in-Chief of the LORD'S heavenly hosts and earthly army of Christians. On the contrary, Jesus Christ has commanded His army of Christian soldiers to conquer the world with His love. Here are some of His military commands to His army of Christian soldiers:

In the Gospel of Matthew, He said to them, *"All power is given unto Me in heaven and in the earth. Go ye therefore, and teach all nations, baptizing them in the name of the Father, and of the Son, and of the Holy Ghost: teaching them to observe all things whatsoever I have commanded you: and lo, I am with you always, even unto the end of the world. Amen."* (Matthew 28:18-20 KJV)

In the Gospel of Mark, He said to them, *Go ye into all the world and preach the gospel to every creature. He that belie-veth and is baptized shall be saved: but he that believeth not shall be damned. And these signs shall follow them that believe: In My name shall they cast out devils; they shall speak with new tongues; They shall take up serpents; and if they drink any deadly thing, it shall not hurt them; they shall lay hands on the sick, and they shall recover."* (Mark 16:15-18, KJV)

In the Gospel of Luke, He said to them, *"Love your ene-mies! Do good to those who hate you. Bless those who curse you. Pray for those who hurt you. If someone slaps you on one cheek, offer the other cheek also. If someone demands your coat, offer your shirt also. Give to anyone who asks; and when things are taken away from you, don't try to get them back.*

Do to others as you would like them to do to you...Then your reward from Heaven will be very great, and you will truly be acting as children of the Most High, for He is kind to those who are unthankful and wicked. You must be compassionate, just as your Father is compassionate. Do not judge others, and you will not be judged. Do not condemn others, or it will all come back against you. Forgive others, and you will be for-given. Give, and you will receive." (Luke 6:27-38 NLT)

In the Gospel of John, He said to them, *"A new command-ment I give you: Love one another. As I have loved you, so you must love one another. By this all men will know that you are My disciples if you love one another."* (John 13:34-35 NIV) And He commanded Simon Peter and His army of Christian soldiers to feed His sheep and His lambs of the lost human race that have gone astray with His Word of love! (John 21:15-17)

So, we see here that love is the insignia by which Christ's disciples and Christian soldiers are known by the world, and love is the non-lethal weapon by which they conquer the world and win souls for Christ. Love conquers all evil by not repaying evil with evil, but evil with love; and love disarms all its enemies by loving it enemies, blessing those that curse, doing good to those that hate, praying for those who are despiteful and persecute. These are Christ's commands to His Christian soldiers and disciples. The souls of men, women, and children are the most precious trophies of Christ!

Wow! This kind of love is way out of this world! It's height, depth, width, and length are too great for any human mind to fathom. And it is this same mighty conquering and vanquishing power of the love of Christ that continues to overthrow, dethrone, and to cast Satan out of the hearts of men, women, and children all over the world! It continues to conquer and to disarm sinners at the Cross!

Love continues to preach the Good News to the poor and meek in spirit; to heal the brokenhearted, the bruised, and hurting; to proclaim freedom and liberty to the captives; to open prison doors and to set the captives free; to proclaim the acceptable year of God's salvation to all sinners; to comfort all those who mourn; to give them beauty in exchange for their ashes; to give them the oil of joy in exchange for their mourning; to give them the garment of praise in exchange for the spirit of despair and hopelessness; to heal the sick; to open blind eyes; to open deaf ears; to heal the lame and the cripple; to cleanse the lepers; to raise the dead; to cast out devils; and to gather the great harvest of souls from every nation, every kindred, every tongue, every tribe, every race, and every people from the ends of the earth! (Isaiah 61:1-3; Luke 4:14-19; Mark 16:15-19)

The kingdom of Heaven is not by war but by love! It is not by force but by power! And it is not by violence but by influence! Neither can the world be conquered by any force of violence or war, but by love alone that is in Christ Jesus. Yes! Jesus Christ, the poor carpenter from Nazareth, has conquered the world with His love! He said to His disciples: *"These things have I spoken to you, that in Me you may have peace. In the world you will have tribulation; but be of good cheer, I have overcome the world."* (John 16:33 NKJV)

Since it is Love that conquers the world and the hearts of all men, therefore, there is no heart too hard and stony that Love cannot break and melt. There is no heart too stubborn and rebellious that Love cannot conquer and tame. There is no heart too sinful and evil that Love cannot forgive and redeem. There is no heart too lost and hopeless that Love cannot find and rescue.

There is no heart too dark that Love cannot lighten and brighten. There is no heart too dead, rotten, and stinking that Love cannot resurrect and make alive. There is no heart too broken, shattered, and scattered that Love cannot gather and put together. There is no heart too wounded and hurting that Love cannot heal and restore. And there is no heart too filthy and ugly that Love cannot purify and beautify!

This is that Amazing Love of Christ that conquers all and loves all! The Bible says that the sting of death is sin. This means that sin has got a sting like that of a poisonous serpent or scorpion. Therefore, just as sin is the sting of death, killing and maiming its victims, so also is Love the antidote to the venom of sin and hatred, bringing healing and eternal life to as many as will receive it. The "bullets" of Love" do not kill or maim their victims, but rather, they save them. Therefore, let us exchange our guns and weapons of mass racial, social media, and political destruction and distortion with the "bullets" of Love. Let us begin to shoot at one another with the "bullets" of Love and not with the canons of racism and hatred.

On the Cross, Christ has already defanged death of its deadly sting, which is sin, so that sin should not have dominion and control over us anymore. For the wages of sin is death.

The Bible says that, *"Death has been swallowed up in victory, therefore, O death, where is thy sting? And O grave, where is thy victory? The sting of death is sin, and the strength of sin is the law!"* (1Corinthians 15:54-57 KJV)

This is that true kind of a God-Love that conquers the world and the hearts of all men; and that conquers the devil and all evil and disarms all its enemies; that breaks down the walls of racial, social, political and societal barriers, enmities, animosities, prejudices, and hostilities; that disarms all militant and warring factions; that demilitarizes all war zones; that neutralizes all weapons of racial, political, and societal injustices and inhumanities; that heals and reconciles all feuding parties; and that saves all sinners!

Therefore, let us take off the mask of racism and hatred and injustice, and let us put on Love! Let us stop pandering the "race card" and let us start playing the "grace card." Let us stop shooting the "hate canons" and let us start shooting the "Love bullets!" Christ has paid a high price. For there is no greater love than this, that a man should lay down his life for his own friends. Christ has demonstrated His highest love toward all mankind by laying down His life as a sacrifice for all races on the Cross. Even while we were yet sinners, Christ died for us all! He that knew no sin was made sin for us; the Just for the unjust! What greater love, and what higher sacrifice! Ponder on this!

O, amazing Love!

How precious thou art, that loves a
wretch like me!
I once was a sinner, but now I am forgiven.
I once was hated, but now I am loved.
I once was rejected, but now I am accepted.
I once was forsaken, but now I am taken.
I once was mistaken, but now I am identified!

O, amazing Love!
How precious thou art, that loves a
wretch like me!
I once was a hater, but now I am a lover.
I once was a racist, but now I am a pacifist.

O, racism, where is thy sting?
For the sting of racism is hate!
O, hate, where is thy venom?
For the venom of hate is unforgiveness!

O, death, where is thy sting?
For the sting of death is sin!
O, grave, where is thy victory?
For death has been swallowed up in victory.

And I thank God who has given me the victory
through Christ Jesus!
For His Amazing Love has conquered me and
has set me free!
For he that the Son sets free, is free indeed!
And I am free indeed! Free at last!
For he that has the Son, has life,
And I have the Son, and I have life!

Praise God, hallelujah!
O, amazing Love!
How precious thou art, that loves a
wretch like me!

This is that Amazing Love that has conquered the world! And in the fullness of time, when all the history of mankind and of this world shall come to an end, LOVE shall put all His enemies under His feet, and the last enemy to be destroyed is death! (1 Corinthians 15:24-28) And then every knee shall bow, and every tongue shall confess that Jesus Christ is LOVE and LORD, to the glory of God the Father! (Philippians 2:10-11)

And then Christ shall establish His kingdom of LOVE, where there shall be no more sin, no more devil, no more evil, no more hate, no more curse, no more racism, no more discrimination, no more prejudice, no more injustice, no more death, no more sorrow, no more crying, no more pain, and no more suffering. And God shall wipe away every tear from their eyes. (Revelation 21:1-7).

This is that all-conquering, all-vanquishing, all-triumphing, all-victorious, all-overcoming, all-redeeming, all-saving, all-healing, all-reconciling, all-liberating, and all-eternal life-giving Love that Loves All, And Conquers All! Has This Love Conquered You Yet?

CHAPTER THIRTEEN

A Call For Racial And National Repentance With Unconditional Love And Forgiveness!

More than ever before, we are living in a very hateful, intolerant, offensive, resentful, revengeful, and an unforgiving world, and America is not only deeply broken, wounded, and hurting, but it is also deeply divided, offended, hateful, intolerant, resentful, revengeful, and unforgiving! And America must return back to God in repentance and with unconditional love and forgiveness in order for any peace, unity and reconciliation to take place!

From its very inception, America was referred to as a "melting pot." According to Wikipedia, the melting pot is a monocultural metaphor for a heterogeneous society becoming more homogeneous, with the different elements "melting together" with a common culture.[23] This means that even though America was made up of different cultures from all over the world, but then these different cultures began to melt together into a homogeneous society that formed the American culture.

This "melting pot" was meant to have melted and blended all the different cultures and races and colors of people together into a unique culture marked by unity in diversity. And I would like to think that perhaps it was because of this cultural, religious, and political homogeneity or blending that America is referred to as "one nation under God, indivisible, with liberty and justice for all," which became the patriotic Pledge of Allegiance to the indivisibility and invincibility of America as a great nation and a world super-power.

However, it seems as if that "melting pot" that once homogenized America as "one nation under God, indivisible, with liberty and justice for all," has now become a boiling cauldron seething with racial, social, political, cultural, and ideological tensions, divisions, and polarization. This "melting pot" has become like a pressurized cooker, and the tragic death of George Floyd in particular, was like lifting off the lid from that pressure cooker and letting off a violent hot steam leading into street protests, rioting, looting, burnings, shootings, killings, chaos, lawlessness, anarchy, and destruction.

We saw how a very violent hot steam of deep-seated subterranean anger, hatred, bitterness, resentments, malice, grudges, intolerance, offenses, revenge, and unforgiveness was vented out and spilled into our streets all over America, and even over-spilling to other nations around the world. It became a worldwide anger and protest.

And the truth is that America has become even more politically, racially, socially, culturally, ideologically, and denominationally broken, wounded, hurting, divided, polarized, and antagonized. And Jesus said that *"Every kingdom divided against itself is brought to desolation, and every city or a house divided against itself will not stand."* (Matthew 12:25 NKJV) The Bible also says that *"A brother offended is harder to win than a strong city. And contentions are like the bars of a castle."* (Proverbs 18:19 NKJV)

And this is exactly the situation in our nation. America is deeply wounded, offended, hurting, and divided. There is a call for racial and national healing, reconciliation, peace, and unity, but how is that going to happen? In this chapter, we are going to talk about what needs to be done and how it should be done in order for any healing, restoration, reconciliation, peace and unity to take place.

What Needs to Be Done!

As it was in the beginning, so it is now, and so it shall always be: God's template for healing any fallen and back-slidden nation is repentance with unconditional love and forgiveness! And this is where America stands, and this is what America desperately needs to do. If we are talking about racial, social, societal, and national healing, restoration, reconciliation, peace, and unity, then this must come with repentance.

What America desperately needs is not a political reset button, but a spiritual repentance and a returning back to God her Founder and Providence! Godly repentance with unconditional love and forgiveness always precedes personal, congregational, racial, and national healing, restoration, reconciliation, peace, and unity. This is God's pattern. And this is how the nations of Israel and Nineveh reacted when they were confronted with national calamities and the imminent judgments of God. They would come together as a nation and proclaim a period of prayer and fasting, humbling themselves before God in repentance, confessing their sins and begging God for mercy and deliverance.

From the kings, priests, leaders, down to the men, women, children, and even down to the animals, they fasted and humbled themselves before God in deep repentance. And when they did, God heard them, answered their prayers, averted His judgments, and healed their land. (Joel 2:12-32; Jonah 3:1-10) And God Himself has made this pre-conditional requirement very clear in His Word when He said, *"If My people who are called by My name will humble themselves, and pray and seek My face, and turn from their wicked ways, then I will hear from heaven, and will forgive their sin and heal their land."* (2 Chronicles 7:14, NKJV)

As we have seen from the above scripture, repentance is the pathway back to God and to any personal, congregational, racial, and national healing, restoration, reconciliation, peace, and unity. And this is what needs to be done in America if we are really being serious about national healing and reconciliation. But will America humble herself before God? This is the big question.

And I would have to say that without this, there is not going to be any true healing, reconciliation, peace, and unity in America. For no true healing, reconciliation, peace, and unity will ever take place in a heart that is sinful and prideful. No true healing will ever take place in a heart that is full of hatred, racism, anger, bitterness, resentments, malice, grudges, revenge, and unforgiveness. These are barriers and roadblocks that will cause some "spiritual blood clots" in the heart, thus blocking God's healing to flow.

Moreover, how can a heart that is offended, angry, hateful, unloving, and unforgiving make peace and reconciliation? It is impossible! We must understand that repentance with unconditional love and forgiveness are divinely and intricately interwoven. Where there is no repentance, there is no forgiveness, and where there is no forgiveness there is no love, and where there is no love, there is no healing, reconciliation, peace, and unity!

America has been offended, broken, wounded, and hurting ever since its inception. To conquer the New World, brutal acts of racial, social, and political violence, injustices and inhumanities were committed, especially against the indigenous Indians. To industrialize the New World, brutal acts of racial, social, and political acts of injustices and inhumanities were committed, especially against the Blacks held in slavery.

And when America became prosperous and a world superpower militarily, economically, financially, scientifically, technologically, culturally, and politically; and when she grew fat and forgot the God that founded and prospered her and started worshiping strange gods that her founding fathers never knew, gross acts of iniquities, evils, immoralities, perversions, idolatry, injustices, and wickedness have been and are being committed!

So, we are talking here about both past and present deep-seated generational, ancestral, racial, social, political, and national wounds, hurts, pain, anger, offenses, hatred, bitterness, resentments, distrust, divisions, and unforgiveness.

Reparation, defunding the police, street protests, rioting, burning, looting, shooting, killing, toppling down historical statues, or any other structural or institutional reform is not the answer. None of these can heal the deep-seated wounds and hurts and offenses in people's hearts. It's going to take the supernatural act and finger of God, and not the natural act of man, to heal America. Only God can heal and change the heart of our nation by the supernatural act of godly repentance and unconditional love and forgiveness through His Son, Jesus Christ, who is our Master-Forgiver!

Understanding the Nature of Offenses and Forgiveness from a God Perspective!

In terms of offenses, man was the first to offend and to hurt God, thereby becoming the "first offender." And in response to man's offenses against God, Jesus became our "First Responder." And since that first day that man first offended God, not only has man become just a 1st, 2nd, 3rd, 4th, 5th, 6th, 7th, offender, but he has become a million and a billion times offender, constantly offending God for over six thousand years now. In fact, the moment Adam and Eve sinned, God was the first to respond by coming down and calling out to him, "Adam, where are you?" And by killing the first animal to cover their nakedness.

And it is this same God who first responded to man's first offense in the Garden of Eden that has also responded on the Cross at Calvary by offering His own Son Jesus Christ to be killed in order to cover the sins and shame and nakedness of the human race. Thus, man became the "first offender," and Christ became our "First Responder," and the Cross is His "universal recall center" to all sinners and offenders.

God is the one that has been most offended and hurt by us humans. The whole wide world, including you and I have all greatly offended and deeply hurt God our Creator by our dis-obedience, rebellion, and sins. That's why the Bible says that we all have sinned and fallen short of the glory of God. Sin is not only an offense, but it is also an abhorrence and an abomi-nation to God, which is punishable by death. For the wages of sin is death, but the free gift of God is unconditional love and forgiveness and eternal life through Jesus Christ our Savior. Just think about the million times you and I have offended God in our lifetime.

And it was because of our sins and offenses against God that Jesus came to die on the Cross to love and to forgive us unconditionally. Christ is our classic and perfect example and role model for unconditional love and forgiveness. Nailed to the Cross and dying for the sins and offenses of the whole world and being mocked by the very people that He came to save, Jesus looked down from that rugged Cross on lost humanity, and with unconditional love and forgiveness, prayed, *"Father, forgive them, for they know not what they do."* (Luke 23:34 KJV)

That was an irrevocable unconditional love and forgiveness offered to an undeserving sinful and an ungrateful world. In describing the helpless and hopeless sinful condition of the human race and God's unconditional love and forgiveness, the Bible says, *"When we were helpless, Christ came at just the right time and died for us sinners. Now, most people would not be willing to die for an upright person, though someone might perhaps be willing to die for a person who is especially good. But God showed His great love for us by sending Christ to die for us while we were still sinners."* (Romans 5:6-8 NLT)

This is what unconditional love and forgiveness is. It is unmerited and undeserved love, mercy, grace, and forgiveness! Furthermore, the Bible says, *"If we say that we have no sin, we deceive ourselves, and the truth is not in us. If we confess our sins, He is faithful and just to forgive us our sins and to cleanse us from all unrighteousness. If we say that we have not sinned, we make Him a liar, and His word is not in us.*

"My little children, these things I write to you, so that you may not sin. And if anyone sins, we have an Advocate with the Father, Jesus Christ the righteous. And He Himself is the propitiation for our sins, and not for ours only but also for the whole world" (1 John 1:8-10; 2:1-2 NKJV)

Again, this is unconditional love and forgiveness that keeps loving and forgiving the sinner and offender.

Offenses Are Inevitable!

It has been said that "To err is human, and to forgive is divine." So true. However, I have come to realize that there are two things under the sun that are the hardest and the most difficult for a person to do in this world: The first is to love your enemies and those who hate you; and the second is to forgive those who have so badly wronged and hurt you. I find these two things the hardest and the most difficult to do under heaven. It is very hard to love your enemies and to forgive those who have hurt you. By our fallen and sinful human nature, man is unloving, unkind, hateful, resentful, unforgiving, and revengeful.

The Lord Jesus said offenses are inevitable, "Woe to the world because of offenses! For offenses must come, but woe to that man by whom the offense comes!" (Matthew 18:7 NKJV) He went further to say, *"And many will be offended, will betray one another, and will hate one another...And because lawlessness will abound, the love of many will grow cold."* (Matthew 24:10, 12 NKJV)

From the above Scriptures, we see that even Jesus has made it abundantly clear that offenses will come, and that they are inevitable. This means that whether we like it or not, offenses will come. Not only have we offended God, but we have also offended others, and others have offended us. In fact, the Bible even says that we all do offend, either in words or in deeds. (James 3:2) And that means, one way or the other, we have offended others, and others have offended us.

The reality of this life is that there is no man or woman or child or husband or wife or father or mother or human or any marriage or family or home or community or nation that is perfect. Even within the same family circle: husbands, wives, fathers, mothers, children, siblings, relatives, etc., have all offended one another.

We live in a fallen, sinful, evil, wicked, broken world full of hatred, injustices, inhumanities, offenses, hurts, pain, sufferings, and unforgiveness. We are living in an imperfect world full of imperfect people in which offenses are inevitable. I have offended my wife and others, and my wife and others have offended me. As long as we are living in this fallen, broken, hurting, and wretched world, offenses are inevitable. But the question is, how do we respond to offenses when they do come? Do we hold on to them or do we let go of them? That's the discussion of this chapter because until we learn how to repent, love and to forgive unconditionally, there will be no healing, peace, joy, reconciliation, and freedom in our personal lives, in our nation, and in the world.

What Is Unconditional Love and Forgiveness?

If we are to move forward as individuals, as a people, as a nation, and as a world, and go past our racial, religious, political, and societal divides, we must choose to love and to forgive one another unconditionally. I know it's easier said than done, but that's what Jesus, our Master-Forgiver said, and that's what God said, and that's what the Bible says. Unconditional love and forgiveness are the only way you and I can overcome offenses and hatred. The Bible says that love covers multitudes of sins: *"Above all, love each other deeply, because love coves over a multitude of sins."* (1 Peter 4:8 NIV) This means that perfect and fervent love, which harbors no offenses or grudges, will cause you to forgive multitudes of offenses by forgiving the person that has offended you.

Firstly, unconditional love and forgiveness means that you choose to voluntarily forgive and "forgo" the offenses and to "let go" of the offender with no preconditions. This means that you willfully decide to forgive and to forgo the offense or wrong done to you and to release and let go free the offender from inside your heart with no strings attached. It is a volitional act of your own free will as a free moral agent of which even God Himself cannot violate because He is also a free moral agent Being who acts volitionally. This means that it is in your power to love and to forgive unconditionally without any duress.

Secondly, unconditional love and forgiveness is an act of acquittal whereby you choose not only to forgive but to also release and set free unconditionally all the people whom you have held prisoners in the dungeon of your heart. By so doing, you are not only releasing them, but you are also releasing all the anger, bitterness, resentments, hatred, malice, grudges, enmity, hurts, pain, unforgiveness, and any thoughts of revenge that you might have harbored in your heart.

Just as a judge would acquit and set free an offender, and just as a probation officer or a prison warden would open the prison door and unlock the handcuffs that have bound the prisoner and set him free, so also must you do. When you forgive unconditionally, you must not only forgive, but you must also release all the people whom you have held prisoners in the dungeon of your heart as "Prisoners of Offenses" (P.O.O). You must unlock their handcuffs which are the offenses, and open their prison doors which is your heart, and release them.

Thirdly, unconditional love and forgiveness is both a spiritual and a judicial act. In this case, you become both your own judge, your own grand jury, and your own prison warden or probation officer in whose power it is to forgive, acquit, unlock, unchain, release, and set free your own "Prisoners of Offenses" (P.O.O). This was exactly what Jesus came to do. He did not only come to forgive our sins and offenses, but to also open the prison doors and to set the captives free from the bondage of sin and the devil. Jesus Himself declared: *"The Spirit of the Sovereign LORD God is upon Me, for the LORD has anointed Me to bring good tidings to the poor. He has sent Me to heal the brokenhearted and to proclaim liberty to the captives, and the opening of the prison to those who are bound."* (Isaiah 61:1-3 NKJV)

Did you hear that? Not only have we all sinned and fallen short of the glory of God, but we have also become slaves to sin and captives to the devil. Therefore, Jesus came not only to forgive our sins, but to also open the prison doors of our imprisonment by sin and by the devil, and to set us totally free; for he that the Son of God sets free is free indeed!

Fourthly, unconditional love and forgiveness is motivated by sympathy, empathy, and compassion. Hatred, racism, anger, bitterness, resentment, revenge, envy, jealousy, will make you not to forgive, but sympathy, empathy, and compassion driven by love will motivate you to forgive. It is an act of compassion and not an act of compulsion whereby you feel compelled to do so. Love does not compel. Love convicts and convinces. And that's the work of the Holy Spirit whom God has sent to convict the world of sin, of offenses, of righteousness, and of judgment. (John 16:7-11)

Fifthly, unconditional love and forgiveness is an act of grace and not an act of race. Grace forgives, racism does not. You do not love and forgive because the person is black or white or brown or red, but you choose to love and to forgive unconditionally because of grace. Grace is unmerited favor, and that means that the person that has hurt you does not deserve your forgiveness, but you choose to be merciful and to forgive even when they have not apologized or asked for forgiveness. Jesus said, *"Blessed are the merciful, for they shall obtain mercy"* (Matthew 5:7 KJV). He also said, *"If you forgive anyone his sins, they are forgiven; if you do not forgive them, they are not forgiven."* (John 20:23 NIV)

In fact, the Old King James Bible uses the word retain, and that means that if you hold on to the offenses and wrongs that people have committed against you and you refuse to forgive them, then you have become a retainer of their sins, wrongs, hurts, and pain. That means you have become a "record-keeper" and a "store-keeper" of your offenders and their offenses. You record them and store them in the storage of your heart.

And imagining the power of the brain and its memory, some people may store up to a hundred, a thousand, a million, a billion, or a trillion gigabytes of offenses. And some may even be running out of storage and you urgently need to delete those offenses in your heart. It's a very dangerous, toxic, and destructive thing to do to store up offenses. That is why the Bible says that unconditional love and forgiveness does not keep records of wrongs or offenses. There is no room or storage for that!

How This Could Be Done and Why You Must Love and Forgive Unconditionally!

First, you must love and forgive unconditionally because God has already loved and forgiven you unconditionally through His Son Jesus Christ over two thousand years ago on the Cross. The Bible says that even when we were utterly helpless, Christ came at just the right time and died for us sinners. Now, most people would not be willing to die for an upright person; someone might perhaps be willing to die for an especially good person. But God showed his great love for us by sending Christ to die for us while we were still sinners. (Romans 5:6-8)

Did you see that? Over two thousand years ago, even before you were ever born, and even before you ever committed any sin, and even after you have committed many sins, God has already demonstrated His unconditional love and forgiveness toward you by sending His Son Jesus Christ to die for you on the Cross. This is what I would call a *"Prepaid Unconditional Love and Forgiveness!"* This is even so true because when Jesus cried on the Cross, "It is finished!" that signified that everything concerning man's forgiveness and redemption has been fully paid for by the shedding of His blood.

Yes! Your redemption and forgiveness have already been prepaid for with the blood of Jesus Christ. All you need to do now is to receive His unconditional love and forgiveness with repentance. The Bible says, *"For God made Christ, who never sinned, to be the offering for our sin, so that we should be made right with God through Christ"* (2 Corinthians 5:21 NLT).

"For Christ also suffered once for sins, the just for the unjust, that He might bring us to God, being put to death in the flesh but made alive by the Spirit." (1 Peter 3:18 NKJV)

The prophet Isaiah said, *"But He was wounded for our transgressions, He was bruised for our iniquities; The chastisement for our peace was upon Him...All we like sheep have gone astray; we have turned everyone, to his own way; and the LORD has laid on Him the iniquities of us all"* (Isaiah 53:5-6 NKJV)

On the Cross, God laid on Jesus the sins of the whole wide world. And it was while hanging on the Cross that He looked down upon lost humanity, and with unconditional love and forgiveness, He prayed, *"Father, forgive them, for they do not know what they are doing!"* (Luke 23:34 NIV) And you and I were also included in that prayer, for all have sinned and fall short of the glory of God.

Second, you must love and forgive unconditionally because Jesus said that if we do not forgive those who have sinned against us, our Heavenly Father will also not forgive us our own sins. In the LORD's Prayer, He said: *"Our Father in heaven, hallowed be Your name, Your kingdom come, Your will be done on earth as it is in heaven. Give us today our daily bread. Forgive us our debts, as we also have forgiven our debtors. And lead us not into temptation but deliver us from the evil one...For if you forgive men when they sin against you, your heavenly Father will also forgive you. But if you do not forgive men their sins, your Father will not forgive your sins."* (Matthew 6:9-15 NIV)

So, we see in the LORD's Prayer how Jesus said that you must forgive those who have sinned against you even as the Father in heaven has forgiven you, but that if you refuse to forgive others, then your Heavenly Father will also not forgive you because it would be unfair and unjust for you to ask God to forgive you when you are refusing to forgive others.

To further illustrate this truth, Jesus told this story of the unmerciful servant who would not forgive his fellow debtor:

"Then Peter came to Him and asked, 'LORD, how often should I forgive someone who sins against me? Seven times?' 'No, not seven times,' Jesus replied, 'but seventy times seven! Therefore, the Kingdom of Heaven can be compared to a king who decided to bring his accounts up to date with his servants who had borrowed money from him. In the process, one of his debtors was brought in who owed him millions of dollars. He

couldn't pay, so his master ordered that he be sold – along with his wife, his children, and everything he owned – to pay the debt. But the man fell down before his master and begged him, 'Please, be patient with me, and I will pay it all.' Then his master was filled with pity for him, and he released him and forgave his debt.

But when the man left the king, he went to a fellow servant who owed him a few thousand dollars. He grabbed him by the throat and demanded instant payment. His fellow servant fell down before him and begged for a little more time.

'Be patient with me, and I will pay it,' he pleaded. But his creditor wouldn't wait. He had the man arrested and put in prison until the debt could be paid in full.

When some of the other servants saw this, they were very upset. They went to the king and told him everything that had happened. Then the king called in the man he had forgiven and said, 'You evil servant! I forgave you that tremendous debt because you pleaded with me. Shouldn't you have mercy on your fellow servant, just as I had mercy on you?' Then the angry king sent the man to prison to be tortured until he had paid his entire debt. That's what My heavenly Father will do to you if you refuse to forgive your brothers and sisters from your heart." (Matthew 18:21-35 NLT)

Did you hear that? Jesus did not only say that you should love and forgive 70 x 7 (which is, arithmetically speaking, 490 times), but that also if you refuse to unconditionally love and forgive others who have done you wrong, then God the Heavenly Father will also not forgive you your sins. And that sounds very dangerous because unforgiveness itself is a damnable sin that could lead you to hell, where you will be tormented forever because you will never be able to repay God back for all the hundreds, and thousands, and millions, and billions, and trillions of the debts of sins and offenses that you have committed against Him and against others since the day you were born!

I have heard people say that they will never forgive those who have hurt or offended them. I frankly do understand where they are coming from. The only danger in that is that there are millions of people in hell right now being tormented because they refused to love and to forgive unconditionally. The Bible says, *"What shall it profit you if you gain the whole world but lose your own soul?"* (Matthew 16:26 KJV)

Third, you must love and forgive unconditionally because unforgiveness will only make your life very miserable. You will live in self-inflicted torture and torment. You will be the most miserable and grumpy person in the world because your soul will be in constant torment and torture because the poison from your hatred, bitterness, anger, and resentments will be fermented into some toxic and noxious waste and taste that will affect your emotions, your spirit, your soul, your mind, and your body. You will be the one losing your sleep and having sleepless nights and nightmares. You will be the one losing your appetite because your palates and taste buds will be made bitter by your own bitterness, and your stomach cannot digest properly because your intestines are full of the bile of anger and hatred.

You will be the one losing your peace of mind and your joy because you will be so stressed out, oppressed, and depressed until you start taking antidepressants! You will be the one losing your health and your wealth. You will be the one whose attitude and behavior will begin to change and affect your husband, your wife, your children, your marriage, your friends, your job, and other people around you.

What bondage and self-inflicted torture and torment will that be! You become your own prisoner and torturer in mental, emotional, psychological, social bondage. You will be in self-incarceration, self-isolation, self-pity, and self-destruction. And you will never be free until your whole man: spirit, soul, body, mind, emotions, and conscience are free from the torture and torment of your sins, anger, hatred, malice, bitterness, resentments, grudges, and unforgiveness. You can only experience total healing, joy, peace, love, happiness, restoration, reconciliation, freedom, and a brand-new life when you choose to repent, love and to forgive unconditionally!

Revenge is not an option either, because you could end up being even more miserable, tortured, and tormented by a guilty conscience, regret, remorse, fear, anxiety, depression, accusations, condemnation, and even suicidal thoughts. Your own very conscience will become your own tribunal. That is why the Bible says that we should repay no evil for evil, but that we must have regard for good things toward all men, and that, if possible, we should live peaceably with all men, and that we should not revenge ourselves, but that we should leave that to the righteous anger of God, and that we should not be overcome by evil, we should overcome evil with good. (Romans 12:17-21)

A Call for Racial and National Repentance with Unconditional Love and Forgiveness!

This is what unconditional love and forgiveness means. And this is what America desperately needs right now in order for her to experience the supernatural healing hand of God. Therefore, I am calling on all my fellow Americans to repent of our own personal sins and of the sins of our leaders and of our nation and let us love and forgive one another unconditionally.

I am calling on all Blacks, Whites, Native Indians, Latinos, Africans, Jews, Asians, Chinese, Russians, Europeans, and all other nationalities and races and colors of people in America to repent and to love and to forgive one another unconditionally for all personal, racial, political, societal, generational, and national sins, offenses, and injustices. As husbands, wives, children, relatives, neighbors, politicians, etc., let us repent and love and forgive one another unconditionally.

And here is what the Bible says about the sum-total effects of our godly repentance with unconditional love and forgiveness not only in our lives, but also in our nation. It says,

"Since God chose you to be the holy people He loves, you must clothe yourselves with tenderhearted mercy, kindness, humility, gentleness, and patience. Make allowance for each other's faults and forgive anyone who offends you. Remember, the Lord forgave you, so you must forgive others. Above all, clothe yourselves with love, which binds us all together in perfect harmony. And let the peace that comes from Christ rule your hearts. For as members of one body, you are called to live in peace." (Colossians 3:12-15 NLT)

From the above passage, we see clearly how love is the spindle from which all the threads of tenderheartedness, mercy, kindness, compassion, goodness, humility, gentleness, tolerance, patience, peace, harmony, unity, and forgiveness spin from to meticulously weave in the intricate patterns and designs of a harmonious life and society. Therefore, let us take off the mask of sin, racism, hatred, injustice, evil, wickedness, anger, resentment, bitterness, grudges, malice, revenge, and unforgiveness, and let us put on the mantle of repentance and of unconditional love and forgiveness!

Let us clothe ourselves with love, walk in love, act in love, talk in love, live in love, and die in love. It is better for you to die in love and forgiveness than to die in hatred and bitterness. It is better for you to die with a heart full of love and forgiveness than to die with a heart full of the poison of racism, hatred, bitterness, and unforgiveness. It is better to live a life of love, forgiveness, and freedom than to live a life of hatred and bondage.

Unconditional love and forgiveness do not wait for an apology that may never come. Therefore, go ahead and give yourself this precious gift of unconditional love and forgiveness by forgiving all the people that have offended and hurt you in the past, present, and future. Set yourself a world record not in the Guinness Book of World Records of this world that comes to nothing, but in the "Unconditional Love and Forgiveness Book of World Records" with your personalized name emblazoned in the Lamb's Book of Life in heaven!

It is the truth that there is a national and a global scarcity of unconditional love and forgiveness. The demand for unconditional love and forgiveness is at its highest peak ever, but its supply is at its lowest ebb ever! There is a universal shortage of unconditional love and forgiveness. The heart of man is impoverished of love. And the reason for this is because men have rejected Love in their hearts, which is Christ Jesus, who is the epitome and embodiment of true unconditional love and forgiveness. Christ is the manifestation and demonstration of God's unconditional love and forgiveness to the world.

The heart of man is the reservoir of unconditional love and forgiveness, and the Holy Spirit is the supplier and replenisher of that reservoir: For the fruit of the Spirit is love! This would mean that without the Holy Spirit inside one's heart, it would be very difficult and if not impossible for one to function in this kind of an unconditional love and Forgiveness.

Therefore, let unconditional love and Forgiveness flow from the reservoir of your heart, cascading with the torrents and currents like those of the great Niagara Falls, and splashing and flooding humanity with the refreshing waters of salvation, healing, deliverance, restoration, peace, joy, unity, and reconciliation! Let the rivers of unconditional love and forgiveness flow out of the dam of your heart to quench the famished and weary souls of thirsty humanity! Let the rivers of unconditional love and forgiveness flow out of the dam of your heart to give life-saving love to a dying and perishing world! The whole wide world is in desperate need of Unconditional Love and Forgiveness. Let's Give It To It!

CHAPTER FOURTEEN

A Call For Racial and National Healing And Restoration!

A merica is broken, wounded, and hurting, and there is a desperate cry for racial, societal, political, and national healing and restoration in our nation. But the question is, do our politicians and leaders and policy makers really understand how badly and how deeply broken, wounded, and hurting our nation has become? Do they understand the nature, depth, complexity, and magnitude of it all? And how do we go about bringing healing and restoration to our nation? These questions must be asked and answered, and that is why in this chapter, we are going to talk about how broken, wounded and hurting America is, and what needs to be done to bring healing and restoration.

First of all, it is my strong belief that it is the health of a nation that determines the wealth of that nation and the wellbeing of its citizens, and not the wealth of a nation that determines the health of that nation and the wellbeing of its citizens. Others may think otherwise, and that depends, if they are looking at it from a scientific, technological, economic, or political point of view. But I am looking at it from a spiritual, moral, emotional, mental, and psychological point of view.

Of course, a nation like America can have all the wealth and riches and latest state of the art scientific and technological breakthroughs and discoveries with the best hospitals, best healthcare system, best welfare system, best educational system, best economic system, best political system, and the best of everything, and yet still be spiritually, morally, ethically, emotionally, mentally, and psychologically sick, broken, wounded, and hurting!

As goes the Latin phrase, *"Mens sana in corpore sano,"* being translated, *"a healthy mind in a healthy body,"* so therefore a nation and its citizens are never made healthy by its mere abundance of wealth, or riches, or material possessions. A man may possess this whole wide world and still be spiritually, morally, ethically, emotionally, mentally, and psychologically bankrupt and sick. That is why the Lord Jesus asked the question what shall it profit a man if he gains this whole world and yet losses his soul in the end? (Mark 8:36) In another scriptural passage, He said that a man's life does not consist of the abundance of his possessions. (Luke 12:15)

America is spiritually, morally, emotionally, mentally, psychologically, racially, socially, economically, politically, and pandemically sick, broken, wounded, and hurting. Millions of lives, homes, and families are broken, wounded, and hurting. Our communities are broken, wounded, and hurting. Our government is broken, wounded, and hurting. Our politicians are broken, wounded, and hurting. Our congress is broken, wounded, and hurting. The White House is broken, wounded, and hurting. Our supreme court is broken, wounded, and hurting. Our police are broken, wounded, and hurting. Our economy is broken, wounded, and hurting. Our businesses are broken, wounded, and hurting. Our schools, colleges and universities are broken, wounded, and hurting. Our churches are broken, wounded, and hurting. Our society is broken, wounded, and hurting.

The precious souls of men, women, children, teenagers, husbands, wives, fathers, mothers, parents, old, young, black, white, red, brown, dark, are all broken, wounded and hurting!

And America is broken, wounded, and hurting! The whole of humanity is broken, wounded, and hurting! And the whole wide world is broken, wounded, and hurting!

It seems as if the Devil himself has descended on the American soil and has put both feet on America's neck, and America is being racially, socially, politically, economically, and spiritually asphyxiated, and is gasping for breath! It seems as if the poem by Emma Lazarus, at the base of the Statue of Liberty in New York that says, *"Give me your tired, your poor, your huddled masses yearning to breathe free,"* and the final heartbreaking words of George Floyd, *"I can't breathe,"* are, to me, spiritually speaking, symbolic and symptomatic of the state of condition of our sick nation.

But America's brokenness, wounds and hurts are not just emotional, mental, psychological, racial, social, and political, rather they are also moral and spiritual in nature. There is yet a more virulent and deadly disease that is plaguing our nation, and that has infected and affected the whole fabric of the American society, and that virulent and deadly disease is sin.

In fact, America's problems, like the rest of the world, are not so much political or racial or economic or social or cultural, but rather it is a sin problem. All the problems we are facing in America and in the world are as a result of sin. Sin is the universal cancer of the human race and is deeply seated in the heart of man where no cardiologist or psychologist or psychiatrist or physician, or scientist, or politician can fathom, only God can.

In fact, we could trace all the symptoms of America's disease and sickness in the heart. It is the heart of man that is diseased, sinful, evil, wicked, and corrupt that desperately needs healing. A man cannot change if his heart is not changed, and a nation cannot change if men are not changed from inside their hearts. Before kingdoms can change, men must change first from within and not from without. The Bible says that as a man thinks, so he is. (Proverbs 23:7) Jesus said that out of the abundance of the heart, the mouth speaks: *"A good person produces good things from the treasury of a good heart, and an evil person produces evil things from the treasury of his evil heart. What you say flows from what is in your heart."* (Luke 6:45, NLT)

America is sick in the heart therefore it is the heart of man that is sinful and evil that desperately needs healing. And that is why America cannot be healed, be united, be reconciled, and be at peace unless the heart of its citizens is healed first.

Therefore, no amount of presidential executive orders, or congressional bills, or government programs, or social welfare benefits, or healthcare programs, or reparation programs can ever bring true healing and restoration to our racially, socially, politically, governmentally, culturally, economically, denominationally, spiritually, morally, and ethically broken, wounded, and hurting nation! Only God can! And this can only happen through the cleansing and healing power of the blood of Jesus Christ. Without this, all else will be political rhetoric and media cosmetics!

This is that broken, wounded, hurting, and sicken state of condition of our nation and society. God has diagnosed the problem with the heart of man and has already given His report in His own "Spiritual Journal of Medicine," the Bible. And here is what it says: *"The human heart is most deceitful of all things, and desperately wicked. Who really knows how bad it is? But I, the LORD, search all hearts and examine secret motives. I give all people their rewards, according to what their actions deserve."* (Jeremiah 17:9-10, NLT)

This is how bad and wicked the human heart is. And if you think that doesn't sound convincing enough, then listen to Jesus' analytical diagnosis of the human heart:

"Then Jesus called to the crowd to come and hear. "All of you listen," He said, "and try to understand. It's not what goes into your body that defiles you; you are defiled by what comes from your heart..." And then He added, "It is what comes from inside that defiles you. For from within, out of a person's heart, come evil thoughts, sexual immorality, theft, murder, adultery, greed, wickedness, deceit, lustful desires, envy, slander, pride, and foolishness. All these vile things come from within, they are what defile you." (Mark 7:14-23, NLT)

Did you hear that? This is God's and Jesus' diagnosis of the human heart, and who can dispute that? And who can heal it, but God! Right now, America's spiritual, moral, racial, social, cultural, political, and national state of condition is like that described by the Lord Jesus as that of a whitewash tomb appearing beautiful on the outside, but inside is full of dead men's bones and all uncleanness: *"Woe to you, teachers of the law and Pharisees, you hypocrites! You are like whitewash tombs, which look beautiful on the outside but on the inside are full of dead men's bones and everything unclean. In the same way, on the outside you appear to people as righteous, but on the inside you are full of hypocrisy and wickedness."* (Matthew 23:27-28, NIV)

This is the state of condition of our nation. America outwardly appears to be normal and beautiful on the outside, but inside her is full of iniquity and wickedness and all kinds of sins of sexual perversions, immoralities, abortion, idolatry, racism, injustices, and of all kinds of evils.

Our nation desperately needs healing, and no president, or congress, or government, or hospital, or World Health Organization, or pharmaceutical company, or drugs, or vaccine, or programs, or police reform, or legislative reform, or executive orders, or Center for Disease Control guidelines, or any man, or any other thing is able to heal the deep-seated racial, social, political, and national wounds and hurts and pain, and hatred, and racism, and bitterness, and anger, and resentments, and unforgiveness and brokenness that our nation is facing right now. No man, but God!

It is the heart of man that desperately needs healing, transformation, and reformation! And there is no man-made drugs or cure for the heart. These are not physical wounds that need medical cure, but rather, they are spiritual, moral, emotional, mental, psychological, racial, political, and societal wounds. They are heart wounds, hurts, pain, and brokenness.

Bitten by Fiery Serpents!

The entire human race is bitten by the fiery serpents of sin, just like the disobedient children of Israel were bitten by fiery serpents in the wilderness. The Bible says, *"And the people spoke against God and against Moses: 'Why have you brought us up out of Egypt to die in the wilderness? For there is no food and no water, and our soul loathes this worthless bread.' So, the LORD sent fiery serpents among the people, and they bit the people, and many of the people died. Therefore, the people came to Moses, and said, 'We have sinned, for we have spoken against the LORD and against you; pray to the LORD that He take away the serpents from us.' So, Moses prayed for the people.*

Then the LORD said to Moses, 'Make a fiery serpent and set it on a pole; and it shall be that everyone who is bitten, when he looks at it, shall live' So, Moses made a bronze serpent, and put it on a pole; and so, it was, if a serpent had bitten anyone, when he looked at the bronze serpent, he lived." (Numbers 21:5-9 NKJV)

From the above passage, the Bible tells us how sin and rebellion against God brought about the fiery wrath of those serpents upon the children of Israel, and how they acknowledged their sins and cried out to Moses to intercede for them before God. Moses did, and God told him to make a serpent of bronze and lift it up on a pole so that the people could see it, and that whosoever looks upon the brazen serpent, even though he has been bitten by these fiery serpents, he will be instantly healed. Moses did as the LORD commanded, and as many as obeyed and looked upon the brazen serpent on the pole were miraculously healed.

The typology of this is that the pole was a type of the Cross, and the brazen serpent was a type of Christ in two ways: First, the serpent represented sin, and second, the serpent was a cursed beast of all creatures made by God. And so, therefore, on the Cross, Christ became both sin and a curse for us, and took upon Himself the sins of the world. The Bible says, "Christ has redeemed us from the curse of the law, having become a curse for us (for it is written, *"Cursed is everyone who hangs on a tree")*, *that the blessings of Abraham might come upon the Gentiles in Christ Jesus, that we might receive the promise of the Spirit through faith."* (Galatians 3:13-14 NKJV)

Moses was also a type of Christ. For just as the people cried out to Moses for him to intercede and mediate between them and God, so also has Christ come to intercede and to be the mediator between God and man, so that through Him alone all men might be saved.

This is that same serpent that had bitten Adam and Eve in the Garden of Eden and caused them also to die, and has brought death, sicknesses, diseases, pain, hurts, sufferings, and untold miseries upon the entire human race. Satan, who is the devil, is also called the dragon and that old serpent:

"And he laid hold on the dragon, that old serpent, which is the devil, and Satan, and bound him a thousand years, and cast him into the bottomless pit…" (Revelation 20:2 KJV)

And so, we also, in our own rebellion against God, have brought upon ourselves the wrath of these fiery serpents of sin in our lives. And you must understand that these fiery serpents represent sin and its deadly poison in our lives. The Bible says, *"Death is swallowed up in victory. O death, where is thy sting? O grave, where is thy victory? The sting of death is sin, and the strength of sin is the law. But thanks be to God, who giveth us the victory through our Lord Jesus Christ."* (1 Corinthians 15:56-57, KJV)

Yes, sin has got a sting more poisonous and more deadly than COVID-19 or any other virus. For the sting of sin is death, and the wages of sin is death! The Bible gives us an example of how the fiery serpents of sin can affect the whole human body when it says:

"Who has woes? Who has sorrow? Who has contentions? Who has complaints? Who has wounds without cause? Who has redness of eyes? Those who linger long at the wine, those who go in search of mixed wine. Do not look on the wine when it is red, when it sparkles in the cup, when it swirls around smoothly; At

the last it bites like a serpent, And stings like a viper. Your eyes will see strange things." (Proverbs 23:29-35 NKJV)

This is the miserable zombie-like condition in which the deadly poison of sin degrades and depraves a man! Could you imagine from the time you were born to now the hundreds or thousands, or even millions of snake bites and of the stings of sin that are inside your body and the deadly poison of those sins in your life?

It is for this purpose that Christ came to take away our sins and the venom of sin in our lives, and to destroy the power of sin, death, hell, and of the devil. And this Christ has already accomplished by the shedding of His blood on the Cross. It is through the power in His blood that we are healed and set free from every broken-hearts and wounds, hurts, pain and suffering that sin has caused in our lives.

Only His blood shed on the Cross at Calvary has got the power to heal, save, and to deliver, and nothing else in the whole wide world can do that. That is why Jesus said, *"And as Moses lifted up the serpent in the wilderness, even so must the Son of Man be lifted up, that whosoever believes in Him should not perish but have eternal life. For God did not send His Son into the world to condemn the world, but that the world through him might be saved."* (John 3:14-17 NKJV)

Yes! Christ was both that brazen serpent on the pole in the wilderness and on the Cross at Calvary! Again, talking about His crucifixion, Jesus said, *"And I, if I be lifted up from the earth, will draw all men unto Me."* (John 12:32 KJV)

From those two scriptural passages, we see a divine pattern that God has set in place for the redemption, healing, and restoration of the human race: and that is, all those who have been bitten by the fiery serpents of sin must look up to the Cross for healing and deliverance. They must look up to Christ on the

Cross at Calvary for their healing, salvation, and deliverance. Just as Moses erected the brazen serpent on a pole in the wilderness so that whosoever looked upon it was miraculously healed and delivered, so also has God erected the Cross at Calvary Hill so that whosoever will look at Christ crucified on the Cross will likewise be miraculously healed, saved, delivered, and restored!

And if America and the world and all those who have been bitten by these fiery serpents of sin want to be healed, saved, delivered, and restored, then they must likewise look up to Christ crucified on the Cross on Calvary Hill!

O, my dear friend, I want you to understand that every sin in your life represents the poisonous and deadly stings of so many fiery serpents that have bitten you, such as the fiery serpents of racism, hatred, bitterness, resentment, malice, grudges, envy, jealousy, corruption, lustfulness, cheating, stealing, lying, adultery, fornication, pornography, prostitution, rape, sexual perversion and immorality, murder, abortion, drugs, cocaine, alcohol, smoking, etc.

And for every single sin that you commit, the fiery serpent of that sin will strike you with the lethal poison of death. And the venom of each sin will poison your whole body, spirit, soul, and mind, and will begin to affect not only you, but your marriage, wife, husband, children, home, family, loved ones, friends, neighbors, communities, society, the nation, and the world. These are the devastating ramifications and multiplying effects of sin.

The Healing Power in the Blood of Jesus Christ!

Like I have already said that only God can heal America, and that healing can only happen through the power of the blood of Jesus Christ! The Bible says of the Lord Jesus that,

"He is despised and rejected by men, A Man of sorrows and acquainted with grief. And we hid, as it were, our faces from Him; He was despised, and we did not esteem Him.

Surely, He borne our griefs and carried our sorrows; Yet we esteemed Him stricken, Smitten by God, and afflicted.

But He was wounded for our transgressions, He was bruised for our iniquities; The chastisement for our peace was upon Him, And by His stripes we are healed. All we like sheep have gone astray; We have turned, everyone to his own way; And the LORD has laid on Him the iniquity of us all. He was oppressed and He was afflicted, Yet He opened not His mouth; He was led as a lamb to the slaughter, and as a sheep before its shearer is silent, so He opened not His mouth." (Isaiah 53:3-7 NKJV)

On the Cross, Christ was bruised, wounded, hurt, broken, shattered, crushed, despised, rejected, smitten, stricken, beaten, oppressed, depressed, discouraged, betrayed, afflicted, chastised, punished, spat upon, mocked, abused, violated, molested, shamed, dishonored, forsaken, abandoned, insulted, falsely accused, acquainted with griefs, sorrows, and sufferings, judged, condemned, crucified, died, buried, and on the third day rose again triumphant!

The Bible tells us how God anointed Jesus Christ with the Holy Spirit to heal all those that are brokenhearted, wounded, bruised, rejected, oppressed, depressed, molested, abused, addicted, sick, and hurting. Jesus Himself has declared, *"The Spirit of the Lord God is upon Me, because He has anointed Me to preach the gospel to the poor; He has sent Me to heal the brokenhearted, to proclaim liberty to the captives, and recovery of sight to the blind, to set at liberty those who are oppressed; to proclaim the acceptable year of the LORD."* (Luke 4:18-19 NKJV) And this is what He wants to do in America, and in the world, and in your life.

To All Those Who Are Wounded, Bruised, Hurting, and Brokenhearted!

There are those of you who have been spiritually, emotionally, mentally, psychologically, physically, sexually, racially, socially, politically, maritally, relationally, financially, economically, and pandemically broken, shattered, bruised, crushed, wounded, bleeding and hurting. There are those of you whose bodies are afflicted with all kinds of sicknesses and diseases and pain. There are those of you who are filled with all kinds of fears, anxieties, and worries. There are those of you struggling with all kinds of alcohol, drugs, sex, pornographic, and other addictions. There are those of you going through all kinds of oppression and depression.

There are those of you whose lives are being haunted by the past with accusations, guilt, regret, condemnation, shame, rejection, and suicidal thoughts. And there are those of you who are thinking that life in this world is meaningless, worthless, useless, hopeless and is not worth living anymore, and are contemplating suicide and giving up on yourself, on life, and on this world.

Many marriages, families, homes, and relationships are broken, wounded, and hurting from physical, emotional, mental, psychological breakdowns, sexual and domestic abuse, marital breakdowns, COVID-19 lock downs, and shutdowns. Millions have lost their jobs, their income, their businesses, their homes, their savings, their investments; and millions are unemployed and are going through severe financial distress. The whole nation is being distressed by the racial, social, political, civil unrest, the economy, and by the pandemic.

Whoever you may be, wherever you may be, and whatever you may be going through in life, there is hope for healing, deliverance, and restoration for you. There is only one Person who knows exactly what you are going through. And that Person is Jesus Christ. He knows your every pain, and hurt, and wound and heartache and brokenness and suffering. He knows and counts every tear that you have shed. It is just for someone like you that He came to die on the Cross to save, heal, and restore. Would you therefore invite Him into your life and ask Him to heal and to restore your spirit, soul, body, mind, marriage, family, home, finances, job, etc.? He is waiting for you to do just that.

A Clarion Call for Racial and National Healing and Restoration in America!

As we have already seen, America is broken, wounded, hurting and limping. Also, we have seen that the only hope for healing and restoration is through the saving and healing power of the precious blood of Jesus Christ. And this is what America desperately needs right now. It doesn't require any scientific or pharmaceutical research or trials, neither does it require the approval of the Food and Drug Administration (FDA), nor does it require any guidelines from the Center for Disease Control (CDC), nor the approval of any congressional bill, nor any presidential executive order.

And it doesn't cost anything. It's already been paid for over two thousand years ago on the Cross. And its power is vicarious and victorious enough to heal every manner of sin and sickness and disease and brokenness and wounds and hurts and hate and pain! The only thing it requires is humility, repentance, with unconditional love and forgiveness.

And this is the clarion call that I am making to all my fellow Americans. If we are to experience personal, congregational, racial, societal, political, governmental, and national healing and restoration in America, then we must start with personal, congregational, racial, societal, political, governmental, and national repentance with unconditional love and forgiveness towards one another.

This is the only pathway to healing and restoration. Only this can heal and restore back civility, nobility and dignity in our conversations, communications, relationships, and friendships. Only this can heal and restore back the broken bridges, broken foundations, and broken umbilical cords of our common brotherhood, sisterhood, neighborhood, and nationhood. And only then will we become our brother's and sister's and neighbor's and promise keepers and lovers!

For God has said that, *"If My people who are called by My name will humble themselves, and pray, and seek My face, and turn from their wicked ways, then I will hear from heaven, and will forgive their sins, and will heal their land!"* (2Chronicles 7:14)

This is God's promise, and this is God's only pathway to the healing and restoration of our racially, socially, politically, culturally, economically, pandemically, denominationally, spiritually, morally, and nationally broken, wounded, hurting, and backslidden America! Therefore, let us run to the Cross of Jesus Christ to receive healing and restoration from Emmanuel's veins! For He was wounded for our transgressions, was bruised for our sins, and by His stripes, we are healed!

CHAPTER FIFTEEN

A Call For Racial And National Reconciliation, Peace And Unity!

America is on edge and is pent-up, and is racially, socially, culturally, politically, and denominationally divided, polarized, antagonized, and terrorized! America is facing a "perfect storm" of gigantic proportion with dark cumulonimbus clouds of racial, social, and political thunderstorms and thunderbolts rumbling over her skies with gushing winds of civil unrest blowing across the land and dumping hailstorms of street protests, rioting, looting, toppling, burning, shooting, killing, anarchy, and lawlessness!

Not only that, but America has also become a racially, socially, culturally, politically, denominationally, and nationally divided nation and a house divided and turned against itself, and up in arms against itself, with her greatest enemies being the very members of her own household. The America that we know as one nation under God, indivisible and *"invincible"* with liberty and justice for all, has now become a nation under many competing and confusing *gods* and *goddesses, patrons,* and *matrons,* divisible and *"vincible"* with partisan politics and racial and societal injustices for many!

The land of the free and of the brave has now become the land of her own slaves and of her own demise and of her own grave, prepared by her own politicians and physicians, and sounding her own death knell! America has become her own very existential threat! The Lord Jesus has said that a house divided against itself cannot stand, and America is not only a house that is already divided against itself, but it is also a house that has turned against itself, and up in arms against its own, and is already standing on a precipice, tilting precariously!

Racism and the race issue, especially in America, has become highly sensitized, highly politicized, highly divisive, highly polarized, highly antagonized, highly volatile, and highly explosive! The racial, social, cultural, and political atmospheric tension is saturated with a thick smog of anger, offenses, hurts, pain, hatred, bitterness, resentments, hostilities, divisions, disunities, polarizations, distrusts, suspicions, intolerance, grudges, unforgiveness and revenge. Great fears, anxieties, perplexities, uncertainties, and hopelessness have gripped the hearts and minds and homes of many!

And it seems as if the enemy has thrust a sharp double-edged sword deep inside the very soul of our nation causing a great rift, division, disunity, and distrust. The foundations and bridges of our relationships, friendships, fellowships, communions, communities, and communications that once held us together as families, neighbors, friends, colleagues, and as one nation under God, seem to have all been broken and fallen apart. The umbilical cords of maternal, paternal, brotherly, sisterly, neighborly, communal love and affection for one another and for God and for country all seem to have been brutally severed!

It seems as if the center can no longer hold, and things are falling apart because the falcon can no longer hear the falconer even as described by William Butler Yeats in his epic poem, "The Second Coming!:" *"Turning and turning in the widening gyre, The falcon cannot hear the falconer; Things fall apart; the centre cannot hold; Mere anarchy is loosed upon the world, The blood dimmed tide is loosed, and everywhere The ceremony of innocence is drowned; The best lack conviction, while the worst Are full of passionate intensity."*[24]

This poem by Yeats is predictive of the age we are living in right now, and clearly describes the very situation and condition in which America currently finds herself. For America as the falcon, has flown too far away both out of sight and out of hearing from her falconer, God! America as a nation has not only departed from God her Founder, but America has rejected God her Providence!

And by rejecting and departing from God, America has destroyed her own very godly and Christian heritage upon which her spiritual, moral, educational, cultural, political, governmental, ethical, marital, family, and biblical foundation was built. And as a result, America is left broken, shaken, divided, antagonized, polarized, and terrorized! America is not only polarized internally, but she is also terrorized by enemies within and without, just like the nation of Israel. Why? Because both sisters have rejected and departed from the God of their Patriarchs and Founding Fathers!

The aftermath of the destruction of these biblical foundations is a massive collapse and disruption of society marred by political, racial, social, cultural, economic, geopolitical, global, pandemic, and environmental upheavals and disasters. Right now, our nation is broken and divided, our government is broken and divided, our congress is broken and divided, our supreme court is broken and divided, our White House is broken and divided, our churches are broken and divided, our families are broken and divided, our marriages are broken and divided, our homes are broken and divided, our schools and colleges are broken and divided, our communities are broken and divided, our society is broken and divided, people's hearts and lives are broken and divided.

America is now a broken and divided nation! The center can no longer hold, and things are falling apart because the foundations have been broken and destroyed! As a result, America is right now a nation that is tottering in steps and stuttering in speech and is losing both her national and global equilibrium!

Our politics and politicians have not helped. There is an African proverb that says when two adult elephants are locked in a fight, it is the grass underneath them that will suffer the most because it is being trampled under the massive feet of these two heavyweight mammoths.

And so, it is in the world of politics. When politicians and their political parties are locked in a fight for political power, control, and leadership, it is usually the masses who suffer. And this African proverb is so true in the case of our politics in America, especially between the Republican and the Democratic Parties. It is interesting that the symbol for the Republican Party is that of an elephant and for the Democratic Party is that of a donkey, and so whenever the elephant and the donkey get into a political fight, it is the masses that suffer the most from the ensuing political infightings and bickering of their leaders. The masses are the ones being trampled and trodden underfoot by these two rival political mammoths!

We live in a badly broken and painfully hurting and sinful world, where all the spiritual, moral, marital, family, relational, political, governmental, economic, cultural, intellectual, racial, social, societal, brotherly, sisterly, communal, and national bridges and relationships that once held us together as a loving and caring community of people and as one nation under God, indivisible with liberty and justice for all, are now crumbling and tumbling downhill into a national and global crisis that is now apparently beyond the ability of any man or government to fix, but God alone.

Bridges are meant to foster interpersonal relationships, fellowships, communions, connectivity, communications, cohesion, peace, and unity. But if these bridges that are meant to keep our marriages, families, neighborhoods, communities, churches, races, societies, governments, and nation together are broken and destroyed, then everything else will be disrupted because there will be a massive collapse and crumbling of society. And America is currently going through what seems an unstoppable massive racial, social, economic, cultural, pandemic, and political avalanche with devastating consequences that only the hand of God can stop!

And the only answer and solution to our broken and divided nation is peace, unity, and reconciliation through the Cross of Jesus Christ. It is the Cross that unites and reconciles us back to God and to our fellow human beings. We must understand that there will be no lasting peace and reconciliation between and among all the races and colors of people unless there is first peace and reconciliation between God and man at the Cross of Jesus Christ that makes peace and reconciles and unites. The Cross is the universal bridge for racial, social, societal, political, and national reconciliation, peace, and unity in America and in the world. The Cross is the universal center for world peace!

The Cross Is the Bridge for Reconciliation Between God and Man

It is sin that has caused separation and enmity between God and man, and it is the Cross that has bridged the enmity between God and man. When Adam and Eve sinned, it brought an eternal separation between God and man. The implosion and explosion of sin in man caused a great chasm and enmity between God and man. Sin made us enemies of God. And since all have sinned and fallen short of the glory of God, therefore, all have also become enemies of God through transgression. Therefore, every sinner is an enemy of God.

And it was for this purpose that Christ came to die on the Cross to forgive our sins and to make peace between us and God, and to reconcile us back to God. The Bible says,

"For it pleased the Father that in Him all the fullness should dwell, and by Him to reconcile all things to Himself, by Him, whether things on earth or things in heaven, having made peace through the blood of His cross. And you, who were once alienated and enemies in your mind by wicked works, yet now He has reconciled in the body of His flesh through death, to present you holy, and blameless, and above reproach in His sight." (Colossians 1:19-22 NKJV)

The Bible also says, *"For if, when we were enemies, we were reconciled to God by the death of his Son, much more, being reconciled, we shall be saved by his life."* (Romans 5:10 KJV)

Sin has not only brought death to the entire human race, but it has also brought enmity between God and man and between all the races. And that is why Jesus came to die to make peace between God and man by nailing the enmity to the Cross. This is very important to know, because there will never be any lasting peace and reconciliation between the races of people until there is first peace and reconciliation between God and man. And this peace and reconciliation between God and Man is only made possible through the Cross of Jesus Christ who is the Peace Maker between God and Man. And the Bible says that if a man dies without making peace with God while he is alive, then that person will die as an enemy of God and will continue to be an enemy of God forever in hell!

The Cross Is the Bridge for Racial and Societal Reconciliation Between All the Races of People!

At the destruction of the Tower of Babel, we saw how sin and rebellion brought about not only the destruction of the idolatrous tower, but it also brought the confusion of their language, their separation and scattering abroad, and the division of the earth into the different continents and nations. (Genesis 11:1-9)

But then on the Cross, Christ died to bring back all the races together as one family under God, indivisible and invincible. On the Cross, Christ has broken down the middle wall of racism and racial partitions, divisions, and enmity between not only the Jews and Gentiles, but between all the races and colors of people in the world and has made peace and reconciliation. The Bible tells us how Jesus was able to accomplish that when it said:

"Don't forget that you Gentiles used to be outsiders. In those days you were living apart from Christ. You were excluded from citizenship among the people of Israel, and you did not know the covenant promises God had made to them. You lived in this world without God and without hope. But now you have been united with Christ Jesus. Once you were far away from God, but now you have been brought near to Him through the blood of Christ.

For Christ Himself has brought peace to us. He united Jews and Gentiles into one people when, in His own body on the Cross, He broke down the wall of hostility that separated us. He did this by ending the system of law with its commandments and regulations. He made peace between Jews and Gentiles by creating in Himself one new people from the two groups.

Together as one body, Christ reconciled both groups to God by means of His death on the cross, and our hostility toward each other was put to death. He brought this Good News of peace to you Gentiles who were far away from Him, and peace to the Jews who were near. Now all of us can come to the Father through the same Holy Spirit because of what Christ has done for us. So now you Gentiles are no longer strangers and foreigners. You are citizens along with all of God's holy people. You are members of God's family...We are carefully joined together in Him..." (Ephesians 2:11-22 NLT)

From the above account, the Bible makes it very clear that on the Cross, Christ has broken down the middle wall of racial partitions, divisions, barriers, prejudice, discrimination, separation, and segregation between Jews and Gentiles, and between all the races and colors of people in the world.

Secondly, it was at the Cross that Jesus has washed away every racial and color line and has made peace between Jews and Gentiles and between all the races of people, thereby uniting them as one new man in Himself.

Thirdly, it was at the Cross that Christ took upon Himself all the ugliness and filthiness of our sins of racism, hatred, discrimination, prejudice, strife, injustice, anger, bitterness, revenge, malice, envy, unforgiveness, and enmity and nailed them to the Cross, and with one stroke of His blood, He crossed them all out, blotted them all out, and wiped them all out!

Fourthly, it was at the Cross that Jesus has gathered all the strayed and scattered lost sheep of the human race as one flock of the Good Shepherd. There, He has called all the prodigals, vagabonds, and the spiritually homeless and fatherless to come back home to their heavenly Father. The Bible says, *"For you were like sheep going astray, but have now returned to the Shepherd and Overseer of your souls."* (1 Peter 2:25 NKJV)

Fifthly, it was at the Cross that Christ has called all sinners, all races, all peoples, all tribes, all tongues, all nations, and the whole wide world as one people and as one race under God. Jesus said, *"And I, If I Am lifted up from the earth, will draw all peoples to Myself."* (John 12:32-33, NKJV)

So, we see that Christ must have to die on the Cross in order to break down the middle wall of racial hatred and partition and abolishing in His flesh that old time enmity that has been in existence for over six thousand years, and then making peace by reconciling man first to Himself, and then to God, and then to one another as one new man and one new body and one new race under God. The Bible says that we are no longer strangers, or aliens, or foreigners from another race, ethnic group, tribe, or nationality, but that we are all now fellow citizens and brothers and sisters of the household of God.

That is why the Bible says, *"For ye are all the children of God by faith in Christ Jesus. For as many of you as have been baptized into Christ have put on Christ. There is neither Jew nor Greek, there is neither bond nor free, there is neither male nor female: for ye are all one in Christ Jesus."* (Galatians 3:26-29 KJV)

God is no respecter of persons. His love is no respecter of persons. His Cross is no respecter of persons, and His blood is no respecter of persons. This means that God does not show any partiality or favoritism. Every man, woman, and child are entitled to His love, and has free equal access to His Cross, regardless of who they are or what they may or may not have done. *"Then Peter opened his mouth and said: "In truth I perceive that God shows no partiality. But in every nation whoever fears Him and works righteousness is accepted by Him."* (Acts 10:34-35 NKJV)

In Christ there are no Jews, nor Greeks, nor Blacks, nor Whites, nor Latinos, nor Asians, nor Africans, nor Europeans, nor Indians, nor Chinese, nor Arabs, nor Russians, nor male, nor female, nor slaves; but we are all one in Christ, bought and redeemed by His blood and His love on the Cross at Calvary!

It is the power of the love of Jesus Christ on the Cross that is the gravitational pull and centripetal force that draws all the races of people together as one. The Cross is the bridge for all racial, societal, political, cultural, and denominational reconciliation, peace, and unity in America and in the world.

It is at the Cross of Jesus Christ that all the racial, social, political, cultural, communal, societal, national, and denominational barriers, divides, tensions, enmity, hostilities, animosities, hatred, and the strongholds of racism are supernaturally broken and destroyed. It is at the Cross that the blood of Jesus Christ has washed away every racial, cultural, political, and denominational line and divide!

The Cross of Jesus Christ is not racist! It is colorless and raceless. It is neither black, nor white, nor brown, nor pink, nor yellow, nor green, nor red, nor blue. The Cross of Jesus Christ was darkened by our sins. God is Spirit, and is neither black, nor white, nor brown, nor pink, nor yellow, nor green, nor red, nor blue. The Bible describes His appearance as a brilliant light of His glory, which shines like the sun, of which no man can approach. (1Timothy 6:15-16)

The Holy Spirit is neither black, nor white, nor brown, nor pink, nor yellow, nor green, nor red, nor blue. He is the Spirit of the Living God. The Bible is neither a Blackman's nor a Whiteman's Bible. It is the Word of the Living God: For in the beginning was the Word, and the Word was with God, and the Word was God, and the Word became flesh, and dwelt among Men!

Christianity is neither a Blackman nor a Whiteman's religion. It is the religion of Jesus Christ and His followers from every nation, and people, and kindred, and tongue. The apostle John said: *"You are worthy to take the scroll, and to open its seals; For You were slain and have redeemed us to God by Your blood out of every tribe and tongue and people and nation; and have made us kings and priests to our God; and we shall reign on the earth."* (Revelation 5:8-10 NKJV)

As we have seen from the above scriptural passages, Christ died for all mankind, and for all races, and for the whole wide world.

The Bible describes this new unity of the human race in Christ Jesus on the Cross when it says, *"Therefore, if anyone is in Christ, he is a new creation; old things have passed away; behold, all things have become new. Now all things are of God, who has reconciled us to Himself through Jesus Christ, and has given us the ministry of reconciliation, that is, that God was in Christ reconciling the world to Himself, not imputing their trespasses to them, and has committed to us the word of reconciliation."* (2 Corinthians 5:17-19 NKJV)

This is that new nature and new life of anyone who has both been reconciled to God and to Christ. It is through the Cross of Jesus Christ that all men are reconciled, and without Him, there is no reconciliation, peace, and unity. Therefore, if we want peace, unity, and reconciliation in America and in the world, then the Cross is the universal bridge for racial, political, and national reconciliation. The Cross is the bridge through which all the races must cross over from the other side of the racial, cultural, and political divide to Christ the winning side!

All other bridges and foundations are broken bridges and foundations, and they are sinking sand. On Christ alone, the Solid Rock we stand! On His Cross He bore the sins of the whole wide world; in His hands He's got the whole wide world; and in His heart He bore the Father's love for the whole wide world!

And that is why I am calling on all my fellow Americans for us to run to the Cross where we can be united as one nation under God. Let us grow out of our petty politics and pity parties and selfishness and let us become patriots putting God and country first above politics and self-aggrandizement!

The things that unite and bind us together are far greater and precious than the things that divide and set us apart. We are all brothers and sisters, friends and neighbors, families and relatives, citizens, and countrymen of the same human race, regardless of our skin color or political ideologies or beliefs. We are all humans, and we are all Americans! Therefore, let us come together in unity with cords that cannot be broken!

The Bible says, *"How can two walk together, unless they are agreed."* (Amos 3:3) In other words, the Bible is saying that two people must learn how to negotiate and navigate their disagreements and difficulties in order for them to reach a place of agreement to agree or to disagree in love and peace.

We will not always agree on everything but let us learn how to negotiate and navigate our differences and difficulties with love and respect and with dignity and integrity without hostility. And in our presently racially, socially, culturally, politically, and denominationally broken, divided, antagonized, polarized, and terrorized nation, America must learn how to negotiate and navigate our differences and difficulties in our race relations, in politics, in government, in society, and in life!

At this very juncture, America has a painful but a gainful choice to make: It's either united we stand, or divided we fall! And how are the mighty fallen! The choice is ours to make. We do not need the United Nations or any outsider to come resolve our internal problems and disputes. We are an American Family, therefore let us sit down and talk as a family. Let us have an American Family Meeting at the Cross where all our Problems and Disputes will be Dissolved and Resolved!

CHAPTER SIXTEEN

A Call For A National And International Day Of Unconditional Love And Forgiveness!

L ike I have already said in the previous chapters that if America is to experience a supernatural healing, restoration, reconciliation, peace, and unity, then we must be willing and ready to repent, love and to forgive unconditionally. And it is along this same line that I am calling for a nationwide and a worldwide "NATIONAL AND INTERNATIONAL DAY OF UNCONDITIONAL LOVE AND FORGIVENESS" to be observed all over America and all over the world and in every state, city, town, school, college, university, workplace, prison, hospital, home, etc.! It would be a very special day when all Americans and all nationals will be encouraged to offer their unconditional love and forgiveness willingly and voluntarily to each other and to all the people that have wronged, offended, and hurt them in life: past, present, future. It would be a very special day when all the Blacks, Whites, Indians, Jews, Africans, Asians, Latinos, and all other nationalities and races and colors of people will be encouraged to offer their unconditional love and forgiveness to each other and to all the people that have wronged, offended, and hurt them in life: past, present, future.

It would be a very special day when all peace-loving and patriotic Americans and nationals will be encouraged to become or act as special "ambassadors" of unconditional love and forgiveness who will reach out to all the people they can in their families, neighborhoods, communities, workplaces, schools, colleges, universities, hospitals, nursing homes, the prisons, malls, restaurants, and everywhere, sharing with them the message of unconditional love and forgiveness.

And I strongly believe that if we do this as a people and as a nation and as a world, it could bring about a great spiritual, moral, racial, societal, cultural, political, governmental, national, and worldwide revival of love, repentance, forgiveness, healing, deliverance, salvation, reconciliation, peace, joy, restoration, restitution, transformation, reformation, freedom and many other blessings not only in people's lives, but also in their homes, families, marriages, communities, neighborhoods, schools, colleges, universities, workplaces, businesses, institutions, governments, in the nations and in the world as a whole.

Supernatural miracles and healings will take place and dead love, dead joy, dead peace, dead happiness, dead dreams, dead visions, dead hopes, dead health, dead marriages, dead families, dead homes, dead relationships, dead friendships, dead economies, dead finances, dead jobs, dead businesses, dead communities, dead governments, dead nations, and a dead world will be revived and restored again!

For God Himself will heal our land and nations according to His promise that says, *"If My people who are called by My name will humble themselves, and pray and seek My face, and turn from their wicked ways, then I will hear from heaven, and will forgive their sins and heal their land."* (2 Chronicles 7:14 NKJV)

I believe that this could be replicated in other nations of the world and could even become both a national and an international event to be observed annually and be celebrated globally. And this could help bring about a worldwide awareness of the power of God's unconditional love and forgiveness and could help bring about an end-time Holy Spirit fire global soul-harvest revival and worldwide evangelism that will help bring in the greatest One Billion Soul Harvest for Christ that the world has ever seen!

And that is why I am calling on all my fellow Americans: Blacks, Whites, Africans, Hispanic, Jews, Indians, Asians, Europeans, Russians, Chinese, and all other nationalities and races and color of people in America and in the world for us to love and to forgive one another unconditionally!

Let us love and forgive unconditionally, and let us be our brothers', our sisters', and our neighbors' keepers! Let us not hate and kill one another like Cain, who was angry at his younger brother Abel and slew him.

Let us all love and forgive unconditionally 70 x 7, which is 490 times, and let us forgive even the 499th time! Let us love and forgive like Christ loved and forgave unconditionally. Let us not repay evil for evil, but rather, let us overcome evil with good, revenge with mercy, racism with grace, hatred with love, and violence with peace!

And of course, I know very well that this is going to be the toughest, hardest, and most difficult thing to do for many people: to love and to forgive their enemies and the people who have so badly wronged and hurt them. I clearly understand the hurts, the pain, the wounds, the bruises, the brokenness, the sufferings, the anger, the resentments, the bitterness, the traumas, the shame that they carry, and I do sympathize and empathize with them even as I myself have been there.

But I want you to understand that what I am sharing with you may seem practically impossible with man, but with God all things are possible. The Bible says, is anything too hard for the LORD? (Genesis 18:14) For nothing is impossible with God. (Luke 1:37) In fact, forgiveness is not a natural act of man, but a supernatural act of God, and He will give you all the grace that you need to do what He is calling you to do. The same Jesus who said to the apostle Paul, *"My grace is sufficient for you, for My strength is made perfect in weakness,"* (2 Corinthians 12:9 NKJV) is the same Jesus whose grace will be sufficient for you. *"For it is not by might nor by power, but by My Spirit, says the LORD!"* (Zechariah 4:6 NKJV)

Let me talk to you a little bit about myself. I am one that has also been badly offended, hated, rejected, despised, broken, wounded, bruised, shattered, and hurt. I am one who has experienced great afflictions, adversities, trials, testing, temptations, injustice, marital breakdown, divorce, betrayals, church split, hurts, pain, sufferings, agonies, traumas, sicknesses, spiritual attacks, witchcraft, back-stabbings, slanders, persecutions, false accusations, character assassination, cursing, anger, resentments, bitterness, disappointments, discouragements, debts, stress, financial distress, oppression, depression, car accidents, eviction, homelessness, fears, anxieties, doubts, hopelessness, suicidal attacks, etc.

From childhood through teenage-hood and adulthood, I have suffered all these things. I arrived in America deeply wounded, broken, hurting, bruised, crushed, and bleeding. I was spiritually, emotionally, mentally, psychologically, and physically weary and exhausted. But then in 2002, in Houston, Texas, God spoke to me through a lady pastor that I have never met or known. God revealed to her that I have been badly hurt and wounded by people, but that she saw God putting His hand deep down inside my heart and removing all the hurts and pain and junk in my heart, and that God was going to heal me completely and use me for His glory.

And then in 2003, in Ashland, Virginia, another pastor whom I have never met before looked at me straight in the eyes with a shock and asked me whether I am a pastor, and I said yes. He then said to me that God just showed him that I have been very badly hurt and wounded by people that I love, but that God is asking me to forgive them all unconditionally. He said I should forgive and release them all from my heart because God is going to heal and restore me, and that He has great plans for my life, but that I must forgive and let go, and let God!

And to be honest with you, at that time, I had just been freshly backstabbed and deeply wounded and hurt by my own pastor that I had served so faithfully. My heart has been freshly stabbed and I was badly wounded, hurting, bleeding, and weeping. I was even going to pick up the phone to call the pastor to vent my anger, but God told me not to, but that I should leave that pastor with Him to deal with.

So, when this strange pastor told me that God said I should forgive, it was very hard for me, but I listened and obeyed. I forgave all of them unconditionally without waiting for an apology that never came. And when I did, something supernatural happened: there was a supernatural release of healing and restoration that took place in my life. God healed all the wounds, brokenness, pain, hurts, anger, resentments, bitterness, shame, stress, depression, oppression, disappointments, discouragements, fears, doubts, anxieties, insecurities, hopelessness, and suicidal thoughts. He healed my body, spirit, soul, and mind, and filled me with His love, compassion, joy, peace, hope, and strength. He gave me a brand-new heart of love and a brand-new life with a brand-new beginning and a brand-new hope and future.

Not only that, but God also told me to marry, and He showed me the woman that I should marry, and He blessed me with the most beautiful, wonderful, precious, virtuous, loving, caring, and God-fearing wife! And we've been married now for fifteen wonderful years! Not only that, but God has also blessed us with a wonderful ministry and with wonderful children.

One of the great lessons that I have learned when you decide to love and to forgive unconditionally is that the blessings of God that follow you will far outweigh all the suffering you've been through in all your life. The gain of unconditional love and forgiveness will far exceed the pain and the hurts that you've been through! It does not only bring freedom, liberty, healing, restoration, reconciliation, peace, love, joy, happiness, hope, health, strength, etc., but it also brings new open doors, spiritual blessings, physical blessings, material blessings, financial blessings, marital blessings, doors of opportunities, promotions, divine health, divine provision, divine connections, divine favor, divine relationships, and supernatural breakthroughs. But over and above all, it brings you into a new level of a deeper intimate love relationship, fellowship, communion, and walk with God!

In fact, it was after I have obeyed God to love and to forgive unconditionally, that years later that my wife and I attended a camp meeting service in the same Ashland, Virginia, and there again God spoke prophetically to me through the same man of God, Apostle Jeff Johns. The LORD said to me through him that He is going to remove all the hardness in my heart and fill me with His own heart of love to feed His sheep and His lambs. And He gave me the scripture passage in the gospel of John where the Lord Jesus asked Simon Peter three times whether he loves Him, and for him to feed His sheep and lambs. Here is that discuss between the Lord Jesus and Simon Peter. The Bible said,

"So, when they had eaten breakfast, Jesus said to Simon Peter, "Simon, son of Jonah, do you love Me more than these?" He said to Him, "Yes, Lord; You that I love You." He said to him, "Feed My lambs." He said to him again a second time,

"Simon, son of Jonah, do you love Me?" He said to Him, "Yes, Lord; You know that I love You." He said to him, "Tend My sheep." He said to him the third time, "Simon, son of Jonah, do you love Me?" Peter was grieved because He said to him the third time, "Do you love Me?" And he said to Him, "Lord, You know all things; You know that I love You." Jesus said to him, "Feed My sheep." (John 21:15-17, NKJV)

This is that same command and charge that the LORD has given to me to feed His sheep and lambs of the lost human race with His love. This is the message and command that He has given me for the world. And that is why God is sending me to you today with this message of unconditional love and forgiveness!

For *"The LORD is my shepherd; I shall not want. He makes me to lie down in green pastures; He leads me beside the still waters; He restores my soul; He leads me in the paths of righteousness For His name's sake. Yea, though I walk through the valley of the shadow of death, I will fear no evil; For You are with me; Your rod and Your staff, they comfort me. You prepare a table before me in the presence of my enemies; You anoint my head with oil; My cup runs over. Surely goodness and mercy shall follow me all the days of my life; I will dwell in the house of the LORD forever!"* (Psalm 23:1-6, NKJV)

This is what Jesus, the Great Shepherd of your soul and of the whole human race wants to do for you! Are you willing to obey and to love and to forgive unconditionally, and let Jesus become your LORD and your Great Shepherd who will lead you to green pastures and to still living waters?

What Does It Mean to Be an Ambassador of Unconditional Love & Forgiveness?

According to the Merriam Webster dictionary, the word ambassador means "an official envoy, especially a diplomatic agent of the highest rank accredited to a foreign government or sovereign as the resident representative of his or her own government or sovereign; or a plenipotentiary appointed for a special and often temporary diplomatic assignment."[25]

From this definition, we see that the word ambassador could also mean an agent, delegate, emissary, envoy, legate, minister, or representative. It could also mean a "goodwill ambassador who advocates for a specific cause or global issue on the basis of their notability as a public figure. They generally deliver goodwill by promoting ideals from one entity to another, or to a population."[26]

It is this same word that Jesus used in sending His disciples to the world. He said to them, *"So now I Am giving you a new commandment: Love each other. Just as I have loved you, you should love each other. Your love for one another will prove to the world that you are My disciples."* (John 13:34-35 NLT)

In other words, Christ was saying to them that the one outstanding characteristic by which the world would recognize you as My ambassadors is when you love one another as I have loved you. In short, Christ was saying to them that I am sending you as My ambassadors to conquer the world for Me with My unconditional love and forgiveness.

The apostle Paul expounded on this same theme when he wrote to the Corinthian Christians, saying: *"This means that anyone who belongs to Christ has become a new person. The old life is gone; a new life has begun! And all of this is a gift from God, who brought us back to Himself through Christ. And God has given us this task of reconciling people to Him. For God was in Christ, reconciling the world to Himself, no longer counting people's sins against them. And He gave us this wonderful message of reconciliation. So, we are Christ's ambassadors; God is making His appeal through us. We speak for Christ when we plead, 'Come back to God!'"* (2 Corinthians 5:17-21 NLT)

The entire Bible is about this wonderful and amazing unconditional love and forgiveness of God toward sinful mankind as demonstrated on the Cross through His Son, Jesus Christ! Therefore, as Christ's ambassadors of unconditional love and forgiveness, you are a goodwill ambassador, a plenipotentiary, who is bringing and sharing God's love, forgiveness, redemption, salvation, deliverance, healing, righteousness, justice, truth, hope, peace, reconciliation, freedom, and the Good News of the gospel of Jesus Christ and of the Kingdom of God to the people around you: your family members, communities, neighborhoods, schools, colleges, prisons, hospitals, workplaces, the market place, villages, towns, cities, the nations, the world, the highways and byways, and anywhere, and anywhere you go!

And that is why I am appealing to all my fellow Americans and to the whole wide world for us to turn all our hatred into love and compassion for one another, and all our enmity and animosity into friendship and fraternity!

Let us turn all our racism, terrorism, and extremism into patriotism and pragmatism. Let us turn all the sounds of violence and fury in our communities and nations into sounds and rhythms of violins and value for life!

Let us turn all our street protests and rioting into community projects, prospects, progress, and prosperity! Let us turn all our malice into mercy, our bitterness to sweetness and our resentments into investments!

Let us turn all our hatred and anger into brotherly and sisterly love and let us be our trusted brothers' and sisters' and neighbors' promise-keepers! Let us do no hurt or harm to them, but let us love, protect, safeguard, support, and defend one another! Let us not be like wicked Cain, who could not protect or defend his own brother, but hated and killed him!

For the sake of our children and future posterity and prosperity, and for the sake of the peace, unity, healing, reconciliation, development, progress, and advancement of our communities, our nation, and the world, let us seek the peace and welfare and wellbeing of every man, every woman, every child, every elderly, and every unborn baby!

Let us turn all our pistols into peace-tools, and our guns into peace-corps! Let us turn all our gossip into a gospel of love, joy, and peace in the Holy Ghost; and let us turn all our jealousies and envies into zeal for God and for good works toward mankind!

As Christ's ambassadors of unconditional love and forgiveness, let us forgive past, present, and future hurts and offenses, and let us strive ahead into a better and brighter future. Let us put politics and race aside and let us politely race toward a new dawn of hope, love, joy, happiness, peace, security, healing, reconciliation, unity, justice, equality, freedom, liberty, prospect, progress, advancement, achievement, and prosperity for all!

Let us forgive and forget all those things which are behind us and let us look forward to those things which are before us and let us press on toward the goal for the heavenly prize which has been set before us. For on that day, we shall all receive our eternal rewards and awards from God, according to all the things that we have done and said here on earth, whether good or bad!

Therefore, let us turn all our strife into strides towards peace and development, and let us lay aside every weight and every sin that so easily ensnares and entangles us, and let us run with endurance the eternal race that is set before us, fixing our eyes unto Jesus, who is the Author and Finisher of our faith and our race, who for the joy that was set before Him endured the cross, disregarding it shame, and is now seated at the right hand of the throne of God! (Hebrews 12:1-4 KJV)

Let us take up our own crosses and let us strive to cross and to crisscross every racial, political, cultural, and generational lines and divides, and let us, together, rebuild the broken bridges and foundations of our lives, our families, our communities, our societies and of our nations that have been destroyed!

This is what it means to be an ambassador of unconditional love and forgiveness, and this is what the "National and International Day of Unconditional Love and Forgiveness" stands for and aims to achieve! Are you therefore willing to become an ambassador of Christ's Unconditional Love and Forgiveness? America is waiting and counting on you! The world is waiting and counting on you! And the souls of men, and women, and children are waiting and counting on you! The voices of the oppressed are waiting and counting on you! And JESUS is waiting and counting on you!

CHAPTER SEVENTEEN

Love's Tender Loving Care Special Invitation To You!

After all that has been said and done, we now come to the conclusion of the matter, which is the crux of the matter and the final point of this book. And the truth of the matter is that you will never be able to experience true eternal love, eternal peace, eternal joy, eternal forgiveness, eternal justice, eternal freedom, eternal healing, eternal reconciliation, eternal redemption, eternal salvation, eternal hope, eternal life, and eternal rest in your life unless you invite this Eternal Love, which is Jesus Christ into your heart as Lord and Savior! And this is because love is eternal and Jesus Christ is everything eternal, and in Him dwells all the fullness of the Godhead bodily, and we are complete in Him alone! (Colossians 2:9-10)

The truth of the matter is that everything else in this world and in this life is temporal! All the problems and issues in life and in this world are all temporal! All the racism, hatred, politics, protests, rioting, looting, burning, shooting, killing, are all temporal! All your needs and wants and cares and desires in life and in this world are temporal! All your jobs, homes, cars, money, bank accounts, investments, riches, wealth, treasures, and pleasures are all temporal! All your education, achievements, accomplishments, employments, attainments, entertainments, and enjoyments are all temporal! Everything else in this life and everything else about you in this world is temporal! Life itself is temporal and is a fleeting shadow!

Everything else in this world is fading away, and all is vanity upon vanity! There is only one thing that is eternal in you, and that is not temporal, and that you will have to take with you when you die. And that one thing is your SOUL! All else will be left behind, even your own very body and flesh that you have labored all your life to entertain and to gratify and to satisfy, will be left behind in a casket and in the grave, while your soul, which is eternal, slips into eternity. Naked we came into this world, and naked we shall return. We brought nothing into this world, and we will take nothing out of this world.

That is why the Lord Jesus posed this eternal question:

"And what do you benefit if you gain the whole world but lose your own soul? Is anything worth more than your soul? For the Son of Man will come with His angels in the glory of His Father and will judge all people according to their deeds." (Matthew 16:26-27, NLT)

This is a "life-investment" question that Jesus asked for every man, woman, teenager, and child to ponder about. In fact, the Bible has made it very clear that life in this world is an investment and that you will surely reap what you have invested or sown into your life. It is an eternal law of sowing and reaping. The Bible says, *"Do not be deceived, God is not mocked; for whatever a man sows, that he will also reap. For he who sows to his flesh will of the flesh reap corruption, but he who sows to the Spirit will of the Spirit reap everlasting life."* (Galatians 6:7-8 NKJV)

When It Is All Over!

Like I said, this is the crux of the matter: When all is said and done about your life here in this world; when all the noise of violence of politics, racism, hatred, protests, rioting, looting, shootings, killings, and burning are over; when all the sound of partying and merrymaking is over; when you have mounted this world's temporal stage and played all your acts and your parts and the curtains of your life are drawn to a close and you dismount this world's stage; when the candlelight of your life blows out its last flickering and smoldering flame; when your eye brows grow dim to the last rays of the sunshine of this world; when your ears grow deaf to the last sounds of the birds singing.

When your lips stutter to mutter their last words; when the shadow of your life begins to fade away; when the last ticking of the clock of your life stops at midnight; when you have inhaled and exhaled your very last ounce of breath and all your vitals shut down and you give up the ghost; when it is all over: where will your soul be? Where will you spend eternity? Will your soul take a celestial flight towards heaven? Or will your soul take a subterranean descent towards the bottomless pit of hell?

Now that all the sounds and fury of the raging storms of this life have ceased and it's all over, and all the temporal things of this world have passed away, and now you are face-to-face with eternity and with reality. But which eternity and which reality will you be face-to-face with? Is it eternity and reality in heaven, or eternity and reality in hell? When the epitaph on your tombstone will read, "May His or Her Soul Rest in Perfect and Perpetual Peace," will your soul be actually resting in perfect and perpetual peace or in eternal and perpetual torment?

And that is an eternal question that you would have to answer for yourself and make the right decision before it is too late, because in hell there will be no eternal peace nor eternal rest, but eternal torment and eternal regret!

In hell there will be no more politics, no more racism, no more protests, no more resistance, no more assistance, and no more partying nor merrymaking, but eternal torment! There will be no more anything of this world. No more! It's all over! That is why right now, while you are still alive and breathing, there is resistance and assistance for you. You can resist sin and the devil right now by fleeing to the Cross to Jesus to receive assistance and eternal life. That is why the Bible says for you to, *"Seek the LORD while He may be found. Call upon Him while He is near. Let the wicked forsake his ways, and let him return to the LORD, and He will have mercy on him; and to our God, For He will abundantly pardon."* (Isaiah 55:6-7, NKJV)

O, my friend, remember that this life is not your own and this world is not your home. We are all pilgrims and wandering strangers here in this fallen and wretched world. What shall it profit you then if you gain this whole wretched world and then lose your soul in the end? Do you realize that you and I are living a borrowed life here in this world, and that one day, God, the Creator and rightful owner of your life is going to require of it someday, somehow, anytime, anywhere? Do you know that there is just one breath between you and eternity, and that you are walking on a thin veil between life and death? And do you know that one last breath could snap out of you at any time and slip into eternity?

O, hear me, my friend: There is no procrastination in seeking God for your life because death may come at any time that you least expect it. You are not guaranteed any tomorrow. Your tomorrow may never come! The Bible says today is the day of God's salvation, and therefore you should not harden your heart when you hear the still small voice of the Holy Spirit calling and wooing you to God. And remember, my friend: this world is not your own and is not your home! All we, are as pilgrims and strangers passing through this world. This world is a temporal stage on which each one of us mounts and play our parts and act our acts and bow out. And how you and I perform on this world's temporal stage will be judged by the Eternal Judge, Jesus Christ. When He would have put down all rebellion and injustices in this world, you and I will have to face the eternal justice of a just God. Perfect peace and eternal rest and eternal life are found in Christ alone!

The Emptiness and Meaninglessness of This Life Without Christ!

The truth of the matter about the reality of our human existence is that life is nothing but empty, void, worthless, useless, hopeless, and meaningless without Christ! For you see my dear friend, when Adam and Eve sinned, there was a spiritual implosion and explosion of sin in the soul of man like that of a volcanic eruption that has left a deep spiritual and moral crater in the soul of man.

It is a spiritual and moral chasm, a hole, a vacuum, a void, an emptiness, a bottomless pit of hell that can never be filled or be satisfied by anything man-made! It cannot be filled or satisfied or gratified with drugs, or alcohol, or sex, or pleasure, or money, or riches, or wealth, or power, or fame, or celebrity, or education, or success, or by anything else in this world. It can only be filled and be satisfied and be justified by Christ alone!

Anything you try to do to fill that hole in your soul is like a child trying to fill a hole with water in a sandy beach. You can gratify the body, but you cannot gratify the soul. The soul can only be justified and not gratified! And it can only be justified by the blood of Jesus Christ, the Redeeming Lamb of God who takes away the sins of the world!

The Bible says that this life without Christ is nothing but a shadow: *"Ask the former generations and find out what their fathers have learned, for we were born only yesterday and know nothing, and our days on earth are but a shadow."* (Job 8:8-9 NIV) This describes the brevity of the human life!

And for many of you, life may seem void, empty, vacant, a vacuum, meaningless and worthless, full of sound and fury, signifying nothing, as aptly described by William Shakespeare in his epic literary work, "Macbeth:" *"Life's but a walking shadow, a poor player that struts and frets his hour upon the stage and then is heard no more. It is a tale told by an idiot, full of sound and fury signifying nothing."*[27]

And there is some truism in this: For life indeed is but a walking shadow that first appears short at sunrise, grows tall at midday, and grows shorter at sunset, and then fades away in the horizon of eternity.

The world indeed is a stage where men mount and strut and fret and play their parts and act their acts and at the end of the scene they dismount and are heard no more. It's all over! Indeed, life in this poor wretched and miserable world is full of the sounds and furies of the raging storms of life battering humanity. And indeed, without Christ in this world and the hereafter, life is, but like a fairy tale as told by an idiot, full of emptiness, wastefulness, uselessness, worthlessness, hope-lessness, meaninglessness, vacant and void! *"It is all vanity of vanities, says the Preacher, vanity of vanities; all is vanity!"* (Ecclesiastes 1:2 KJV)

The human soul is like a wasteland without Christ! It is like an arid wilderness full of nothing but the sounds and fury of the desert storms of life at daytime and the sounds of cracking and exfoliation of life at nighttime! And in that vast wilderness, the soul finds itself in solitary confinement, lonely, languishing, thirsting, restless and perishing! And so, it will be restless in this world until it finds rest in Christ, and so it shall be restless in hell without Christ!

The soul of man may take its flights to the highest stars. It may take its flight to the farthest ends of the earth. It may take its dive into the deepest oceans, and still will not find peace and rest! The soul of man will never find peace and rest until it returns and alights in the very hands of God its Maker!

Love's Tender Loving Care Invitation to All Those Who Hunger and Thirst for the Bread of Life and for the Fountain of Living Water!

Life is made of past, present, and future. However, life in this world is not determined by your past, but by your present and your future. You cannot recover the past, but you can discover the present and determine the future. The decisions that you make are not based on your past, but on your present and future. It is the present and the future that corrects and rectifies the past and gives meaning for the present and hope for the future. The past is history!

In this life, there are many decisions that we make: some good, some bad, some temporal, and some eternal. And we have all made some bad choices and some terrible mistakes in the past. But you cannot dwell in the past. You have to take charge of your present and your future.

However, the greatest and the most important decision that you could ever make in your entire lifetime is an eternal decision, and not temporal. And that eternal decision centers around Jesus Christ: your acceptance or your rejection of Him. This is the greatest and the most important eternal life changing decision that you could ever make. And it is this decision that will determine your past, present, and future life in this world and after you die and slip into eternity.

It is in Jesus Christ alone that our past, present, and future is secured and guaranteed. Outside of Him, your past, present, and future will be dark, empty, lonely, meaningless, hopeless, and restless.

Right now, there are those of you whose lives are broken, empty, void, vacant, worthless, useless, meaningless, and hopeless. You feel that life is not even worth living anymore. And you have tried to fill this chasm, this void, this hole, this emptiness, this bottomless pit of hell inside your soul with sex, pornography, alcohol, drugs, smoking, gambling, material possessions, money, riches, wealth, fame, celebrity, popularity, publicity, power, education, success, partying, and with all kinds of pleasures and indulgence, but yet still each time you are left even more empty, dissatisfied, frustrated, depressed, and suicidal.

But what you may not understand is that you are made of three parts: the spirit, soul, and body. The body you can feed with natural foods and drinks and canal pleasures, but not so with your spirit and soul. Your body is natural, but your soul is spiritual, so therefore it cannot be satisfied or be gratified with natural foods and drinks and sex, drugs, alcohol, and other carnal things. Your soul is spiritual and can only be justified and be satisfied with spiritual things. And it can only be justified and be satisfied with Christ alone, who is the Bread of Life and the Fountain of Living Water!

And that is why the Lord Jesus Christ Himself is extending this special love's tender loving care invitation to all those of you who are hungry and thirsty for this eternal life and eternal peace and rest. He is saying,

"Ho! Everyone who thirsts, come to the waters; And you who have no money! Come, buy and eat. Yes, come, buy wine and milk without price. Why do you spend your money for what is not bread, and your wages for what does not satisfy? Listen carefully to Me, and eat what is good, and let your soul delight itself in abundance. Incline your ear, and come to Me. Hear, and your soul shall live; and I will make an everlasting covenant with you – The sure mercies of David. Seek the LORD while He may be found. Call upon Him while He is near. Let the wicked forsake his way, and the unrighteous man his thoughts; Let him return to the LORD, and He will have mercy on him; And to our God, for He will abundantly pardon." (Isaiah 55:1-3, 6, 7 NKJV)

With outstretched arms, Jesus is tenderly inviting all those of you that are spiritually hungry, thirsty, empty, weary, fainting, helpless, and hopeless to come to Him and eat of His eternal bread of life and drink of His fountain of living waters of life that can satisfy your spirit and soul. Why spend or waste your money on things that do not satisfy your spirit and soul? Only Jesus can satisfy the hungry and thirsty soul. In Him alone the spirit and soul of man is justified and satisfied.

And that is why He said to the Jews, *"Most assuredly, I say to you, he who believes in Me has everlasting life. I am the bread of life. Your fathers ate the manna in the wilderness and are dead. This is the bread which came down from heaven, that one may eat of it and not die. I am the living bread which came down from heaven. If anyone eats of this bread, he will live forever; and the bread that I shall give is My flesh, which I shall give for the life of the world.*" (John 6:47-51 NKJV)

Jesus is that living bread that came down from heaven, and in Him alone is eternal life so that whosoever eats of that bread shall not die but shall have everlasting life. Figuratively speaking, that living bread is His body that He gave for the life of the world when He died on the Cross for the sins of the world. On the Cross, He shed His blood for the remission of the sins of the world.

The soul of man is desperately craving for something spiritual and eternal. And this thirsting and hungering and craving of the soul can only be filled and be satisfied by Christ alone! That is why He said to the Samaritan woman at the well, *"Whoever drinks of this water will thirst again, but whoever drinks of the water that I shall give him will never thirst. But the water that I shall give him will become in him a fountain of water springing up into everlasting life."* (John 4:13-14 NKJV)

Here, Jesus is comparing temporal and eternal things. He told the woman that she could drink of that natural water and drink of all the desires of the pleasures of this life, and she will still thirst again. In other words, all those natural and temporal things in life can never satisfy her. She will be craving for more. This is the truth concerning sex, alcohol, drugs, food, money, clothing, material possessions, riches, pleasures, power, and all other things in this world. You may have all of these things and yet still you are not satisfied and content. You keep craving and lusting for more.

Only Christ alone can extinguish the flaming fires of hell and quench the fiery thirsting and hungering of your famished and anguished soul! Only Christ alone can fill that empty void, that chasm, that bottomless pit of hell in your soul! And that is why He said, *"Blessed are those who hunger and thirst for righteousness, for they shall be filled."* (Matthew 5:6)

Christ alone is the firm foundation of life and the Solid Rock upon which we stand! All other rocks and foundations are quick sinking sand and sink holes ready to crumble underneath and sink you down to the bottomless pit of hell! Today, consider the poverty of your soul and the impoverishment of your life. Consider the emptiness, worthlessness, meaninglessness, helplessness, and hopelessness of your soul! Do you feel empty, void, dissatisfied, confused, anxious, restless, fearful, sleepless, worthless, meaningless, helpless, and hopeless deep down inside your soul? Do you feel there is something missing in your soul? Do you feel one or two or many pieces of the puzzle of your life are missing?

Are you searching for answers? Are you searching for true meaning in life? Are you hungry and thirsty for true eternal love, eternal peace, eternal joy, eternal satisfaction, eternal hope, and eternal life? Jesus Christ is the answer, and He is saying to you, *"It is done! I am the Alpha and the Omega, the Beginning, and the End. I will give of the fountain of the water of life freely to him who thirst."* (Revelation 21:6, NKJV)

LOVE'S tender loving care is tenderly inviting you to come and eat of the bread of life because Jesus is the Bread of Life, and to drink of the waters of life because Jesus is the Fountain of Life. He said, *"Come to me, all you who are weary and carry heavy burdens, and I will give you rest. Take my yoke upon you. Let me teach you, because I am humble and gentle at heart, and you will find rest for your souls. For my yoke is easy to bear, and the burden I give you is light."* (Matthew 11:28-30 NLT)

The Lord Jesus said to the apostle John, *"Do not seal the words of the prophecy of this book, for the time is at hand. He who is unjust, let him be unjust still; he who is filthy, let him be filthy still; he who is righteous, let him be righteous still; he who is holy, let him be holy still. And behold, I am coming quickly, and My reward is with Me, to give to everyone according to his work. I am the Alpha and the Omega, the Beginning and the End, the First and the Last. Blessed are those who do His commandments, that they may have the right to the tree of life, and may enter through the gates into the city. But outside are dogs and sorcerers and sexually immoral and murderers and idolaters, and whoever loves and practices a lie.*

I, Jesus, have sent My angel to testify to you these things in the churches. I am the Root and the Offspring of David, the Bright and Morning Star. And the Spirit and the bride say,

'Come!' And let him who hears say, 'Come!' And let him who thirsts come. Whoever desires, let him take the water of life freely." (Revelation 22:10-17 NKJV)

This is LOVE'S tender loving care special invitation to you. Will you accept His invitation or not? Jesus is right now standing at the front door of your heart and of your home, gently knocking, patiently waiting, and tenderly calling, *"Behold, I stand at the door and knock. If anyone hears My voice and opens the door, I will come into him and dine with him, and he with Me."* (Revelation 3:20 NKJV) Just take a moment to listen attentively to His still small whispering voice tenderly pleading with you to let Him in.

Oh, my dear broken, shattered, crushed, bruised, wounded, bleeding, hurting, abused, molested, shamed, rejected, dejected, weary, fainting, weak, fearful, heavy burdened, empty, void, helpless, hopeless, and restless one, would you please open the door of your heart and of your home and invite Jesus to come in and have dinner with you today? And the dinner He wants to share with you is His Holy Communion of Love through His body that was broken for you for your healing and restoration, and His blood that was shed for your redemption and remission of your sins.

Jesus wants to fill the emptiness of your heart and to satisfy the hunger and thirsting of your soul. He wants to give you eternal love, eternal peace, eternal joy, eternal freedom, eternal healing, eternal reconciliation, eternal justice, eternal meaning, eternal hope, eternal satisfaction, and eternal life!

This is that true Love that conquers the world and the hearts of all men, women, and children! This is that true Love that conquers the devil and all evils and that disarms all its enemies! This is that all-powerful, all-conquering, all-triumphing, all-vanquishing, all-victorious, all-consuming, all-overcoming, all-redeeming, all-saving, all-healing, all-reconciling, all-liberating, and all-eternal life-giving LOVE that is inviting you to come and taste and see the goodness of the LORD!

Christ wants to freely share with you His already "Prepaid" and "Preprepared" meal of the bread of eternal life and of the fountain of living waters. Are you going to open the door of your heart and ACCEPT Him into your life, or are you going to shut the door of your heart and REJECT Him out of your life? And remember, my dear friend, when all is said and done here in this world; and when the final scroll of the chronicles of this world and of the human race is wrapped up and brought to a close; and when in the final culmination and consummation of time and space; and when it is all over; only LOVE will triumph!

Has this LOVE conquered you yet? Even as I close the final page of this book, I would like to leave you with one thing for you to remember and to ponder about, and this is that one thing: **Always Remember That In The Whole Wide World There Is No One Else That Can Love You More Than JESUS, For There Is No Greater Love Than His, And There**

Is No Greater Lover Than Him! And It Is This Love That Is Standing At The Door Of Your Heart Gently Knocking, Patiently Waiting, And Tenderly Pleading For You To Open The Door Of Your Heart And Invite Him In. Your Acceptance Or Rejection Of Him Will Determine Where You Will Spend The Rest Of Your Life In Which Eternity: Heaven Or Hell! The Decision Is Yours! SHALOM!

Endnotes

1   Allen, Austin. "Emma Lazarus: The New
    Colossus." Poetry Foundation. November 22,
    2017. www.poetryfoundation. org/articles/144956/
    emma-lazarus-the-new-colossus.

2   Merriam Webster's New World Dictionary. 1988. Third
    ed. New York: Simon & Schuster, Inc.

3   Anderson, Austin. "The Dark Side of Darwinism/
    Philosophy for the Many." November 16, 2016. https://
    sites.williams.edu/engl-209-fall16/uncategorized/
    the-dark-side-of-darwinism/.

4   Branch, Andre J. "Deculturalization: Diversity &
    Consistency, Sociology of Education." May 31, 2012.
    sk.sagepub.com/reference/diversityineducation/n190.xm.

5   Wikipedia. 2020. "The Free Encyclopedia; Master Race."
    Last modified October 19, 2020. https://en.wiwkipedia.
    org/ wiki/Master race.

6   Wikipedia. 2020. "The Free Encyclopedia: Eugenics."
    Last modified October 19, 2020. https://en.wiwkipedia.
    org/ wiki/Master race.

7   "Bob Marley & The Wailers Lyrics: The Redemption Song." https://www.azlyrics.com/lyrics/bobmarley/redemptionsong.html.

8   Merriam Webster's New World Dictionary. 1988. Third ed. New York: Simon & Schuster, Inc.

9   Shakespeare, William. 2013. Macbeth. New York: Simon & Schuster Paperbacks.

10 "Declaration of Independence: A Transcription." The National Archives. Accessed July 24, 2020. www. archives. gov/founding-docs/declaration-transcript.

11 Orwell, George. (1906) 1996. Animal Farm. Reprint, New York: Signet Classics.

12 Josephus – The Complete Works, Translated by William Whiston, A.M; Copyright © 1998 by Thomas Nelson Publishers.

13 Alfred Wegner's Theory of Continental Drift, WIKIPEDIA, www.en.m.wikipedia.org. Last edited February 7, 2021 by GenQuest. Website visited February 10, 2021.

14 Ethnologue Languages of the World, www.ethnologue.com, 2rd Edition, by Gary Simon, February 21, 2020. Website visited February 5, 2021

15 Lincoln, Abraham. "Lincoln's Second Inaugural Address." March 4, 1865. https.//www.nps.gov/linc/learn/history-culture/Lincoln-second-inaugural.htm.

16 The Citizen's Almanac. Washington: U.S. Department of Homeland Security, 2007.

17 Wikipedia. 2020. "The Free Encyclopedia: Jim Crow Laws of Racial Segregation." Last modified October 16, 2020. https://en.wikipedia.org/wiki/Jim_crow_laws.

18 Carson, Clayborne, ed. 1998. The Autobiography of Martin Luther King, Jr. New York: Grand Central Publishing.

19 Carson, Clayborne, ed. 1998. The Autobiography of Martin Luther King, Jr. New York: Grand Central Publishing.

20 Carson, Clayborne, ed. 1998. The Autobiography of Martin Luther King, Jr. New York: Grand Central Publishing.

21 "Declaration of Independence: A Transcription." The National Archives. www.archives.gov/founding-docs/declaration-transcript.

22 "Napoleon Bonaparte Quotes." www.azquotes.com/author/1621-Napoleon_Bonaparte.

23 Wikipedia. 2020. "The Free Encyclopedia: Melting Pot." Last modified October 19, 2020. https://en.wiwkipedia.org/ wiki/melting pot.

24 William Butler Yeats, The Second Coming, WIKIPEDIA, www.en.m.wikipedia.org. Last edited January 25 2021 by JamesLucas. Website visited February 10, 2021.

25 Merriam Webster's New World Dictionary. 1988. Third ed. New York: Simon & Schuster, Inc.

26 Wikipedia. 2020. "The Free Encyclopedia: Ambassador." Last modified October 4, 2020. https://en.wiwkipedia.org/ wiki/Ambassador.

27 Shakespeare, William. 2013. Macbeth. New York: Simon & Schuster Paperbacks.

CPSIA information can be obtained
at www.ICGtesting.com
Printed in the USA
BVHW050733150721
611786BV00007B/81

9 781662 806124